WHEN SHE WAS BAD

WHEN SHE WAS BAD

Violent

Women

& the

Myth of

Innocence

PATRICIA PEARSON

RANDOM HOUSE OF CANADA

Canadian Cataloguing in Publication Data

Pearson, Patricia, 1964-
When she was bad
ISBN 0-394-22430-2

1. Female offenders.   2. Violent crimes.
3. Violence.   4. Women—Psychology.
I. Title.

HV6046.P42 1997   364.3´74   C97-930809-7

This book is printed on acid-free paper.

Printer in the United States of America
Set in ITC New Baskerville
Designed by Pei Koay

For Geoffrey and Landon,

who gave me life and

filled it with love

ACKNOWLEDGMENTS

Writing a book is a strange job.

"Here you go," a publisher says at the outset, handing you a salary of sorts, and a deadline, "we'll see you in two years." And there you go indeed, in a state of high alarm, without any day-to-day ballast—no appointments, no tasks assigned each morning, no office colleagues to act as sounding boards, no clue as to what you are doing: equipped solely with a single idea, which you cling to like driftwood in a great, dark sea.

Under the circumstances, which in my case led to hiding beneath my bed for rather long stretches of time, all assistance rendered is most gratefully received.

And so I offer my thanks to:

Sarah Lazin, my agent, who is also my beloved friend, for editing the proposal in the autumn of 1993 when it resembled a set of IKEA furniture instructions, shepherding me through the world of publishing with alacrity and wry asides, defending my interests with a genuine passion, and encouraging me to learn how to spell.

Doug Pepper, editorial director at Random House Canada, who first encouraged me to write this book and continually supported me thereafter; Alice Wood at Little, Brown UK, who came on board early and provided astute commentary along the way; Jane von Mehren at Viking Penguin, my principal editor, who fielded neurotic questions with grace and patience, edited each draft with subtlety and precision, and reiterated her faith in the project whenever I misplaced mine.

For their lighting the way intellectually, I am indebted most specifically to Candice Skrapec, for her insights into the commission of extreme violence; Coramae Richey Mann, for her research on female homicide offenders; Allison Morris, on female criminality; Alice Miller and Landon Pearson, on child abuse and cycles of violence; Kaj Björkqvist and his Finnish colleagues, for their excellent work on female aggression.

For long conversations that served to refine my ideas, I'm grateful to my mother, Landon; Michael DeCarlo; Candice Skrapec; Pier Bryden; Diana Bryden, with whom I shared the horror of Bernardo's trial; Barbara Moon; Diana Symonds; and Kate Fillion, who went through it all alongside me as she wrote her own book.

For research in the field, I am immensely thankful to everybody who gave so freely of their time, resources, and expertise, including: Dr. Fred Mathews; Leroy Orozco; Donna Stewart; Stuart Asch; Bill Tillier; Toby Wong; Eric Hickey; Cedric Southerland; Justice Michael Corriero; the men in Steve Easton's support group; Murray Straus; Michael Thomas; Reena Sommer; Kim Rossmo; Detectives Gierasch, Rice, and Cabrera; the staff of the Suffolk County district attorney's office; court officials in Schenectady, San Jose, and San Francisco; Beth Valentine; the staff at New York Legal Aid, Juvenile Division; William Wood; Precious Bedell; Arlene Mohammad; Marti Salas-Tarin; and all the women at Miracle House, who were so welcoming one early spring weekend.

For making sure the research was *correct*, a special thanks to my fact-checker, Geri Savits-Fine. All remaining errors in this work are mine to shamefacedly claim.

Finally, I thank my parents, my siblings, and my friends for their love throughout this taxing time, and my husband, Ambrose, whose warm, surrounding presence keeps me sane.

CONTENTS

I have to recant, give up the old belief that I am powerless and because of it nothing I can do will ever hurt anyone.

MARGARET ATWOOD, SURFACING

WHEN SHE WAS BAD

GIRLS WILL BE GIRLS

The Nature of Female Aggression

Everyone starts out totally dependent on a woman. The idea that she could turn out to be your enemy is terribly frightening.

LORD ASTOR, British philanthropist, 1993

This story of violence begins with a war. It was America's war, the razzle-dazzle one in the Persian Gulf, where the desert was a proving ground for a new generation of heroes. Stormin' Norman Schwarzkopf came out of that war, and General Colin Powell, and CNN, and high-tech missiles. And the soldiers who died on the sand, who were injured, taken prisoner, whose names we never caught—for them, yellow ribbons bedecked the nation's trees. They were the heroes to whom one little girl, ten-year-old Tina Killie, of Wrightstown, Wisconsin, carefully penned a letter, at the instruction of her teacher, to support the troops of Operation Desert Storm. Tina addressed her envelope to "any soldier," and her teacher mailed it to the United States Army.

Months went by, the war wound down, and Tina Killie was dreaming up what to wear for Halloween when all of a sudden she received a reply. All the talk in her school and on television about the courageous men of war had distilled into a living human being, a hero with a heartbeat, with the desert in his boots and the sun in his eyes, crouched over a canteen table writing personally, to her. "Don't be misled by my handwriting," the letter began. "I am a guy— I just have fairly decent penmanship because I once took up calligraphy as an art." The soldier seemed to know that he had to explain away, at once, the stereotypes of manhood and apologize for being nothing more or less than a person. "I shall [begin] what I hope will be a continued pen pal between us," he wrote in his lovely script, "by giving a quick description of myself. I have been in the army ever since graduation [from high school in Las Vegas]. I am 6′1″ and 165 pounds. I love to run . . . I used to run track in high school."

Army Specialist Anthony Riggs, one rank shy of sergeant, nicknamed "Slowpoke" by his buddies because he was gentle and hard to rile, had gone into the army because he couldn't afford to go to college. He was stationed with the Forty-third Air Defense Artillery, D Battery, a unit that operated Patriot missiles in Saudi Arabia. Over the next four months, as America's precision war gave way to a jagged peace, Riggs sent Tina more than a dozen letters. He included tokens of his adventure abroad, like a Pepsi bottle with Arabic script, and she sent him reminders of comfort, like carefully packaged boxes of chocolate chip cookies. "I hope you don't mind me calling you Angel," he wrote in one of his last notes. "It's because you're so nice to me and yet we've never met. It's nice to know there are people like you still growing up in America."

Riggs's surprise at her kindness was curious. It measured, perhaps, the distance American soldiers had traveled since World War II, when Yankees were so famous for their optimism. Now it was the end of the century, and Riggs was an African American who lived in the bleak heart of downtown Detroit, where optimism had been subsumed by a stalwart determination to simply survive. "I have no intentions of becoming one of this war's casualties," he wrote to his mother in Las Vegas. "With the Lord's grace and his guidance, I'll walk American soil once again."

On March 16, 1991, Specialist Riggs strode jubilantly across the airport tarmac in Fort Bliss, Texas, and gave his twenty-two-year-old wife, Toni Cato Riggs, a tentative "D'ya still love me?" hug. Toni had driven across the country to welcome him home with her three-year-old daughter, Ambere. For that, and for being home, he was immensely relieved. After spending several months equal parts scared and bored senseless, he'd made it to safe ground. He craved what was heartening: some french fries, a little romance, and when he got back to Detroit, a move *out* of there, to a small house being offered by the army on a base in Warren, Michigan.

While Riggs was away, Toni had returned to the childhood home where her grandmother, Joan Cato, had raised her—a small wooden house on once-genteel Conley Avenue in Detroit. The yellow ribbon she had tied to the porch slumped in the cold March rain as the couple slogged back and forth between the house and Riggs's Nissan Sentra, filling it up with their belongings, on their first day back in the city. By two in the morning, the car was crammed with old furniture, Ambere's toys, Toni's school books, Anthony's army stuff, just one more haul to do, then a weary stretch of the shoulders and a fitful sleep. Anthony was still outside when Joan Cato noticed that the porch light had gone out. Toni went to the doorway to switch it back on. She stopped in mid-stride, jerked into stillness by gunfire. In Detroit, this was dismal and predictable terror, not shocking so much as depressing. When it stopped, Joan and Toni peered through the screen. They saw the Nissan pulling away. Oh, Lord, this was violence coming right on home. Anthony was on the ground. He was hit. Just like the war. That impersonal. Within moments, he was dead.

It didn't take long for the dispiriting irony of this veteran's urban murder to be grasped by every politician and columnist in the nation. Within twenty-four hours, Detroit City Council's president Maryann Mahaffey had pegged it "the great American tragedy." In Washington, at the Senate subcommittee hearing on the Brady Bill, mandating a seven-day waiting period for handguns, Specialist Riggs arose repeatedly as the day's bitterest case in point. Never mind Saddam Hussein. American men were dying at *one another's* hands, in their own home-grown "combat zones." The statistics spoke plainly. "During every 100 hours on our streets, we lose three times more young men than were killed in 100 hours of ground war in the Persian Gulf," Health and Human Services secretary Louis Sullivan had testified. "Where are the yellow ribbons of hope and remembrance?" he wanted to know. A spokesman for Detroit's mayor Coleman Young gave a statement. "A new war needs to be fought on the home front," he said, ". . . so this gallant young man would not have died in vain."

Seven hundred citizens filed into Detroit's Little Rock Baptist Church to honor the life of Anthony Riggs. Congresspersons Barbara Rose-Collins and John Conyers flew in from Washington to attend. The Reverend Jesse Jackson's voice resounded from the pulpit, memorializing a man he did not know, who had been "any soldier" and was a different sort of hero now. "What is the redeeming value in this tragic loss of life?" Jackson asked. "Somehow Anthony has brought us together. By his blood a nation could be saved. Not Kuwait, but America. He illuminates and illustrates, by living and dying, the crisis and challenge of a generation of young African-American men. There's a need to cry out: 'Stop the violence.' "

Detroit's greatest soul singer, Aretha Franklin, her voice as eloquent as the preacher's, led the congregation in a hymn, and Jackson escorted Toni to the coffin to pray. A bugler played taps while an American flag was lifted from the casket, ceremoniously folded, and handed to the solemn young widow. Toni wasn't as articulate as the pundits and scribes who'd swept her husband up into their symbolic world, but she managed to echo their point: "I can't believe I've waited all this time for him to come back and he does, and then I lose him again," she lamented.

The community rallied swiftly and emphatically around Riggs's family. Tina Killie sent Anthony's mother, Lessie, a sweatshirt that said, "Somebody in Wrightstown loves you." A local Honda/Jeep Eagle dealership offered Toni a car. The NAACP posted a ten-thousand-dollar reward for information leading to the killer's arrest. On March 23 homicide detectives found Anthony's stolen car parked on a residential street about a mile from where he died. Strangely, the family's packed belongings were still inside. It wasn't a robbery. So what was it? Something gang-related? Riggs gunned down as a message? Mistaken for somebody else? Detectives also found a .38-caliber pistol in a Dumpster near the car, matching the bullets in the fallen soldier. They put through a registration trace. The ownership came back to someone named Antonio Shelby, who proved to be a local street tough and a crack dealer, currently on probation. Hauled in and grilled, Shelby told a story that turned this senseless urban murder on its head. He had lent his gun, he said, to nineteen-year-old Michael Cato, who was his friend. Cato was also, as it happens, the son of his godmother, Paula, and the brother-in-law of Anthony Riggs. Cato was the shooter, Shelby said. But it wasn't his idea. The idea belonged to Toni.

Michael Cato was arrested on March 25, on the strength of Shelby's confession. Swiftly giving in to his predicament, having no talent for lies, he explained what had happened. Toni Cato Riggs, older sister, the smarter and tougher-minded of the two, who had protected Michael since they had been neglected as children by their drug-addicted mother, had asked him to murder her husband. She would split with Michael, she said, her two-hundred-thousand-dollar payoff in life insurance. Then they could get out of the neighborhood, do something better. So Michael borrowed Antonio's gun, and the plan went into motion.

Detroit was stunned. The pundits were speechless. What eulogies were there to fashion about this little twist? The killer was family. The violence had nothing to do with men at all, it had been arranged by a woman. Instantly, the voices of anguish fell silent. In place of a nation's impassioned pleas for reconciliation came a couple of news stories reporting the gossip of neighbors. Toni Cato Riggs was promiscuous. She had been "runnin' around with a lot of men." It was whispered that she had herpes. Another rumor was that she was pregnant. "That's a fact," a Conley Avenue neighbor named Ollie Hicks told *USA Today*, though it wasn't. "I always knew she was selfish and self-centered," said Anthony's mother, Lessie.

Army Sergeant Gary Welliver told a reporter that, come to think of it, when Toni met Anthony in Fort Bliss she'd told him she wanted a divorce. "An interesting way to get greeted," Welliver said sarcastically. Reporters unearthed the unsavory fact that Toni was already married to another man when she married her soldier. She still hadn't divorced Marcus Butler, Ambere's father. They also found

out by interviewing her cousins and girlfriends that Toni was a restless, disconsolate woman who didn't love Anthony and didn't want
to be an army wife in the suburbs. Anthony himself had described
Toni's unhappiness in a letter to his mother from the war. "Toni has
wrecked my car again," he wrote Lessie; "I don't know what's on her
mind. . . . Mom, I would put my head through the neck of a hot
sauce bottle to please her."

A reader sifting through the details from the papers, now offered
up as unimportant true crime fluff, might begin to glimpse the discord in Toni and Anthony's marriage, how one man was being hurt,
one woman stifled, and both were trying to assemble new lives from
what shreds of opportunity the inner city provides. Anthony took the
legitimate route and joined the army. Toni went the illicit route and
arranged a shooting, like the ones she saw around her every day.

But the fact that Riggs was embroiled in familial rancor and fell
victim to it held no meaning for the citizenry of Detroit. "What I did,
I did for a soldier," the Reverend James Holley of Little Rock Baptist
Church said, referring to his arrangement of the funeral. "What
bothers me is that those of us who live here felt one hundred percent the way the media did, that this was the kind of . . . violence
we've grown used to." Reverend Holley did not mean the violence in
his community in which women are principal players, as mothers
and lovers and sisters and daughters. He wasn't referring to child
abuse, infanticide, spousal assault, or school yard and girl gang
aggression. He did not take, for his reference point, the eighty thousand women arrested for violent crime in America the year that
Riggs died or the thousands of others whose violence was invisible
and went unremarked upon. He meant masculine violence, permissible or illicit, heroic or profane, but publicly engaged in and
displayed. "It makes me think I need to take a long look at myself,"
he concluded, of his initial assumption about Riggs's fate. "Have
we come to the point that we just automatically perceive ourselves
this way?"

What a society perceives about violence has less to do with a fixed
reality than the lenses we are given through which to see. Before the
twentieth century, the man who beat his mule or his child was not a

violent man. Nor was the woman who lashed her dog or, in some eras, abandoned her newborn to die of exposure. Rape is violent, but only in the last twenty years have we perceived that a husband might be his wife's rapist. The violence that words inflict is newly perceived, and so is the violence of "harassment" and "hazing." Our perception of violence is selective, and changeable. What the citizens of Detroit had "grown used to," as Reverend Holley put it, was one dimension of destructive human behavior. Boys were gunning down boys, to be sure. But girls and women were contributing their share to the cycle of rage, and injury, and pain.

Women commit the majority of child homicides in the United States, a greater share of physical child abuse, an equal rate of sibling violence and assaults on the elderly, about a quarter of child sexual abuse, an overwhelming share of the killings of newborns, and a fair preponderance of spousal assaults. The question is how do we come to *perceive* what girls and women do? Violence is still universally considered to be the province of the male. Violence is masculine. Men are the cause of it, and women and children the ones who suffer. The sole explanation offered up by criminologists for violence committed by a woman is that it is involuntary, the rare result of provocation or mental illness, as if half the population of the globe consisted of saintly stoics who never succumbed to fury, frustration, or greed. Though the evidence may contradict the statement, the consensus runs deep. Women from all walks of life, at all levels of power—corporate, political, or familial, women in combat and on police forces—have no part in violence.

It is one of the most abiding myths of our time.

The notion that women are a homogeneous species of nurturant souls has myriad wellsprings, but the deepest, perhaps, has to do with our basic conception of the body.

Violence, we believe, is implicit in the construction of the male: the chest-beating ape evolved into the soldier, the rapist. Men are propeled into conquest by a surge of testosterone, and build their blocks of power on the strength of their physique. Research may show that women are tougher, longer-living, more tolerant of pain, but research is dry and pedantic. Literature rejoices in the docility of female flesh, its yielding form, its penetrability. The female body fosters life itself. Women do not physically thrust and strut and dominate. To picture women's aggression, men would have to picture women's bodies bereft of the erotic, the maternal, the divine. No such sacrifice is required in conjuring male aggression. Muscle and hormone are the twin pillars upon which all our darkest human urges stand: lust, rage, jealousy, revenge, the craving for power, the quest for control. Dark urges, and yet the capacity to express them is also held up as a matter of masculine strength and of valor. "It is highly probable," wrote Anthony Storr, one of this century's most famous theorists on violence, "that the undoubted superiority of the male sex in intellectual and creative achievement is related to their greater endowment of aggression." Masculinity, according to sociologist James Messerschmidt, "emphasizes practices toward authority, control, competitive individualism, independence, aggressiveness, and the capacity for violence."

A 1996 book about the primate origins of human aggression, *Demonic Males*, made it clear in the title that, whether we began as creatures of earth or as creatures of God, it is men who wreak the havoc. Men destroy, women create. Men are from Mars, women are from Venus. The gender dichotomy is remarkably enduring, and surprisingly crude.

So what is its basis in fact?

Over the last twenty years, a host of scientific research projects have zeroed in on the physical underpinnings of human behavior, with results that pose a sharp challenge to the biological maleness of aggression. Testosterone, the oldest chestnut, has fallen into disrepute of late, as laboratory experiments call the causative effect of the hormone into question. One comprehensive literature review pronounced research to date to be utterly inconclusive on the influence of male hormones on violence. A major flaw in the research has been that testosterone, like adrenaline, increases in people exposed to conflict. The populations most often tested for it are prison inmates, who already have higher levels because of where they are—in an edgy, tense, combative cage. "The outcome of aggressive or competitive encounters," noted the reviewer, "can increase or decrease testosterone levels." Elevated levels have been measured in *female* prisoners, as well as in winners of "a cash prize" in a tennis tournament, recipients of medical degrees, and the triumphant competitor in a wrestling match. "Does the hormone modulate the behavior," asks psychologist David Benton, "or does fighting and winning increase the release of the hormone?" For all its celebrity, testosterone is an elusive player in this game. It explains nothing, after all, of Toni Cato, or the mother who pummels her child, or the girl in a gang with a switchblade.

In fact, a more compelling culprit than hormones in violent behavior may be the wiring of the human brain, in a way that does not discriminate one sex from the other. There is fascinating work being done on the effect of head injury on the human propensity for aggression. Frontal lobe damage, for example, can cause perfectly calm people to lose their impulse control, which is usually governed by the cerebral cortex. They revert to the most primal emotions, zooming from annoyance to homicidal fury in a matter of seconds, with no mood in between. We know this in its less extreme form as "hair-trigger temper." Its more voluble expression is called "episodic aggression" or "rage attacks." But why would it affect only men? It doesn't. Pauline Mason of Toronto was driving on a highway in 1992 when a spring flew off a transport truck, smashed through her window, and struck her head. She went amnesiac for some months, was permanently blinded, and grew wildly and erratically violent, to the point where her scared spouse initiated divorce proceedings.

How many other women undergo this Jekyll and Hyde transformation? Thousands? The scientific literature is mum. Men are the standard bearers of violence, and masculine violence the measure.

A study released in early 1996 evaluated the impact of lead ingestion on delinquency in children. According to the study's authors at the University of Pittsburgh, "bullying, vandalism, setting fires and shoplifting" all increased in children exposed to lead-based paints on pipes and plumbing in their homes. The authors cautioned that lead should be considered a serious hazard to children for this reason. But they only studied boys. What about girls? If they're exposed to lead, what happens to them?

Researchers at Johns Hopkins University in Baltimore have discovered that if you breed male mice without the gene that produces nitric oxide—a molecule that allows nerve cells to communicate—they grow up to be the rodent version of soccer hooligans, beating the hell out of each other without provocation. But what do female mice do? The author of the experiment, Dr. Solomon H. Snyder, concedes that the focus of the research has been on males. As he told Natalie Angier of *The New York Times*, "Not much could be concluded about behavioral changes in females."

In 1995, research by the psychologist Adrian Raine and his colleagues at the University of Southern California revealed that juvenile delinquents with low heartbeat and sweat rates, signaling sluggish nervous systems, proved more likely to become adult criminals than fellow juveniles with swift nervous system responses. "If you have chronically low levels of arousal," Raine said, "the theory is that you seek out stimulation to increase arousal levels back to normal." Raine and his colleagues took the pulse rates of adolescent boys. Who knows what happens to girls?

Biological research has gone down several other trails. Seratonin, a neurotransmitter in the brain, may be related to violent behavior. So might the body's electrical impulses, since some violent criminals show markedly erratic electroencephalogram readings. Certain irregularities in brain function show up in the magnetic resonance imaging scans of psychopaths, suggesting a severance in the links between emotion and language. Prozac has recently taken some blame for heightening impulses to suicide. And blood sugar levels have been connected to impulsive aggression, most famously in the so-called Twinkie defense, in which the man who assassinated San Francisco supervisor Harvey Milk and mayor George Mosconi pled not guilty on the basis of temporary insanity because his depression was deepened by eating too much junk food. Biocriminologists will continue to tinker with the physical mechanisms of horrid behavior and haul their findings into court. But at what point will the exclusive application of this research to men cease to hold?

In primate research, all it took was one scholar, the primatologist Sarah Hrdy, to pose the right questions and challenge the myth of exclusively male aggression. Conducting field research in Africa in the 1970s, Hrdy observed that, in monogamous primates, loyalty was imposed by the females, not the males. "Any prospect of polygyny," she wrote, referring to the practice of having multiple mates, "would be precluded by fierce antagonism among females of breeding age. In most monogamous species, rival females are physically excluded from the territory by the aggressiveness of its mistress." Hrdy dubbed this the Hagar phenomenon, a reference to the biblical Sarah, wife of Abraham, who drove her husband's mistress into the desert. "The basic dynamics of the mating system depend not so much on male predilections"—the mythic hairy ape dragging his female away by her scruff—but "on the degree to which one female tolerates another." According to subsequent research by Reijo Holmström, female primates also kill one another's offspring and freeze one another out of feeding groups so that rivals become vulnerable to starvation.

The lesson revealed in this research, as well as in the findings of biocriminology, is that aggression is not innately masculine, but that evidence lies within the eye of the beholder. As long as patriarchs and feminists alike covet the notion that women are gentle, they will not look for the facts that dispute it. Hrdy has suggested that one reason other primatologists continue to assume males are the sole aggressors is that what females do doesn't look like violence. In other words, one reason women dwell outside the discourse on aggression is because of the tendency of scholars to define aggression in a specifically masculine way.

Regardless whether we assign it a positive or negative value, we tend to conceive of violence as a collection of assertive, public acts: fistfights, bar brawls, gun duels, the collision of soldiers on a field. Violence is the spectacle of teenaged boys beating one another up and mobsters blowing rivals away. It is physical; it is direct. The violent person targets his victim head-on. Pow. Boom. Crack. Defined this way, as in-your-face physical aggression, what we are really talking about is a gendered style. Visible physical aggression is a masculine display, which, many parents insist, shows up early in boys. Scholars who study preschool children, however, find that injurious physical aggression is committed equally by boys and girls. A little girl who has been displaced by a new baby is just as likely to thwack the baby over the head with her juice cup as a boy is. The psychologists Anne Colby and William Danon note that "there is very little support in the psychological literature for the notion that girls are more aware of others' feelings or are more altruistic than boys." We all begin our lives as selfish creatures with poor impulse control, out to defend our vital interests as we see them. But what happens to boys at the preschool level is that they begin to engage in much higher levels of "playful aggression" than girls do. What parents are noticing is that their boys have begun to dress-rehearse for gender, engaging in varieties of masculine gesture and display. This sort of aggression, playful in preschool and combative by high school, has nothing to do with the preconditions of criminal *motive*. It has to do with posturing. James Messerschmidt calls it "doing gender." Boys play rough because we expect them to play rough. Seventy percent of respondents to a 1968 survey conducted for the National Commission on the Causes and Prevention of Violence said that "they believed it was important for a boy to have a few fist fights while he was growing up." Evidently, most boys do. Every year since 1976, about half of all men in the United States have answered "yes" to the question "Have you ever been punched or beaten by someone?"

"Where I grew up, in Mississippi and Arkansas," wrote the novelist Richard Ford in 1996, "to be willing to hit another person in the face with your fist meant something." What did it mean? That you were brutish, power-mad, in love with someone else's pain? "It meant you were—well, brave . . . ," wrote Ford. "As a frank, willed act, hitting in the face was a move toward adulthood, the place we were all headed—a step in the right direction."

Aggressive display is a cultural practice, and even within the United States there are cultural variations in the degree to which men deploy it. Researchers at the University of Michigan recently explored the link between elevated violence rates in the southern United States, for example, and "the culture of honor." This southern belief, which endures long past the outlaw of duels, is that insults must be met with an aggressive defense. Theorizing that the culture of honor obliges southern men to behave more violently than northern men, the researchers divided a group of students according to where they'd been raised. The students—unaware of the experiment—were bumped in a corridor and called "asshole." Northerners reacted mainly with amusement, whereas southerners more often got angry. In a second experiment, the students were put on a collision course with the experimenters in the hallway, setting up a game of chicken, to see whether they, or the experimenter, would step out of the way first. Again, northerners were quicker to give way, less inclined to feel that losing the game "damaged their reputation for masculinity."

British men follow a different model for masculinity. Their ideal is more likely to be "a stolid, pipe-sucking manhood, unmoved by panic or excitement," admirable for showing reason and self-restraint. In a review of violence rates in Western countries, anthropologist Elliott Leyton speculated that the British rates are much lower because of these cultural ideals. As Leyton points out, certain factors that contribute to the commission of serious violence—individual pathologies, life stresses, childhood maltreatment, and social upheaval—are constant in every society. But levels of displayed aggression fluctuate, according to cultural norms.

What would happen, then, if women felt entitled or compelled to express themselves physically in a public arena, if standing up to fight were not just a manly ideal but a womanly one as well? Would they resist the opportunity because they are not *inherently* aggressive— neither quick to anger, nor desirous of power, nor keen to brandish their own strength? In fact, the capacity of women to use masculine violence emerges very clearly in those societies that sanction its expression. Anthropologist Victoria Burbank has found that women engage publicly in physical aggression in more than eighty contemporary societies around the world, with other women—their rivals for status, dominance, and resources—the most frequent targets. Like men's, women's aggression differs in severity and purpose from place to place. On Margarita Island, off the coast of Venezuela, the anthropologist H. B. Kimberly Cook "found that women are *more* violent than men in the expression of aggression." They engage publicly in

fistfights and verbal assaults, with "the most common theme underlying fights between women [being] paternity issues" and status.
Against men, they use various techniques of "social control," or what
they call *"parar el macho,"* to quell male machismo. "When I first got
married," one twenty-two-year-old fisherman told Cook, "I used to
talk disrespectfully to my wife. . . . One day my mother took a board
and hit me across the mouth. Blood came out of my lip. I cried and
said, 'Mama, why did you hit me?' She answered, 'So that you learn
respect for your wife.' " Men are slapped, kicked, hit, and berated,
and they don't see such behavior as trivial or unfeminine. It is a point
of pride that, "Yes, my wife knows how to *parar el macho.*" It is also a
point of pride for the women. "A woman's physical strength and
ability to defend herself is . . . central in the self-concept of women."

The same is true of Aboriginal women in Australia. Victoria Burbank observed 174 fights in one community and found that women
started nearly half. When women were physically injured in fights,
their aggressors were women about half the time. Noting that
"Western theories, metaphors and stereotypes of female aggression
and victimization frame our understanding" but do not speak universal truth, Burbank asked the women how they saw their behavior.
They viewed it as natural. Aggression was "the expected, if not
inevitable, outcome of anger," for both men and women, and wasn't
seen as socially deviant.

Anthropologist Maria Lepowsky studied aggressive strategies on
the island of Vanatinai, near New Guinea, where men and women
are held to be equal in economic, political, marital, and sexual relations. "Males and females experience equally strong emotions of
envy, jealousy, frustrated desire and rage," she observed. "There is
no perception that a man's feelings of anger are stronger than a
woman's." But equality in itself doesn't make women physically violent. In that particular culture, both sexes are expected to curtail
verbal and physical aggression. Instead, they may use sorcery or
witchcraft, and indeed that is the most prevalent form of violence on
the island. Lepowsky only witnessed five incidents of physical violence in ten years of field research. Four of the fights were instigated
by women; two of their victims were sexual rivals.

. . .

Every now and then, when scholars in criminology and sociology concede the possibility of female aggression, they hasten to add that women only engage in "expressive" aggression, which means giving vent impulsively to bottled-up feelings. Women do not, these scholars maintain, engage in "instrumental" aggression, the kind that is cool and calculating. By maintaining this distinction between impulsive and strategic violence, the basic paradigm of female virtue holds. But if the distinction is accurate, what are we to make of the women who have hunted and fought battles—with no less ferocity than men—in societies throughout history: in, for example, Libya, Anatolia, Bulgaria, Greece, Armenia, Russia, Celtic England, and northern Scotland? That Western historians have exhibited an almost universal tendency to ignore such women does not, in itself, render them freaks of nature. The British writer Antonia Fraser notes that several powerful female rulers have mysteriously disappeared from history books. We have heard of Cleopatra, more as femme fatale than as the shrewd queen she was, but not of her contemporaries: Dynamis of Bosphorus, who starved her husband to death, assumed control of his kingdom, and conquered adjoining regions; or Artemisia, a queen who conducted a brilliant military campaign against the Greeks. Amid the forgotten warriors there do remain some legends: Joan of Arc; Catherine the Great of Russia; Elizabeth I of England; the great Celtic Queen Boadicea; Lucrezia Borgia; Catherine de Médicis; the Nazi leader Irma Grese, sadistic administrator of a female concentration camp; Madam Mao of China's Gang of Four; and Sarah Kyolaba, soldier-wife of Ugandan dictator Idi Amin.

None of these women were strangers to cruel governance or instrumental aggression. Were they anomalous because they were operating at the top of the political hierarchy, using violence to survive in a masculine world? Not really. Ordinary women have proven to be just as militaristic, supporting the continuance of war, shaming men who would dodge the draft, screaming for blood in a mob, fighting alongside their brothers and sons when they could, acting as snipers, as fighter pilots, as guerrilla soldiers and terrorists. At the height of international terrorism in the 1970s, there were 204 active female terrorists throughout the world, participating directly in 41.6 percent of maimings and 22.5 percent of assassinations. Amid the apocalyptic atrocities in Rwanda in 1995, women all over the country were wielding machetes and lobbing grenades. In fact, one of the largest massacres of Tutsis was allegedly led by Rwanda's minister for women and family affairs, Pauline Nyiramasuhuko. Another massacre was allegedly overseen by the Rwandan minister of justice, Agnes Ntamabyariro. Survivors of slaughter at Rwanda's Kabuye Hill described a former police officer, heavily pregnant, "on her knees, shooting into us." Across the world, militia groups arming themselves in America's northern forests and western deserts count women in their ranks just as surely as women now train in the army. As the scholar Carol Tavris has written, "I have no illusions that women, if drafted in large numbers into the military, will transform that institution; without question the military will transform them."

If women in myriad cultures are capable of direct physical aggression, both expressively and instrumentally, why are Western women perceived, collectively, as angels in their houses, capable only of caring, nurturance, and submission? Are they constructed of a different fiber? Softer and more pliant than other women on the planet? Or might it be that they dwell in a culture that has, traditionally, shaped their aggression in an entirely different way than men's? Shaped differently and named differently, not as violence, with all the force, intentionality, and power implied in that term, but something else?

The history of Western women is a history of subterranean narratives. Through the centuries, we have fulfilled our ambitions and expressed our bids for power in a manner concealed from men. We were taught to bury the secret of our strength, and we did. Intellectual women adopted male pseudonyms; political women advised in the bed chamber; angry women let go the fists they'd made as tomboys and unleashed their wit instead. Excavating the sites of our history, feminist academicians and writers have traced the routes of these subterranean courses—discovering the female names behind the "Anon." signature in poetry and unearthing the reality of how households and castles were run. But they have been considerably less keen to delve into the violence we've done.

Of 314 studies on human aggression published by 1974, only 8 percent focused on women or girls. That basic orientation—still evident in biocriminological research—only began to change in aggression studies in the 1980s. A female-focused field started to grow, populated mainly by anthropologists and social psychologists, who studied what became of those preschool girls who were initially just as aggressive as their brothers. "In our view," noted the psychologists Claudia Frey and Siegfried Hoppe-Graff, "the empirical evidence might be more decisive when the question 'Is there a higher rate of aggression in boys than in girls' is substituted by the more precise question: 'Do girls and boys differ in specific types of aggression?' " Posing the question this way, what the scholars discovered was that, as soon as girls hone their verbal and social skills, at around ten or eleven, they become aggressors of a different kind. They abandon physical aggression, even though their prepubescent hormones are still no different than boys', and adopt a new set of tactics: they bully, they name call, they set up and frame fellow kids. They become masters of indirection.

Indirect aggression, as the Finnish psychologist Kaj Björkqvist defines it, is "a kind of social manipulation: the aggressor manipulates others to attack the victim, or, by other means, makes use of the social structure in order to harm the target person, without being personally involved in the attack." Anyone who has seen an eight-year-old girl smoothly set another child up for undeserved punishment knows what this means. "The more able the aggressor is at staying out of reach of the opponent, and at assessing the opponent's retaliation resources, the better (s)he will be at avoiding counter-attack, and minimizing risks."

When Kaj Björkqvist and his colleagues looked at female aggressive styles during adolescence, they asked girls what they did to express anger or compete with their rivals, and the girls offered strategies like "gossiping, exchanging nasty notes, trying to win others to one's side, and excluding from groups." These were the basic power plays, the objective of which was to gain currency or dominance within the social milieu. A survey of one's own friends adds color to the picture. Anne, a Torontonian now in her thirties, was at the receiving end of girls' aggression in ninth grade, when she found herself to be the object of a classwide "hate club," with its own coded hand signal and password. The club had been formed by girls who felt threatened by Anne's precocious sexual allure. The club members recruited the boys in the class, and Anne was officially "hated." This was in the late 1970s, around the time that Stephen King's novel *Carrie* came out and introduced the world to gothic cruelty in teenaged girls. In a 1993 survey of Ontario high school girls, the community psychologist Fred Mathews put the following question to them: Defining violence as broadly as they wished, who were they most afraid of? Overwhelmingly, they responded, "Other girls."

Ask women what they did in childhood to disrupt the status quo— engaging in subversion—while their brothers, for instance, were running around stealing hubcaps, blowing up frogs, or throwing eggs at the neighbors, and their answers also reveal ingenious forms of indirect aggression. "My father was an obsessive-compulsive type," says Karen, a twenty-four-year-old from Seattle. "Everything had to be in its place. So I spent a lot of time fucking with his head, moving his stuff around, scratching his car with a penknife, so that if he asked me if I'd driven the car, I could honestly say no, just driving him nuts." Shelly, a twenty-nine-year-old actress, ruined the confidence of her little brother once, by telling him that, although he thought he was eight years old, he was actually twelve. He was retarded. His parents hadn't wanted him to know.

What qualitative measure do we possess in our culture to understand injurious behavior that isn't masculine in style? Would Shelly's "retarded" brother have suffered more if she'd struck him on the head? Would Allison's father have been more damaged if she'd crashed his car instead of tormenting him psychologically? Would Anne—to whom relationships were everything—have hurt worse if she'd been made to participate in a frat house haze? Because we have developed a male-centered measure of aggression, we have blinded ourselves to the ways in which girls develop and utilize power. At the same time, we have negated a whole class of injuries—both in scholarly research and political rhetoric—in a manner that is completely counterintuitive: "Sticks and stones may break my bones, but words can never hurt me." Never, that is, if they fly from the lips of a girl.

Anthropologist Ilsa Glazer developed an interest in modes of female aggression when she was working in Zambia and noticed that female political leaders there tended to scapegoat rather than support young educated women. Later, in Israel, she studied interfemale aggression on the kibbutz and found similar tactics at work. Namely, women of higher status used gossip and inside "knowledge" to keep other women out of the game. Could these tactics be described as injurious? Glazer next went to Palestine, where twenty to forty women are murdered each year by their brothers or fathers to "defend family honor." She discovered that other women acted as instigators and collaborators in these murders by setting loose the gossip that spurred accusation and compelled men to respond. Although this is "violence against women," in that men suffer no commensurate fate, it is equally "violence *by* women against women," mediated by a particular value structure. Among North American youth gangs, girls will instigate conflicts by making comments or spreading rumors that oblige their boyfriends to fight. "When I was a leader of a gang," one boy told researchers in Toronto, "my girlfriend went around and picked fights. . . . girls can be badmouthing people because they know that their boyfriends would, whatever, pull a gun, shoot the guy, whatever."

On Bellona, in the Solomon Islands, where the division between the sexes is highly patriarchal, women rarely bloody their own hands through physical aggression. Instead, they "hire assassins," according to the Danish psychologist Rolf Kushel. They target other women through "hair pulling," bringing their victim down to the ground and disfiguring her beauty with fingernail rakes, which is "felt [to be] a serious humiliation." They displace their aggression onto young children, in particular a child highly valued by the target. They commit or threaten to commit suicide, which has serious repercussions from the community for the men who drove them to it. And, because shame and honor are intensely felt on Bellona, they use "mocking songs" to ridicule a person, an extremely potent kind of attack. As with gossip, "the composer would be known only to a few people." The aggressor remains hidden; but the injury is felt. Gossip, as Ilsa Glazer observed, is the "power of the weak." It is not an insignificant power. The fundamental mistake that feminism has made is to equate political weakness with moral innocence.

Men for their part persist in dismissing female aggression as trivial or hapless, amounting to nothing but tongue wagging and cat fights. But there are sound reasons why women use gossip and exclusion as weaponry, and these have to do with the currency of power women trade in. Women in patriarchal societies inhabit a relational universe. Their basic sense of security is tied to their ability to forge relationships—with men, who quite literally feed them, and with their children, through whom they can impress themselves upon the world. The British crime theorist Colin Wilson dismissed any prospect of female aggression on this very basis: "It seems unlikely that female crime will ever become a serious social problem," he wrote in 1973. "The reason is obvious: woman's basic instinct is for a home and security, and it is unlikely she'll do anything to jeopardize that security." Yet violence is often a bid for security, when something of profound value is threatened. That something may be as psychologically inchoate as selfhood, or as concrete as four walls and a roof. Whatever women's "basic instincts" are, relationalism does not, in itself, render them gentler. What it does do is alter the purpose and method of their aggression. Men may flamboyantly display force to promote and defend status in the public realm, but women as surely need their own aggressive strategies to defend, maintain, and control their intimate relations, not just to "defend their cubs," which is the sentimental view, but to defend their aspirations, their identity, and their place on the stage.

In 1950, the psychologist Otto Pollak argued that Western women's crime probably did approach the level of men's but that "the criminality of women is largely masked criminality." He argued that "the lack of social equality between the sexes has led to a cultural distribution of roles which forces women in many cases into the part of instigator rather than . . . performer of an overt act." Modern criminologists denounce Pollak for having been sexist, which he was. But the essence of his insight is correct.

This was precisely the method employed by Toni Cato Riggs. In the autumn of 1991, her brother Michael, the shooter, went to trial for the murder of his brother-in-law, was convicted on his own confession, and was sentenced to life in prison. But U.S. District Court Judge Vesta Svenson had already dropped all charges against Toni Cato Riggs, ruling that Antonio Shelby's testimony against her was hearsay and that Michael's confession was inadmissible on the grounds of the Fifth Amendment—the right to avoid self-incrimination. She could not be directly connected to the crime. So she collected Riggs's insurance money, returned to college, and disappeared from view.

What is clearly discomfiting about indirect strategies of aggression is that they bestow upon women ignoble traits: hysteria, duplicitousness, manipulation, cunning. At least, we think, a male villain is straightforward. His aggression mirrors that which is valiant in other arenas, such as in war. Female aggressive strategies are never valorous, for they are by necessity underhanded, and partly because of that, they run completely counter to the way women want to view themselves. We cringe when we hear a man deriding our sex as sneaky and two-faced. As a result, our inclination is to deny the intention as well as the strategy—to adamantly insist on the absence of feminine malice. We tend to be far more comfortable talking about a different form of female aggression, one that doesn't appear antisocial or malicious, and that is the direction of violence against the self.

Female self-destruction harks back to one of the Western tradition's first heroines, Queen Alcestis, celebrated by both Homer and Euripides as the virtuous and beautiful queen who volunteered to die in place of her husband, King Admetus. By self-destructing to promote the career of her man, Alcestis won the esteem of generations of male scribes. Shakespeare's romantic heroine, Ophelia, gained her currency by flinging herself into a river and drowning. The outlaw heroines Thelma and Louise in Hollywood's 1991 film hurled themselves into a canyon. Self-destructive heroines are far more memorable within our culture than female warriors, and they teach white Western women that the most acceptable and admirable way to take a last stand in defense of their worth is to turn against themselves.

New England psychologist Dusty Miller treats an array of self-injuring patients who were sexually abused as children and need to vent their unresolved rage. She calls their behavior "trauma reenactment syndrome." Men who have been traumatized, Miller says, "are socialized to act aggressively and to fight back." But the sort of white, middle-class women that Miller sometimes treats have been taught to be "feminine" about their feelings. Being "hurt or humiliated is far more socially acceptable." So they cut, they starve, they drink, they shoot drugs, they attempt suicide, they throw up. Although Miller characterizes this behavior as a syndrome, what women are doing is no less aggressive than punching walls or picking a fight. The violence is equally willful, the consequences equally drastic for family and community, and the motive arises from a similar place. One of Miller's patients wrote in her journal: "Today a doctor humiliated a patient. I wanted to grab his head and pound it against the bed rail until he bled. I wanted to rip him to shreds." But she didn't. She force fed herself and then just as forcibly vomited. One woman who had cut her arms and wrists with razor blades in college called it "incredibly satisfying," because it "opened a pressure valve." Self-mutilation has been described as tattooing one's rage on one's skin—bringing blood to the surface to make the wounds plain.

We don't see what women do to themselves as aggressive or violent because we don't perceive self-destruction as something that we willfully direct. Our leading popular feminists blame eating disorders, for example, on the fashion industry, and have even called anorexia a form of "genocide," perpetrated on women by the misogynists on Seventh Avenue. The manifold causes of eating disorders notwithstanding, the point that is always missed in this discourse is that aggressive gestures are directed by cultural expectation: more often inward if you're female, more often outward if you're male. Because we don't recognize the commonality in these two directions, we tend to pathologize self-destruction, to peg women as afflicted and mentally ill, while understanding men as willful, immoral, and antisocial.

Whenever there's an increase in female drug abuse or drinking, an expert in addiction research invariably chimes in with an explanation that points to external pressures, such as social coercion, as if women were never reckless and wild of their own accord. Much of what is intrinsic to the concept of aggression—a willingness to be extreme, to go to the wall, to up the ante for something we want or believe in—is presumed missing in the female psyche. Self-injuring women are frequently mislabeled, according to Dusty Miller, as "schizophrenic, depressed, obsessive-compulsive, narcissistic, histrionic, borderline, multiple-personality disordered."

In essence, what is lost in the way we view female aggression is its moral and rational content. Women are not responsible actors imposing their will upon the world. They are passive and rather deranged little robots who imperil themselves on cue. Suicide statistics provide an interesting window through which to look at this. In 1992, 34 percent of Latina high school girls and 24 percent of white high school girls in America said they had considered suicide at some point that year. This leads us to believe that our young women are wandering around in despair, as Mary Pipher argues in her 1995 best-seller, *Reviving Ophelia.* Young women between the ages of fifteen and nineteen are two and a half times more likely to attempt suicide than are young men. But young men are *five* times more likely to actually kill themselves. The highest rate of suicide in America belongs to the scions of the privileged patriarchs: 16.1 of one hundred thousand white adolescent males end their own lives. Are girls less competent at self-obliteration? According to the Centers for Disease Control in Atlanta, boys use more instantly lethal methods, like firearms, whereas girls tend to swallow pills, so that death arrives less certainly. Yet, in America's prisons, where neither sex has access to firearms, eighty-eight males committed suicide in 1993, and no females did. Is it possible that some girls are using gestures of self-destruction as a form of empowerment and a language of protest?

"I dare you to prevent me."

"I command you to rescue me."

"If you leave me, I will die."

Male coercion takes the form of saying, "Do this, or I will harm you." Sometimes the man succeeds. Sometimes he courts retaliation in kind, starting a fight in a bar and getting stabbed, or battering his wife and paying with his life when she shoots him. For women, on the other hand, coercion may take the form of saying "Do this, or I will harm myself." Sometimes the woman succeeds. Sometimes she becomes the architect of her own destruction. Who, male or female, is more coercive?

Ultimately, the effect that indirect strategies have on our understanding of female behavior is to erase the connection between one form of aggression and another. We can trace the arc from ape to male, follow the line from fistfights to warfare, see a continuity of intent in willed aggression. All men are *not* killers, but the potential is there: We see the capacity to use force. This is why battered women's advocates talk of escalation theory: A man who hits his lover could very well kill her one day. As a matter of intent, there may be no truth to that at all, but as a matter of potential, there is. With women, on the other hand, the gestural connection in aggression is obscured. If a woman slices her skin or fashions her words into weapons, how clear is it that she can shift direction and suddenly engage in overt violence? It isn't clear at all. That is why criminal women wind up so radically isolated from their own sex, cast out as sexual deviants, dykes, witches. Feminist criminologists have tried to bring them back into the fold by recasting them as victims, arguing their violence away. But the truth is, although few of us will ever encounter women who are blatantly evil, strategies of aggression and violence are culled from a shared cultural repertoire. Just as Richard Ford shares a gestural language with Anthony Riggs and Michael Cato, so Toni Cato has a language in common with her putative sisters. The violent woman differs from other women in character and propensity but not in modus operandi. Instead of insisting on her innocence, we might insist on the capacity of all women to bring their force of will to bear upon the world.

.   .   .

In the early spring of 1993, two years after her husband's death, Toni Cato went for a job interview. The job was narcotics trafficking. The men who were offering it were undercover agents for the Drug Enforcement Administration who were unaware of Toni Cato's prior infamy; they stumbled across her when she got involved in a ten-kilo cocaine run to Texas with a friend, on a study break before college finals. Her friend was caught and arrested by Texas state troopers, but Cato, who says she was merely accompanying him on the trip, had already flown back to Detroit: "I'm paying to go to school, this is coming out of my pocket, and I'm not going to miss my finals," she later explained to the undercover agents. Hoping to crack the trafficking ring, the agents tapped Cato as a potential unwitting informant. Lured by the prospect of money and travel, she agreed to a series of meetings.

Her conversations with them took place in a small, stripped-down office stocked with a couple of hard wooden chairs and a desk. A surveillance camera was high up in the wall, providing a view of a young, sturdily built, attractive woman attired neatly but casually, resting her hands in her lap. On these videos, Cato looks focused, purposeful, and calm. She isn't terribly interested in flattering or flirting with these big-money drug dealers. If they can offer her a way to make serious money without much risk, she'll consider it. "I'm not afraid of anything," she tells them at one point, and her matter-of-factness makes you inclined to believe her.

Toni Cato grew up young. Her mother, Paula, in love with her drugs, as Cato recalls, left her children alone for hours at a time and as often as not returned home without food. At the age of five, Toni was farmed out to relatives, ultimately winding up with her grandmother on Conley Avenue. But her little brother, Michael, stayed behind "and spent the majority of his time left alone in the house." His lifeline was Toni, who talked to him on the phone when their mother was gone, often reading stories to him over the line. Brother and sister remained close throughout school and beyond, eventually "turning to the streets [together] without our family knowing."

As the meetings progressed, Cato began to feel she might rely on these dealers to help her out. The word on the street about her involvement in Anthony's murder had not wholly subsided. "My name is coming up constantly," she told them. "I'm not in an uproar, I'm not nervous or anything. It's just that my name is on everyone's lips." The source of the innuendo was Antonio Shelby, the man who first tipped Detroit detectives off to the murder-for-insurance scheme. "Antonio Shelby came forward and said that I offered him money," Cato explained to the agents, neither confirming nor denying that Shelby had spoken the truth. "[The prosecutors] had to prove that I had knowledge of what happened [to my husband], and they have no proof of that. They have some motive, because we had marital discord or whatever, but that's *all* they have. That's why the judge let me go." Her fear, however, was that sooner or later, the cops were going to find a way to make Shelby's statement stick. For that, there seemed only one solution.

"From the very beginning when we were going through the preliminary hearings," she told the agents, "me and my brother were thinking about it."

"So you think extreme action is necessary," one of the agents replied, masking his astonishment. This was, after all, just a minor drug investigation until Cato raised the fate of Riggs.

"M-hmm," she replied, rather dispassionately.

"What do you want done?"

"I want him eliminated, period. No coming back, no nothing."

Cato sounded for all the world like a mafia boss or a secret agent, commanding the fate of a man in a perfunctory and impersonal way. In reality there was probably a great deal of personal upset. Shelby had been family; he betrayed her. Perhaps what was worse, after he sang to the cops, she bumped into him visiting with her mother— "the man who was responsible for sending my brother to prison standing there in my mother's living room laughing and talking as if nothing had happened." That had to hurt. Could it be she was striking back at her mother?

She and the agent discussed a fee: fifteen thousand dollars if she wanted it to look like an accident. Did she have enough money for that? She said she did. They talked about it like they were arranging a bank transaction and settled the affair with nods of the head. "That's our job, solving problems," said the agent, "so we'll take care of it." He did, but not as she expected. He contacted Detroit homicide and gave them their long-sought suspect.

In November, Toni Cato was rearrested, this time for two counts of conspiracy to commit murder. After a two-week trial, she was convicted by her own words. It was June 1994.

If Toni Cato is illustrative of indirect aggression, she is not a tidy example. African-American women have a different social and historical experience of violence than white women do. The historian Laura Fishman points out that slavery and its ceaseless outrages fostered in slave women a much greater need for self-reliance and forceful action. Many slave women developed "a reputation as fighters. . . . They were tough, powerful and spirited." They argued with their masters, sometimes assaulted them, frequently committed arson, theft, even infanticide as indirect forms of protest, and occasionally murdered the slaveholders. White slave mistresses, for their part, could be extremely cruel to black slave women, but they confined their attacks to the privacy of their plantation parlors and appealed to their men for more public abuses. More than a century later, it is still possible to glimpse these differences between races. The differences are apparent in how subcultures of women express themselves in adolescence. On the street outside Public School 119 in New York's Spanish Harlem, a visitor saw two high school girls one day slamming each other with words. "Who you tellin'? Who you tellin'? You gonna beat me up with your umbrella?" one girl shouts. "Ain't nobody gonna do shit to me." For a moment it looks as if the confrontation will escalate, as if one of the girls will produce her "boxcutter," a razor-sharp knife that's the preferred weapon of New York City girls at this moment, good for slashing wincing cuts into one another's cheeks. But there's a storm moving in on this cold November day, wind gusts whipping up the litter on the street, deterring the girls from hanging outside. They gesture their mutual contempt and move off into a sideways slicing rain.

Down in the basement of the school, in an office filled with industrial-size cans of peanut butter, beans, corn, and macaroni for an upcoming food drive, a lanky, well-muscled, middle-aged guidance counselor holds forth on his twenty-three years of trying to prevent students from fighting. "In this community," Cedric Southerland says, "girls and boys are almost interchangeable. We have girls in this school who would wipe the floor with boys their age. They don't think twice about it. Sometimes you can't tell the aggressor from the aggressee. I had a girl last year, she looked like a little angel. She had already slit a girl's face open. I had three girls in here the other day, one of them had her eye blacked and her hair extensions pulled out.

"Yesterday," Cedric says, "I had a girl in. She has this brother, she loves him, but he's a pain in the butt. She tells her parents but they don't do anything. So she stabs him in the hand with some scissors. So she's having a problem with being heard, getting people to believe her." Not for this girl the muzzled, feminine silence we hear so much about in the literature on adolescent females. To reach his kids, Cedric posts a sign in his office that reads: "Tough times don't last. Tough people do." Black girls in his community consider themselves to be tough; there's no feminine currency in being frail, because, in large part, black women hold the community together. They can't look to men for protection: the men aren't around.

"I was never involved in a gang," says Toni Cato, reflecting on the fights between girls in her own high school. "I had been approached a couple of times because I had a reputation for being mean. [But] I didn't associate with too many females because they kept up too much confusion, and if I had wanted, I could have caused enough havoc by myself." Instead, she concentrated, successfully, on staying on the honor role.

"Girls are much quicker to fight than boys at this age," says Southerland. "They'll hit you in a minute. But if you take that to another level, to the street, then it changes. It's the boys that shoot you down." He pulls open a desk drawer and brings out a box filled with freshly sharpened pencils. Tucked in among them is a delicate gold watch, which one of his students stole from someone on Lexington Avenue. "The boys here are little hoodlums in training. Now it's watches, later it's gonna be cars, and then they're gonna need a pistol." As Southerland sees it, the opportunistic aggression of girls will not become their *vocation*; it isn't on-the-job training the way it is for boys. White or black, almost universally in North America this century, girls' aggression has gone underground as they mature, retreating into indirection—or into the private, less remarked-upon realm of the home.

According to data collected on all homicides in the city of Chicago from 1966 to 1996 (there are no comparable data for Detroit), the Chicago citizen at greatest risk of being killed by an intimate partner is the African-American man, at almost double the rate of African-American women and five times the rate of white women. Eighteen percent of black men killed in Chicago in those years died at the hands of their mates. These men, husbands or lovers, were most at risk when the woman was in her teens or twenties. The risk of being killed by a female partner in any racial group peaks when the woman is in her twenties and then declines sharply.

Whether the men provoked their killers or not, assaulted them or not, seems to be highly variable. Sixty-five percent of the men killed by women in Chicago had no recorded history of violence, domestic or otherwise. Does that mean that police simply didn't know about their vile behavior, or that they, like Anthony Riggs, genuinely cared for their mates? Probably both. In eighty-six cases, the woman killed her partner when he tried to leave her; in sixty cases, she killed a man who had left; in eight, the victim was her female lover; and in twenty-four, she used an accomplice or a hit man, removing herself from the scene of the crime. Indiana criminologist Coramae Richey Mann looked at female homicide offenders from six major U.S. cities, including Detroit, and found that 30 percent of the women who killed men had previous arrest records for assault, battery, and weapons charges, and another 38 percent had between one and thirty previous misdemeanor arrests. Alcohol was the most common combustive fuel, leading Mann to suggest as a "conceivable interpretation . . . that both parties were drinking, a domestic fight ensued, and the female homicide offender won."

This is difficult to accept. It sounds wrong. It goes down sour. But it is our frame of reference, our habit of viewing women as put upon, done to, afflicted, that makes us so resistant. The field of criminology has taken, for its reference point, the political agenda of Second Wave feminism, in which the systemic powerlessness of women is the transcendent theme, subsuming within it the intensity and passion of individual females, never allowing that one woman can be more powerful and harming than one man. Women kill only in fear, for survival, to take a last stand. Violence by women, as two criminologists wrote in 1995, is simply "a resource for self-protection." The two criminologists based their conclusion on a review of fifty homicide cases. Eighteen of those cases, or less than half, actually supported their contention. What do they do with the other thirty-two cases in which the victims were children, other women, and patently innocent men? Take them as evidence that violence is human, not gendered? Examine them as a means to further our understanding of what women do, and what is unique to women, and what is shared with men? Or do they put the thirty-two cases aside and never address them, and fall into silence like the pundits in Detroit?

On Thanksgiving Day in 1994, a week or so after Toni Cato was arrested, the Associated Press ran the following stories:

In Peoria, Illinois, thirty-seven-year-old Francine Knox was charged with manslaughter for electrocuting her seven-moth-old nephew with a stun gun.

In Largo, Florida, Christina Rubio was sentenced to thirteen years in prison for poisoning her thirteen-month-old son. She was already on probation for the attempted murder of her three-year-old daughter.

In West Palm Beach, Florida, Naomi Morrison pleaded guilty to aggravated battery, robbery, and auto burglary. In an attempt to steal her victim's wallet and car, Morrison bit the ninety-year-old man in three places, once to the bone, and transmitted the AIDS virus, for which she'd tested positive in 1988.

In Avella, Pennsylvania, a nineteen-year-old college student home for the holidays set her house on fire, killing her father and seriously injuring her mother. Melanie Vicheck was charged with murder and arson.

In New Orleans, twenty-three-year-old Consuella Monique Gaines-Thomas sprung her boyfriend from custody by threatening his guards with a shotgun on the courthouse steps, then carjacked a Cadillac from two elderly women and drove with her boyfriend to the Georgia coast.

In Baltimore, Renee Aulton, twenty-six, was charged with arson and murder in the deaths of her children, Christina, four, and Natalie, two. She had flicked a burning cigarette inside the bedroom closet of her home, left her two girls inside, and gone down to the street to watch the flames consume them.

That same week, in November 1994, three South Florida women carjacked a Toyota on I-95 and assaulted its driver with knives. A young woman in Edmonton, Alberta, was declared a dangerous offender after multiple knife assaults on prostitutes. In Virginia, a beauty queen named Traci Lippard broke into the home of her rival and attacked the girl's father with a hammer.

These, of course, were the headline grabbers, revealing little about the other eighty-seven thousand women arrested for violent crimes in 1994, who were also up to something complicated, idiosyncratic, and human. Some of the violence was conventional and domestic, some of it more public, more recognizably "male." The picture of female violence is a rich and textured tableau that we present to ourselves as monchromatic and stilted. To some, the subject of women's aggression is too threatening. To others, the subject is too trivial, destined only for the True Crime shelves. To others, most notably the academics who define the terms and interpret the data, it's too alarmingly "anti-feminist" to even suggest. Yet, we must suggest it.

Violent crime rates by women have risen at the end of this century. Arrests for aggravated assault climbed from sixteen women per 100,000 in 1960 to fifty by 1992; arrests for robbery quadrupled; the homicide rate increased by a third. Female violent-crime arrests overall grew at more than twice the pace of men's. The cultural shape of aggression, moreover, is rapidly becoming apparent in the shift in behavior for young women, of a new generation, who are the fastest-growing group of violent offenders on the continent. Between 1960 and 1990, the aggravated assault and robbery arrests for girls increased tenfold, more than twice the increase for boys, and both rates soared relative to the actual population. Girls' felony arrest rates jumped 124 percent from 1986 to 1995. In Canada, young women now account for 24 percent of all violent offenses in their age group; in the United States, it is 18 percent. At the same time, suicide rates by teenaged girls have dropped—by 50 percent since 1970.

Clearly, it's high time we provided shade and nuance to the picture. Not only because it makes no sense to talk of all these women as innocent or to pretend that family violence is not, somehow, the responsibility of fully half of its perpetrators. But because if we concede that women are ambitious, like men, and possess a will to power as men do, then we need to concede that women, like men, are capable of injuring others who thwart them. We cannot insist on the strength and competence of women in all the traditional masculine arenas yet continue to exonerate ourselves from the consequences of power by arguing that, where the course of it runs more darkly, we are actually power*less*. This has become an awkward paradox in feminist argument. How do we argue that we can be aggressive on every front—the Persian Gulf, the urban police beat, the empires of business, sports, hunting, politics, debate—but never in a manner that does harm? How do we affirm ourselves to be as complex, desirous, and independent as men without conceding the antisocial potential in those qualities? And what does Toni Cato become if we insist that women are nonviolent players? She becomes Jezebel thrown to the dogs, to be labeled as people see fit and know how, as an unimportant, two-timing whore. Anthony Riggs was emblematic, first of "any soldier," valiant and brave, then of any African-American man, struggling to regain dignity and a rightful place. His wife is a nonwoman, irrelevant, a slut.

MAYBE YOU MISTOOK ME FOR AN ANGEL

Perceptions of Female Violence
& the Vocabulary of Motive

> Messire, I am but a poor village girl. I cannot ride on horseback nor lead men to violence.
>
> JOAN OF ARC, fifteenth century

> If I need to understand what I am doing, if I cannot act without my own approbation ... then I will invent a morality that condones me. Though by doing so, I risk condemning all that I have been.
>
> MARGARET DRABBLE, *THE WATERFALL*, 1969

Sometimes, the truths that we hold to be fixed in our culture develop a fissure, which widens into a crack, and as we watch, the mirror shatters shard by shard, until nothing is left but fragments of prejudice lying in disarray at our feet. This happened to a family, a community, and a nation when a young woman named Karla Homolka walked out of her marital home in Saint Catharines, Ontario, in the bitter midwinter of 1993, her eyes black and her legs bruised, and went home with her upset parents and, at their urging, called the police.

Saint Catharines is not like Detroit. It is a small, bland, conservative city with a tidy downtown. There are few guns. The crime rate is low. Nothing in the landscape resembles a "combat zone." The only war that rages in Saint Catharines is the one that happens everywhere, the one that leapt to mind when the police fielded Karla Homolka's call and made their way to the pretty suburb where she'd lived along Lake Ontario's frozen shore. Another victim of domestic violence. Two cops shook their heads as they slowed their cruiser on a silent, snow-banked street. They knocked on the door of a pink,

Cape Cod–style home, stamping their feet in the cold, and after a moment Paul Bernardo, twenty-eight, preppy-handsome in a collegiate sweater, his hair, like his wife's, dyed Florida blond, ushered them in politely.

Paul Bernardo was a courteous young man, the son of a prominent Ontario family. Above him on his living room wall was a photograph of his wedding: he and Karla on June 29, 1992, radiant, the groom in an expensive tuxedo, the gorgeous bride in white, both of them well-fed and cared-for and smiling.

Now, the picture-perfect wife had an awfully ugly tear. "You're under arrest for assault with a weapon," the officers told Paul. "A flashlight," she'd explained. Paul went along to the station, calm, as if running an errand. He paid his bail, he went back home. The next afternoon, he changed his locks.

Valentine's Day came and went, and no word passed between the couple; their affair was over as fast as it had begun. They'd met in a hotel restaurant when she was seventeen, he, twenty-two, and within hours made love, exhilarated, in full view of the two friends who would become best man and maid of honor at their wedding. He was a young business student, she'd taken a year off from high school to work. They were both headstrong and sexy, intelligent, hungry to take on the world. For the next three years, Paul courted Karla long-distance from Toronto, while she lived at home with her family and aced her way through school. Then they married, throwing an extravagant bash, and settled in Saint Catharines in a house they could barely afford. Appearances, appearances. Look smart, dress sharp, party hard.

Karla Homolka's mother, Dorothy, could not fathom what had happened when she pulled her battered daughter out. She'd seen Karla every week of her marriage; the couple was always over, swimming in their pool, arranging games and parties, hosting barbecues. Karla had a comic genius—she did imitations, her best being Edith Bunker from "All in the Family." Paul was witty and high-spirited. The Homolkas had never seen Karla despondent or injured, and then she'd been *horribly* assaulted. Dorothy Homolka saw her daughter's face that day and "almost had a heart attack."

And that was it. It was over. Except that the story had not yet begun.

On February 16, two officers from the metro Toronto sexual vice squad called Karla Homolka at her aunt and uncle's condo in Brampton, a Westchester-style bedroom community north of Toronto, where she'd gone to escape Paul. Not that he'd pursued her. But, her family had reasoned, abusive men stalk. Karla was safe in Brampton. She was even having fun there—rebounding swiftly from her trauma. Shopping, out to parties, having a fling with a fellow she met in a nightclub.

The vice squad officers had some news. DNA results had come in from the Centre for Forensic Sciences in downtown Toronto. Paul Bernardo appeared to match the genetic fingerprint left behind on the victims of the Scarborough Rapist. This had to be astonishing news. Everyone in Ontario knew the specter of that rapist. A composite sketch of his face rode on buses and subways throughout the 1980s. Like Seattle's Green River killer, he struck repeatedly in the same suburb of metro Toronto, eluding detection for years. Nineteen women raped at knifepoint, many wounded, some mutilated. Wraith-like, he had haunted the streets where Paul had been living, before he moved to Saint Catharines to marry Karla.

In the days that followed this stunning revelation, the Ontario press would report that twenty-one-year-old Karla Homolka, a battered wife, was assisting the police by searching her memory in quest of clues to her husband's nocturnal movements. She couldn't know much, could she, because during the time the rapist struck she was living at home with her parents in Saint Catharines. Nevertheless, media columnists debated the matter of compelled spousal testimony: Was it legal? Would she be able to provide evidence if it was? "Wife a Victim, Too," ran the *Toronto Star* headline on February 22, five days after Paul's arrest. "You know who I really feel sorry for?" a Saint Catharines woman told the *Star*. "It's Karla." Imagine being married to a rapist. "She's a victim," agreed her boss, David Wade, a veterinarian for whom Karla was a full-time assistant. "She can come back to the clinic any time." At Dorothy Homolka's workplace, administrators brought in a battered-woman's expert to help employees understand what their colleague and her daughter went through.

In fact, Karla was refusing to cooperate with the police. She'd retained a lawyer. She had reason to believe that investigators were making a connection between the Scarborough rapes and another set of crimes. In 1991 and 1992, the abduction and demise of two high school girls had gripped the towns and small cities of southern Ontario. The girls were loved and deeply mourned. There was speculation that a serial killer was loose. Citizens told reporters how frightened they felt. Acting on a tip, one of thousands they were sifting through, two Niagara region police officers had interviewed Paul Bernardo in May of 1992. But Bernardo hadn't struck them as a likely suspect. If everyone in Detroit assumed that a black man had murdered Specialist Riggs, nobody thought an affable, well-mannered, married accountant sitting comfortably on his sleek white couch in a fancy Saint Catharines neighborhood could even write bad checks. The investigators looked around, lost interest, and left.

Now, however, assumptions had radically shifted.

If Bernardo was capable of wife assault and serial rape, he was probably capable of murder. Knowing that investigators would question her about it, Homolka confided to her aunt that she was "in serious trouble." Her aunt passed this information on to the police, and they recognized it triumphantly as the break they had been waiting for. They finally seemed to have a witness to a pair of unsolvable slayings. The sadistic bastard's wife could link him to the crimes. It was wonderful news. In short order, the Niagara region crown attorney signaled Homolka's lawyer that they wanted to offer a deal. Whatever her story was—for she'd not said a word—they'd ensure she receive gentle treatment if she agreed to testify against her husband. "We're not here to get you, we need you to get him," a Niagara region investigator told Homolka as the attorneys negotiated. "You're innocent. You're the victim."

What could they, or anybody else, otherwise believe? Within our culture, we are not taught to view well-mannered, pretty young women as possible criminals. Certainly, we are unable to see a woman who has been battered, if only once by her husband, as having ever been his equal in harming someone else. We may not hesitate to arrest a fourteen-year-old male gang member from Detroit, even if he's been beaten, cut up, shot at by others. We'll even arrest a ten-year-old boy who's worked in tandem with another child, as in the infamous British murder of the toddler James Bulger in 1993. But a woman who has been hit, a good woman, good-looking, white, middle class, cannot possibly be culpable in her own right. Police officers have been found to identify female offenders "with their mothers, sisters, or daughters," according to one law enforcement study, and to feel "reluctant" to arrest them. Women of all races are the least likely offenders to be processed beyond the arrest stage.

"Women will try to use their femininity," says retired Los Angeles Police Department robbery-homicide detective Leroy Orozco. " 'Look at me, I'm so small.' Yeah, but you got a big gun. A woman will try to use that on you." Of course they will, because it works. Not until her lawyer had clinched Homolka's deal, a ten-year sentence for manslaughter, with parole after six, did anyone even arrest her. From mid-February until May 18, 1993, Karla Homolka was free to play the public role of Paul Bernardo's wounded wife, mystified and saddened. The police did not even tell the media that she was a suspect in the crimes.

Once in custody, Homolka mistakenly believed that the police had found the videotapes she and Paul had made of their crimes. Although, at first, she'd removed herself entirely from the killings, saying that he'd only told her about them, then conceded she'd been a witness to them, she now decided to confess to far more than her interrogators expected. Why not, after all? She had secured immunity from all further charges as part of her deal. In a series of interviews during the summer of 1993, Homolka told a horrifying tale.

Her account began with December 1990, because that's where she had to begin, to explain the videotapes. On Christmas Eve, Karla Homolka's sister, Tammy Lynn, fifteen years old, had been in the basement of the Homolka family rec room in the company of Paul and Karla, watching a video. She drank too much champagne, passed out, and choked on her vomit. That had been Paul and Karla's official story, long accepted by the family. But now, Homolka revealed a different scenario. Confirmed upon exhumation of the corpse: Homolka had offered her sister to her sweetheart, drugged. Having learned from David Wade how to administer animal anesthetic, she had used her skill to douse her sister with toxic amounts of Halothane and the sedative Halcion, after which she and Paul had raped her.

Karla Homolka explained that she'd been a battered woman. She didn't intend for her sister to die, she said, but she had to rape her. She was under Paul's control: abused by him, threatened, coerced. When everything went wrong, disastrously and tragically, and Tammy Lynn Homolka was buried in the ground, Karla found herself trapped. Paul had a secret with which he could blackmail her. She had to move in with her monster. She had to marry him. She had to help him abduct, rape, and murder.

The rest of the story unfolded like this.

Mid-June 1991, Karla was frantic with last-minute details for her wedding. She and Paul would be the figures atop their white cake. A morning suit, a southern belle gown, pheasant for dinner, and a horse-drawn carriage to whisk them away. Lying awake at night, going over details: What's done? What's left? Did I make the right decision about shoes?

Countdown to the wedding. Relatives shop for gifts. Karla and Paul say, "Money! We just want money!" They throw a Stag and Doe party and get loaded down with yuppie goods, with patio furniture and a barbecue and bottles of Scotch and peach schnapps.

In the nearby town of Burlington, volunteers comb fields and streams for a sign of Leslie Mahaffy, last seen late at night outside her house. Unable to get in, she'd walked to the 7-Eleven and phoned her best friend, looking for a place to crash so she wouldn't have to wake up her parents and admit she'd missed her curfew. Then she had vanished.

June 29, the day breaks fine, the wish of every bride. Karla slips on the taffeta dress she bought across the border in Buffalo after obsessing for months in her wedding planner about where to buy the perfect gown. She teases her hair. She bosses her bridesmaids around.

Michael Doucette, out fishing with his little boy a few miles from the wedding ceremony, wades past a cracked cement block and finds within it a severed thigh.

Leslie Mahaffy had braces and a brand-new boyfriend, she was funky and smart and a bit rebellious, but she had no idea how normal, how just like her, a predator could look. Paul chatted her up, she asked him for a cigarette, he kidnapped her off her front lawn. She lived in the pink Cape Cod house for twenty-four hours, raped repeatedly by both Paul and Karla. The jury at Paul's trial would view the scene on the video that surfaced after Homolka made her deal. Spectators in the courtroom heard the audio portion: a radio in the white carpeted master bedroom plays "I Am Superman" by R.E.M. above the murmurs of a man and a woman and the rise and fall of a girl's voice, wailing.

Late the second night, Leslie Mahaffy was killed. The next day, Karla entertained her parents for lunch.

Kristen French, abducted in daylight outside her high school the following April, was kept alive for Easter weekend. She was dark-haired, sixteen years old, beautiful, and frank, her face, in the newspaper photos, filled with intelligence—everyone in Ontario followed her vanishing and hoped she'd come out alive. Witnesses had seen "two men" pull her into a cream-colored car. Reporters gave up-to-the-minute news. There was no break in the case for fourteen days. Then French was found in a ditch near Leslie Mahaffy's grave. She was naked, curled up as if asleep. Her long hair had been shorn, her body bleached of hair, to erase all trace of fibers. There were ligature marks on her neck. She seemed to have been strangled.

She *was* strangled, Homolka now said. Paul did it, at her urging, because she had to go to her parents' home for Easter dinner. They could no longer have this captive in their house. Questions abounded in shocked minds. Why had witnesses seen "two men" abduct Kristen French? They must have filled in the picture the way they imagined it had to be. It was Homolka undisguised—deliberately, unthreateningly female—who'd called French over to the car. If the investigators were thrown by the idea that all this time, for over a year, they'd been chasing down every lead that involved two men, they were not about to leap to the other end of the spectrum of possibility and see this as two people, male and female, equal partners in a crime. What Karla Homolka was telling them could translate into only one language: that of the present day, the ideology of masculine dominance and feminine submission. If she was involved in these horror stories, it could only have been because she—fair-haired, beautiful, and black-eyed—had no choice.

"For women, violence is a necessary resource for self-protection."

"In this country, women murder mainly as a means of survival."

"The majority of women are in prison because men abuse them."

"You're innocent. You're the victim."

In the months leading up to her plea-bargain hearing, before anyone yet knew the facts, Homolka repeated to friends the investigator's comment to her that she was the victim. "Clearly," wrote Toronto journalists Scott Burnside and Alan Cairns, "those words had become a kind of mantra." Convince the world, convince yourself.

How people come to account for themselves in the aftermath of violent behavior has been called the vocabulary of motive. This vocabulary—a set of phrases or rationales—has less to do with personal truth than with commonly held beliefs. "There exist accounts for behavior which are popularly acceptable as excuses," notes criminologist Allison Morris. People tend to explain what they do according to cultural scripts. A girl who hits her little brother might say to her parents that he hit her first, which is what her parents might expect of boys. Therefore, her motive was self-defense. On the island of Margarita, the same girl could acceptably say that she hit her brother to *parar el macho*. Her motive was to keep her brother in line. Within urban American street culture, a girl could say she hit her brother because he "dissed" her. Her motive was to defend her standing. Whatever the accessible cultural rationale is, we will borrow it to explain ourselves. We use the vocabulary when we know it's not the truth, and we use it when we don't know what the truth is.

Until the 1970s, it was acceptable in Texas for men to say they had killed their wives as retribution for adultery. Now, they cannot as easily use that explanation, even if jealousy was the motive. They must come up with something else, both legally and culturally. So they talk of brain injury or too much sugar or a childhood of abuse. Ted Bundy blamed his attacks on women in the late 1970s in the states of Washington, Utah, and Florida on pornography. More than a few antiporn activists leapt on this confession as gospel truth. In another era, Bundy might have said he was possessed by the devil. The behavior is so complex and unfathomable, even to him, that he grasped at the slim straws provided by popular rhetoric.

Now that it's been named, premenstrual syndrome is an easy explanation for why women get wild and angry. Is it the truth? Or is it just part of the vocabulary of motive? Two studies in England conducted in the mid-1980s found that women reported drastic mood swings related to menstruation only when they thought they were being asked about PMS; when they thought they were simply noting their moods over time, they described far more even tempers. The authors of one study concluded that "the self-reports of depression and aggression due to menstruation were influenced by social expectations."

Criminologist Robert J. Kelly interviewed several inmates at Rikers Island, a correctional facility in New York City, and observed that "in their own words, many inmates experience themselves as putty in the hands of fate." They blamed bad luck, coincidence, unforeseen circumstances—the victim shouldn't have been there, the cops shouldn't have shown up. The inmates could not explain what they did in terms of their own moral choices; they had to explain it in terms of forces beyond their control. It isn't just because criminals aim to get away with their crimes, it's also because they need to live with them. "A frank and sincere acknowledgment of responsibility would result in a collapse of the psyche," notes Kelly. Criminals are compelled to reconstruct events in such a way that the aftermath is bearable. They need to maintain a sense of self-worth. Announcing to themselves in the mirror "I am evil" is not a popular option.

Violent offenders often claim amnesia during crimes, telling the police something like "The next thing I remember, she was lying there on the floor." It is not that they actually black out. It is that they cannot permit themselves to recall what they did. The sociologist Jack Katz argues that this is particularly true of women: "They appear to have a distinct problem in self-consciously acknowledging the . . . rage that they were able to effect." Rage runs contrary to a sense of the feminine self. It surprises, shocks, and ultimately shames the offender. She denies what she has witnessed in herself.

Unlike men, however, women can more plausibly use this refusal to acknowledge what they did as the basis for an insanity defense. Lorena Bobbitt, for example, was able to claim that her inability to remember cutting her husband's penis off was, in itself, evidence of temporary insanity. She was acquitted. In Calgary, Alberta, in 1996, a wealthy, alcoholic divorcée named Dorothy Joudrie was acquitted for shooting and crippling her ex-husband in her garage because she claimed that she'd "dissociated."

Although self-justification is universally human, the vocabulary of motive is different for male and female offenders. Because we won't concede aggression and anger in women, the language we use to describe what they do is much more limited, and much more exonerative. There exist perhaps three or four rationales for the whole, extraordinary diversity of violent acts women commit, and they all play into preexisting prejudices about female nature. The operative assumption is that the violent woman couldn't have *wanted*, deliberately, to cause harm. Therefore, if she says she was abused/coerced/insane, she probably was.

Allison Morris cites the example of premenstrual syndrome. In 1980, Sandra Craddock pleaded not guilty to murdering a fellow cocktail waitress in London on the basis of PMS. Her plea was accepted. Christine English also successfully pleaded guilty to a reduced charge of manslaughter that year, for crushing a former lover against a telegraph pole with her car. Men simply cannot say in court, "I killed a guy because my testosterone levels were too high." He may be playing into the notion that men are governed by their hormones, but he is also working against the belief that men are willfully and rationally aggressive. Therefore his motive is not believable.

On the "Sally Jessy Raphael" show, October 25, 1995, the theme was "My Teen Is a Terror." The three thirteen-year-old girls who came on with their mothers sat cross-armed and sullen, smirking at the audience. One had threatened to kill her mother with a lead pipe and had beaten her little brother, in spite of his brain tumor; a second had sent a sixty-five-year-old babysitter to the hospital; a third had beaten her sister beyond recognition and told the show, "I like to kick ass." The audience responded to these various tales with laughter, derision, and scolding. By the end of the show, they had decided collectively that one girl was "forgiven," "sympathetic," and "understandable" because she burst into tears and plaintively blamed her behavior on a mother who "never disciplined me." The other girls were more stoic, unwilling or unable to express their own hurts, more like boys. They availed themselves of no vocabulary and so were heaped with scorn.

If prejudice about female nature is the gift of misogyny to women who want to get away with crime, it doesn't necessarily follow that women themselves believe in their guilt. The effect of cultural explanation for individual behavior tilts women toward an interpretation of themselves as fundamentally innocent. What they do (what we all do) is to equate powerlessness with innocence. In acts of violence, this is not only an expedient, but a necessary, means of self-justification.

Various guises of madness, coupled with abuse and coercion, are the most prominent rationales within the female vocabulary of motive. A fourth is the concept of failed suicide. A woman will claim that she meant to kill herself but somehow wound up taking someone else's life instead, a claim that arises from a woman's sense that it is more socially acceptable to self-destruct than to be outwardly destructive. Jean Harris and Betty Broderick, both white, upper-middle-class Americans who traveled considerable distances to enter without invitation the homes of their ex-mates and shoot them dead, claimed that they actually intended to kill themselves. In Broderick's case, she was ready to take her own life but suddenly "panicked" and fatally wounded her ex-husband, Daniel, and his new wife, Linda, while they slept in their bed. In Harris's case, the gun "went off accidentally" and doomed the disoriented, pajama-clad Herman Tarnower. The judge at her trial felt moved to apologize to the criminal before him. "It's unhappy that you have to be sentenced, Mrs. Harris," he said, as if it were all some unseemly mistake, "[but] the best of luck to you."

"Many women who kill their abusers start out intending to commit suicide," wrote one battered woman syndrome expert. But they don't. Men are far more apt to kill themselves in the aftermath of family violence. An extraordinarily high number of Chicago men turn guns and knives on themselves after killing their mates: more than 25 percent of white men, about 29 percent of Latino men (who otherwise have a low suicide rate), and 10 percent of black men. Less than 2 percent of women in all race categories do. What may be going on is that women more comfortably label their violent impulses as self-destructive. Suicide is a social script they can follow before they strike, to formulate intent, and after the deed, to provide a rationale.

A striking example of this is the Texas murder case of thirty-five-year old Yolanda Saldivar, who killed the rising Tejano music star Selena with a .38-caliber revolver. The crime took place outside a Corpus Christi, Texas, motel on March 31, 1995. Saldivar had been an avid fan of the Grammy Award–winning singer. She contacted Selena and offered to found a fan club for her, eventually becoming close to both Selena and the singer's extended family. For various reasons, Saldivar was on the verge of being fired by Selena and expelled from the tribe when Saldivar shot her beloved singer in the back. She then got into a tense, ten-hour standoff with police, holding the gun to her head and insisting that Selena's father, Abraham Quintanilla, had raped her and "made me shoot her." This, then, was the first motive that leapt to mind: the popular belief in male coercion. Trying to talk her down, the police offered Saldivar another explanation. "Maybe it was a mistake," negotiator Isaac Valencia told her, "maybe it was an accident." Once he had provided her with this idea and implied that it was acceptable, she adopted it, telling everyone thereafter that she actually meant to commit suicide, "I couldn't live no more," but the "gun went off" accidentally and hit Selena. At her trial, officers involved in the standoff testified that Saldivar was practiced with her revolver, having skillfully cocked it when they approached her pick-up truck, then uncocked it as they backed away. She was too competent to have killed by mistake. Her victim was a widely loved young woman. Saldivar was convicted of murder.

The failed suicide rationale was also raised by Susan Smith as an explanation for why she drowned her two sons in a lake in South Carolina. One of Smith's defense attorneys, Judy Clarke, promoted the claim at her trial: "Hopelessness is not malice. She went to the ramp to commit suicide and take her children [with her], but she failed." Indeed, she did. In *Newsweek* magazine's cover story on the case, reporters picked up on the rationale without examining it logically. "Some severely depressed parents kill their children in a bungled attempt to kill themselves," the story read. "Susan Smith told authorities that's what she had in mind when she drove to the lake. [But] unable to take her own life, she found herself rolling the car with her sons into the lake instead." Notice the implication of passivity in the phrase "found herself."

Newsweek then quoted Northeastern University criminologist James Allan Fox describing the act as "murder by proxy." Well, really it was murder by murder. But how, in any event, does the murder of children accomplish the objective of suicide? *Newsweek* doesn't explain. Perhaps the killing of the child ameliorates the need for suicide, in that the presence of the child is the problem in the first place. Describing what Smith did as "bungled" suicide simultaneously positions women as inept and self-effacing, both qualities that our culture can accommodate.

Newsweek also fit Susan Smith into "the sad subset of mothers who kill their kids in a vain attempt to win approval from their new man." The magazine quoted the sociologist Richard Gelles as saying: "Her identity comes from pleasing the men in her life. The boyfriend says, 'Jump!' and she says, 'How high?' " The magazine didn't offer any statistics on how many men make infanticide a prerequisite for dating, but it did illustrate how limited our vocabulary of motive is for women. We struggle to describe their aggression in tortuous terms, as if speaking a foreign language, not one rich with literature about violence, morality, and crime.

· · ·

Speaking of men in the world wars, the historian John Grey wrote: "It is a crucial moment in a soldier's life when he is ordered to perform a deed that he finds completely at variance with his own notions of right and good. Probably for the first time, he discovers that an act someone else thinks to be necessary is for him criminal. . . . Suddenly the soldier feels himself abandoned and cast off from all security. Conscience has isolated him, and its voice is a warning. If you do this, you will not be at peace with me in the future. You can do it, but you ought not. You must act as a man and not as an instrument of another's will."

In preparation for Bernardo's trial, attorneys for both crown and defense hired a number of forensic psychiatrists to examine Karla Homolka and confirm that she had acted "as a woman," as an instrument of Bernardo's will. The reports they received back were unexpected. Dr. Nathan Pollock described Homolka as an "immature, moody, shallow, rigid, hostile individual preoccupied with themes of violence and victimization." He disagreed with the characterization of her as a battered woman. The evidence, he wrote, "is not sufficient to conclude she was suffering from battered-woman syndrome, or that she was in such a confused and hopeless state of mind that she was unable to govern her own behaviour." Dr. Angus McDonald concurred: "Her presentation clearly suggests a degree of callousness and insensitivity of major proportion. . . . Her behaviour, to my mind, simply cannot be explained solely on the basis of intimidation or abuse from Paul Bernardo." According to a third psychiatrist, Dr. Alan Long, Homolka "views the world as a threatening place and sees herself as having been unjustly blamed for others' problems." Concluded Dr. McDonald, "Karla Homolka remains something of a diagnostic mystery. . . . There is a moral vacuity in her which is difficult, if not impossible, to explain."

Had she been male, the explanation might have been that she was a psychopath or in some other way criminally indifferent to the feelings of others. Intricate theory abounds for male offenders. But she was female. The only available explanation in the 1990s was that she had acted against her own, inherently nonviolent inclinations, either because she was insane or because she had been coerced. None of the psychiatrists were called into court. Their reports were never mentioned.

The weight of evidence cannot tip justice when the weight of prejudice is on the other scale. "If it happens we have to go against each other," Los Angeles murderess Carol Bundy wrote to her co-conspirator, Doug Clark, from jail in 1982, "remember, I look innocent. Impression is worth as much as facts." She announced at his trial: "Mr. Clark had virtual total control over my personality and behavior, my wants, my desires, my dreams."

When Homolka appeared on June 19, 1995, in Room 6-1, Ontario Court, General Division, to blame the sexual assault and slaughter of three young women on Paul Bernardo, her face was as blank as a doll's. She seemed eerily plastic, her hair shiny, her smooth skin artificially tanned, as if everything that made her human had been airbrushed away. Her language, too, had been carefully rinsed of the idioms and inflections that colored her early police statements. It was as if she had taken special note of a book she was reading in prison, *Perfect Victim*, which documents the case of a California teenager who was kidnapped and kept in a box for three years: " 'What made the victim convincing [in court]?' someone asked in the book. [The juror] replied: 'Her deadness. Her stillness.' "

Wherever Homolka was getting her ideas while she ticked away the days of her plea-bargained sentence—*The Battered Woman* by Lenore Walker was another favorite book—the erasure of her character in service to her innocence was well under way by the time she arrived in the courtroom. The young woman that we had been watching for a month of trial proceedings in home videos shot by Paul Bernardo—assertive, vivacious, demanding of the camera's attention, her makeup bright, her body bruiseless—did not exist. What we saw, we were told by crown attorney Ray Houlahan, was an illusion.

There she was on December 23, 1990, prancing about her parents' home, singing out raucously "Christmas is fun!" hours before she and Paul raped, sodomized, and killed her little sister. The video revealed a comfortable, high-spirited woman ordering her boyfriend around as he taped—"Paul! Over *here!*" But, said the crown,

Homolka had merely been "scripted" by Bernardo to perform. In letters and notes entered as evidence, her voice was exuberant, lustful, sarcastic, snobbish about people she worked with ("Secretaries have to be the most boring nowhere people ever"), jealous of her lover's time, angry when he got mad at her "for a fucking ridiculous reason," unmoved when he pouted—"Boo Fucking Hoo"—and often, very often, self-involved and vain.

But, said the crown, this voice was the product of a Svengali ventriloquism. It wasn't Karla's voice. Karla had no voice. Karla was a battered woman. Everything she said and did was at the bidding of her man. "Paul did it," she would say on the witness stand. "He made me do it." "He kept bugging me." "Just do it." We deduced here a plot as densely tragic as of Medea, reduced in its narration to a jingle.

To boost the crown's position that Homolka wasn't to blame (the murders themselves were the only events not recorded on video), Ray Houlahan had her thread complaints of her own mistreatment through an account of horrifying cruelty to her victims. Not only did they drag Kristen French off the street to make her their sex slave for three days and then slaughter her and dump her in a ditch, but Paul hit Karla on the *arm,* and she got a bruise! The documentation of bruises was a fool's arithmetic. How many punches does it take to rape your sister? Nine? Fifty? One thousand and two?

The crown didn't see how Homolka's testimony belittled the courage of the young women she killed, which had become so agonizingly evident in the videos, as French and Mahaffy struggled, fought, refused to perform certain acts. Nor did the crown see how their argument that any woman would have done what Homolka did demeaned the character of an entire sex.

How had we as a society—our attorneys, our cops, our psychiatrists, our politicians—come to this point, that we could find no other way to discuss or position a female offender?

A crucial development in the modern vocabulary of female violence came about in 1977, as a result of the Lansing, Michigan, case of Francine Hughes, a horribly battered woman profiled by Faith McNulty in her book *The Burning Bed* and portrayed by Farrah Fawcett in a TV movie of the same name. Hughes was arrested for setting fire to her ex-husband, James "Mickey" Hughes, after a day in which the police had been called yet again and had left Francine on her own yet again to cope with the increasingly lethal brutality he was raining upon her. Prosecutors saw it as an open-and-shut case. First-degree murder. No plea bargain. There was no understanding of how a woman might snap after years of unrelenting attack, which she had repeatedly tried to escape, only to be dragged back, unable in her poverty to go far enough away to evade an obsessed man, beyond rescue from the entire community, who watched from behind their curtains and refused to acknowledge the grave danger she was in.

From the prosecutor's point of view, all that mattered was that Francine had had time to think about where Mickey kept his gasoline, had found it, sprinkled it around his bed, and, after putting their four children in the car, had set a match to the fuel and fled. It was clearly premeditated murder. The fact that she'd driven straight to the police, in unconsolable upset and terror, was not seen as evidence that her crime was impulsive and reactive. The fact that the entire police force knew Mickey to be a "vicious bastard," as one put it, wasn't considered relevant. Struggling with the legal options, Francine Hughes's defense attorney could see only one way to go: He had to argue "temporary insanity." There was no other criminal category available to exonerate his client.

Advocates from around the country came to Michigan to protest on the courthouse steps that Francine Hughes deserved to be acquitted because of her "right to self-defense." They argued that the concept of "justifiable homicide" had to be broadened to include women who saw no other way to prevent themselves from being beaten. Francine did not have to be considered insane for rational people to agree that she had been trapped, and that she finally took the only action that guaranteed her future safety. What they were saying touched a chord in America's long tradition of vigilante justice: When the law is an ass, take it into your hands and, by your actions, change the law. Judy Sturm of Nebraska, whose murder case predated Francine Hughes's by three years, tried to push this point. At the age of twenty-six, Sturm shot her sleeping husband with her own hunting rifle after a brief marriage in which he persisted in being a sadistic menace. Said Sturm: "I just said to myself, it's not going to happen. I'm not going to be beaten. My kids aren't going to be beaten." She shot him dead, she went to trial, and she presented herself as sane. Her jury recommended probation. Years later, Sturm told an interviewer: "If the man were alive today, I'd probably kill him again."

Francine Hughes's attorney wasn't prepared to employ that argument. His passionate commitment to his client overrode the broader issues that her situation raised. He wanted to fit her into the law as it stood so that she could go free. After a mesmerizing eight-day trial, in which Hughes revealed immense reserves of fortitude, compassion, fair-mindedness, and integrity, she was acquitted of first-degree murder on a plea of temporary insanity.

The long-term result of the *Burning Bed* case, in the context of the vocabulary of motive, has been terribly problematic. We took the legal framework of temporary insanity, which was never meant to explain Hughes but rather to give the jury a way to acquit her, and turned it into a full-blown female propensity. And because, at this critical juncture, we opted to press the view that battered women were psychologically deranged, not situationally trapped, we ventured down a road toward the battered woman syndrome, a specifically female form of helplessness that is increasingly applicable to women in circumstances far removed from those of Francine Hughes.

The cornerstone of the battered woman syndrome is the concept of learned helplessness, which stems from experiments by animal behaviorists in which it has been found that if one repeatedly and arbitrarily shocks dogs, they become so demoralized that they lose the will to escape from their cages. Learned helplessness was first applied to battered women by Lenore Walker, who said, "Only men kill in anger." Women had to have some other reason, something more selfless, perhaps, or innocent, or fundamentally well-intentioned. Women also had to have a reason that would qualify as insanity in a court of law.

Walker has testified throughout the American court system that women, like dogs, are rendered helpless and passive by the randomness of their husbands' assaults, a condition reinforced by feminine conditioning to be submissive. This is why they don't leave their husbands, even if they have opportunities to do so: "Repeated batterings, like electrical shocks, diminish . . . motivation to respond."

By the time Homolka took the stand in 1995, the standard of what degree of brutality a woman must sustain before she succumbs to this "syndrome" had eroded to a point of insulting implausibility.

"When Tammy first died I felt numb," Karla testified. "Then, when Leslie was in the house I felt number. With Kristen I felt even number." If she was hoping to describe the condition of "psychic numbing," as it is called in her battered women books, she was, nevertheless, too preoccupied with deflecting responsibility from herself to keep it consistent. Asked why she could be heard confidently instructing Kristen to fellate Paul on one of their videotapes, she replied, "I didn't want her to be beaten." Sensitive to punches, but numb to abduction. Murdered, okay. But not beaten. She was borrowing from the battered woman syndrome and getting it almost, but not quite, straight.

If learned helplessness is a valid explanation of what happens to abused individuals (who ought to include children, male spouses, and elderly parents, by the way), it has never been clear why this is a homicide defense. Walker and other battered women syndrome experts don't address the contradiction in the formula as it applies to a violent response: If the woman/dog is too listless and disoriented to escape, she will also be too apathetic to attack. A woman cannot simultaneously be stupefied and lethal. According to the scholars who originally identified learned helplessness, domestic violence is not an appropriate example of the condition. From their point of view, the classic case is of elderly patients in a nursing home who are completely deprived of control over their lives, to the point of being unable to water their own plants or go to the bathroom alone. They lose all power of self-determination and, ultimately, become so despondent and demoralized that they pass away. As the law professor Gerald Caplan has written, "[This] reasoning doesn't explain how women who are that helpless manage to stab their husbands repeatedly in the chest."

Karla Homolka, for one, engaged actively and spiritedly in her full-time job, arranged an extravagant wedding for herself, traveled, socialized regularly, raised a Rottweiler dog, moved into and furnished a house, all the while too helpless in one realm only: to make the moral choice not to drug, rape, and kill. Her self-exonerating testimony grew so distressing and offensive over the course of the summer that Paul Bernardo's defense attorney, John Rosen, looked like a folk hero when he jumped up on July 5, 1995, to cross-examine her. He was the first person to put truly probing questions to Homolka since she'd left her marital home, and the effect was strangely exhilarating.

When Homolka testified about her sister's rape, "I didn't believe that her life or physical safety would be in jeopardy," Rosen asked, "Do you still not understand, Ms. Homolka, that her integrity as a *woman* was in jeopardy? That your boyfriend was planning to *rape* her in your parents' home?"

Of course she did, she said, abandoning all pretense of blankness and becoming combative and pedantic, but what could she do? She loved Paul. "A lot of women go through this," she instructed Rosen coldly. "It is not that unusual to be abused and still be in love with the man."

Rosen said, "Ms. Homolka, let's just get this straight. You were in Saint Catharines, you had your parents, you had your sisters . . . you had your friends. You had your co-workers. You had a doctor you could confide in. And the person who's supposedly abusing you is in *Scarborough*, an hour and a half away!"

Homolka glared at him. "You don't have to be physically isolated to be emotionally isolated," she retorted, as if he were a dunce.

Rosen produced a letter she had written in 1991, lecturing a friend to get a restraining order against a violent lover, telling the friend that the situation was "ridiculous." He flung her own words in her face.

The law professor Charles Ewing recently studied one hundred battered women who killed their mates and compared them to one hundred battered women who left them. The difference, he found, was that the women who killed were more situationally trapped. It had nothing to do with their psyches. It had to do with the fact that, every time they tried to get away from their husbands, the man came after them with a closed fist or a shotgun. As the social psychologist Julie Blackman told *Time* magazine, "They don't have personality disorders. They're just beat up worse."

An analogy might be drawn to the fate that befalls men in war. In the First and Second World Wars, men in combat shit their pants with fear. They vomited and cried like babies, because, as one wrote, "Loud and violent death is screaming down from the sky and pounding the earth around you, smashing and pulping everything in the search for you." Men went into the world wars without hope of getting out—they died, went mad, or the war got won. In large part, the atrocities of war are committed as a response to the fear men feel. Terror and humiliation are the combustible fuels of rage. They are striking out blindly against their own predicament. Passivity, if it comes, sinks in later, after the violence is spent. Common wisdom as to when a soldier would fall victim to "shell shock" was two hundred days of uninterrupted horror on the front lines. "Inevitably," wrote one military historian, "all will break down if in combat long enough." And broken down, they'll cease to fight.

"I don't expect anybody to understand," Judy Sturm told a journalist in 1995, about how she had reacted to marital terror, "because you can't imagine, no more than I can imagine being in Vietnam or Saudi Arabia and what the veterans went through." Sturm's daughter had served as an army corporal in the Gulf War, and her comparison is apt. Based on the experience of soldiers and Francine Hughes and Judy Sturm, Lenore Walker's formula is simply too pat. Learned helplessness is not the percursor to violence. It describes, if anything, the shattered spirit in the aftermath, when a woman has fought and failed, and falls, once and for all, to despair.

Judy Sturm cofounded the Nebraska Domestic Violence Sexual Assault Coalition in 1976 and went to work helping other women get out of abusive marriages. "I don't want to seem like I'm endorsing open season on men," she said. "There's less reason to kill them today—there are shelters and support. I didn't have any of that." Sturm was once at the forefront of arguing that women were perfectly capable of defending themselves against male violence, but advocates of psychological derangement ran roughshod over her position. The battered woman syndrome has entered the vocabulary of motive. Cut adrift from the circumstances that gave rise to Sturm's and Hughes's violence, the syndrome is now an entity unto itself, free-floating through criminology research and courtrooms, providing the answer for why a woman, any woman, would commit an act of violence.

One day at the Bernardo trial, the crown brought in an expert witness to state that up to "eighty percent" of women in prison were there because men had abused them. This is a widely held sentiment among feminist criminologists and battered women's advocates. Lenore Walker is more conservative, insofar as she asserts that one half of women in prison committed their offenses—check forgery to pay bills, theft for food denied to them by their husbands—to avoid further battering. Statistically, this picture of women as humble creatures sneaking timidly off to snatch a loaf of bread for their children before the next beating is a bit off target. A survey of California's female prisoners in 1993 found that only 3.1 percent had become criminal "to escape abuse." Another 5.4 percent broke the law "to protect self or children." A sample of 1,880 adult female offenders across the United States found that less than half reported being physically assaulted by a mate in their lifetimes. Fourteen percent had been assaulted one to two times, another 40 percent three to ten times. What that violence had to do with their crimes—heroin dealing, armed robbery, infanticide, prostitution, embezzlement, the whole gamut—wasn't determined. Of 90 percent of the women incarcerated in Florida during August 1985, one quarter stated that they'd been assaulted in violent relationships at some point, with the question of degree and mutuality again unclear. No correlation was made to their crimes.

Like men, most women who commit crimes have no stake in correcting our impression of their innocence, and possess, at any rate, no explanatory language for their actions beyond the vocabulary of motive. It's up to us to disentangle the variables, to see which women are truly violent in self-defense, which ones are genuinely insane, which ones turned criminal because they were, indeed, coerced.

Our ability to interpret what is really going on is confounded, however, by the advent, in feminist scholarship, of "standpoint epistemology." This research framework holds that history must be told
from the standpoint of the woman/victim. Her explanation for what
she does is the true one, because, being oppressed, she possesses "a
more complete view of social reality" than her oppressors, which is to
say, men. We cannot impose an explanation upon her, and we must
listen to her account with respect for "the centrality of consciousness
raising." It is a principle similar to the one that's at work in therapy
circles, where a woman's recovered memory of ritual abuse, for
example, is held by the therapist to be more important than the
actual evidence.

Standpoint epistemology is laudable in certain types of research,
but it tends to collide with the criminal mind in a manner akin to
Bambi meeting Godzilla. A seasoned armed robber who is asked by
earnest interviewers whether she's ever been abused will call to mind
a time when she was. Why shouldn't she? She's being invited to air a
grievance. The assault may have been a defining moment in her life
or an incidental experience, for she has moved through a rough and
hostile world. In either event, it is not the de facto cause of her
crime. Overlooking factors like personality, temperament, moral
judgment, drug addiction, poverty, and cultural milieu as if their
importance were fleeting, the researcher prompts the criminal to
spin the simplest possible tale of her woe. Inmate Veronica Compton, in a guest editorial in *Prison Life* magazine, echoed the typical
view that "violence on the part of women is usually in response to
abuse." Compton didn't mention to her readers that she was serving
time for strangling an innocent cocktail waitress in Los Angeles in
1978. To illustrate the point that women are treated more harshly
than men in prison, she complained that she'd done most of her
time "either in maximum security or the hole"; but she skipped the
fact that she escaped from prison early in her sentence and was a
high-security risk.

In her six-city study, Coramae Richey Mann found that 80 percent
of her sample of women who'd killed claimed they were "not responsible," whether their victims were men, other women, or children. In

cases of self-defense, the provocation often turned out to be verbal—
a taunt or an insult, not a lethal physical attack. In some cases,
the provocation was sexual rivalry. One woman who claimed self-
defense, for instance, was a twenty-eight-year-old Latina humiliated
by the love affair between her younger sister and her husband. When
her sister gave birth to his baby, she went to her sister's apartment
intent on killing them both. The sisters fought, the eldest whipped
out a handgun and fired three shots, killing her betraying sibling.
Then she grabbed her infant niece, stormed over to her husband's
workplace, announced what she'd done, and threatened to kill him,
too. Her husband was able to wrench free the gun. "With no prior
record, she received 10 years' probation." And landed in the data as
an abused woman who'd killed in self-defense.

Once again, the point here is not to suggest that women never act
in self-defense—of course they do. The point is that criminologists
contemplate no other factors. Whereas they once described violent
women as lesbian man-eaters and perverts, we have simply sailed to
the other extreme, from whore to madonna. The old fabric of
misogyny blends seamlessly with new threads of feminist essentialism
to preserve the myth that women are more susceptible than men to
being helpless, crazy, and biddable. The effect, in the case of Karla
Homolka, was startlingly clear in the courtroom. Encouraged to
attribute every move, every want, every look on her fiercely intelligent
face to the machinations of Paul Bernardo, Homolka renounced her
claim to be an adult. She infantilized herself, relinquishing spirit, will,
passion, pride, resourcefulness, and rage. Her wheat-blond hair fell
across her wan face like a curtain as she sat on the stand for three
weeks, and she divested herself of a soul.

The danger posed to female characterological integrity in the
spreading use of abuse rationales has been widely articulated. The
moral logic of these exculpatory defenses concerned feminists of
the nineteenth century. One 1844 manifesto argued, "[Man] has
made [woman], morally, an irresponsible being, as she can commit
many crimes with impunity, provided they be done in the presence
of her husband." Why haven't we made any progress with this view?

. . .

In the past decade, as women began to stream into North American prisons in record numbers, our society, in a coincidence of timing, cottoned on to child abuse as a factor in criminal behavior. It has quickly become the newest rationale for female violence—another point of entry for our understanding and forgiveness. The *Sourcebook of Criminal Justice Statistics*, ostensibly the most objective data about annual American crime rates, now contain a table that cites the percentage of incarcerated women who were abused as children. There is no comparable table for incarcerated men, even though the influence of child abuse on subsequent violent behavior is well documented for both sexes, and more boys suffer physical abuse in childhood than girls. What is implied by the inclusion of one sex and not the other in the table? That a woman who was beaten in grade school might understandably grow up to mug an old man, but a boy who was similarly treated has no such excuse for his crime? As with coercion and self-defense, we clearly seek a preemptive cause for female transgressions that preserves an emphasis on victimization. It is not the effect of abuse on future criminality that truly concerns us. It is the desire to avoid seeing women as wilfull aggressors.

In 1991, criminologist Kathleen Daly studied the presentence investigations reports prepared by probation officers for criminals in New Haven, Connecticut. From the social and family histories garnered in these reports, she found that a larger proportion of women (one third, versus about one tenth of men) was characterized as having been physically or sexually abused as children. Daly wondered if, perhaps, fewer men had been *asked* by the probation officers if they were abused. Sure enough, when she put this question to the probation officers, "some said they were more inclined to probe the women's family histories." Embedded in the facts were presuppositions about women and men, rendering it impossible for even a fair-minded researcher like Daly to draw conclusions about how the sexes might differ in commiting their crimes. In Washington State, therapists who receive board certification to counsel sex offenders are taught that the offender's admission that he was molested or abused as a child is to be dismissed as "rationalization." Ditto in countless other jurisdictions for wife assault. We may leap to insist that women only commit violence because of their own abuse, but we rush in the opposite direction for men.

The distinction we draw between men and women is stunningly evident in popular culture. In 1994, Lifetime Television aired a movie called *Overkill: The Aileen Wuornos Story*, a docudrama about a serial killer from Florida in the late 1980s. Aileen Wuornos was a drifter, armed robber, and sometime hooker who'd had a horrible childhood, utterly without haven. She moved around southern Florida by hitchhiking along I-75, often drunk, usually broke. Over the course of two years, she shot seven of the men who picked her up, and abandoned their bodies to rot in the Everglades. Wuornos also robbed them of various pawnable items—a camera, a watch, a sweetheart ring, a car, which she took for a joy ride and crashed. When she was caught, she claimed self-defense.

The real Aileen Wuornos, rangy, gritty, foul-mouthed, and frighteningly volatile, was nowhere in evidence on television. The actress who played Wuornos, Jean Smart, portrayed her as pensive, kind, needy, and melancholic. The awful rage that the real Aileen Wuornos displayed at her trial, bellowing at jurors that she hoped their daughters were raped, snapping at her victims' widows that they could "rot in hell," was replaced by a TV Wuornos who handed money to homeless women at SeaWorld. The TV character has flashbacks to herself as a pretty blond girl dressing up in pearls before a mirror, trying to be a lady, as if that were all she still wanted for herself—as if the brutality of her life had not transformed her into someone monstrously hardened and destructive. The cops who pursue the TV Wuornos are sympathetic and patient, like Harvey Keitel's character in the movie *Thelma and Louise*. "It's ironic," says the kindly wife of the lead detective, "now the biggest case of your life comes along and you're hunting down a victim of child abuse."

Imagine a TV movie about the Chicago serial killer John Wayne Gacy, assaulted by his father as a boy, containing such a statement. Or the movie *Helter Skelter*, about child abuse victim Charles Manson, pitching him to us as pitiable. From infancy, Manson was unwanted, neglected, mistreated, bounced from one rejecting adult to another. When he was six, his mother was convicted of armed robbery and assault. The Texas serial killer Henry Lee Lucas's mother beat him throughout his early years. Aileen Wuornos shares common origins with these men. Yet by the time they come to public attention through extreme and destructive efforts at self-empowerment, the men are full-blown predators. The woman is a child abuse victim, grown taller. In essence, she is still a child.

What are the consequences for women when we draw such irrationally gendered distinctions in motives and causes of violent behavior? In the interest of pitying women for their relative powerlessness within our society, we reduce them to something less than themselves. Guinevere Garcia, an inmate at Stateville Correctional Center, in Joliet, Illinois, requested in January 1996 that her execution for first-degree murder go ahead as scheduled. Garcia, who is thirty-nine, was on death row for killing her sixty-one-year-old ex-husband outside his condominium while in the company of her new boyfriend. She had been out of prison for four months, having served ten years for smothering her eleven-month-old daughter. Accounts vary as to what happened at the time of the second murder, in July 1991. It may have been an argument over money. Or a robbery. Or it had to do with the fact that her husband, having visited her faithfully in prison very week, assaulted her once she got out. What was clear was that Garcia was drunk and had just come from a confrontation with the uncle who'd raped her as a girl. "I killed George Garcia, and only I know why," she told the prisoner review board. "Do not generically label, package and attempt to justify my actions as that of an abused woman. There is a lot of rage built up inside me and if I am released in the general population that rage will present itself again."

Twenty percent of the men on death row in America in 1995 permitted their executions to go forward. As a culture, we would not grant Garcia the same right to self-determination. Where women are concerned, we are not stern judges but nannies who know best. "The groups fighting on Garcia's behalf say [that] after a life filled with tragedy she is not capable of choosing her own fate," reported National Public Radio. Garcia did not want to take responsibility for her crimes, her advocates argued; she was entertaining a demented urge to commit suicide, and if the state of Illinois executed her, it would become "state-assisted suicide." Garcia was furious. "This is not a suicide," she retorted. "I am not taking my own life. I committed these crimes. I am responsible for these crimes." She added, "Do not consider this petition based on the fact that I am a woman."

Everyone ignored her. Amnesty International sent Bianca Jagger to tell the prisoner review board that "Garcia is the quintessential case of a battered woman and an abandoned child." Garcia responded, "This must be her cause for the week, rather than the Screen Actors Guild or cruelty to animals." But Jagger proved a more effective spokeswoman for Garcia than the inmate was for herself. Jagger's argument got picked up and played nationally by the media. "After enduring fifteen years of his alleged abuse," NPR reported, wrongly, for Garcia had barely been released from prison, "Garcia admits she killed her husband." *The New York Times* wrote, "She was a battered wife who exploded after years of abuse." Amnesty International lawyer Jed Stone said: "This woman is a pitiful, tormented creature. When we kill the John Gacys and the Ted Bundys, there are people who stand by and cheer. But when we kill the Guinevere Garcias, there will be nobody cheering."

Whether anybody should cheer an execution is another argument. The fact is that Guinevere Garcia had the right, and indeed the moral *obligation,* as a sane, intelligent woman, to take responsibility for her violence. She wasn't mentally disabled or in some other way genuinely unable to be held responsible, as some criminals are. As her execution date neared, she told her prison therapist that she'd "started forgiving people whom I had hated, and I started asking for forgiveness from those people who I had not asked . . . before." Not unlike Sean Penn's character in the greatly admired 1995 film *Dead Man Walking,* Garcia was contemplating her life in the face of her death and seeking some measure of redemption. By depicting her as a "pitiable creature," her supporters stole from her an elemental gesture of grace.

On January 16, 1996, Illinois governor Jim Edgar commuted Garcia's sentence to life in prison. He cited evidence of impulse murder, saying Garcia intended to use her gun only to rob her husband, and pointed to mitigating circumstances, such as lifelong hardship and alcoholism. He rejected, correctly, the arguments that she was a "victim of battered woman syndrome."

The American Civil Liberties Union told the *Christian Science Monitor* in January 1996, "Most death row women have killed an abusive husband." In fact, few women are on death row for that reason. Those in Texas, California, Florida, Alabama, and Illinois have all committed savage or calculated crimes. The reality is that chivalry justice is a thriving player in death penalty cases. The reluctance of men to punish women severely—thus admitting that a woman can, in fact, be threatening to them—is alive and well at the end of the twentieth century. Only two of 379 executions in Illinois's history have been women. Of 103 women sentenced to death in the United States since 1977, one has been executed; 47 remain on death row; the remainder were transferred out.

Many feminists, and some criminologists, promote the notion that women are treated more harshly than men for crime: that not only is the violence they commit the fault of others' abuse but that the system further abuses them through punishment. The evidence suggests the contrary: Women are still receiving preferential treatment in the justice system. In 1987, twenty-two out of every one hundred persons arrested for "serious crimes" in the United States were women. Yet only ten out of one hundred persons convicted for serious crimes were women, and five out of one hundred persons imprisoned for those crimes were women. In 1986, 48 percent of New York women convicted of homicide actually went to prison, whereas 77 percent of men did. By 1991, a Phoenix, Arizona, study of 2,500 felony offenders found that men were twice as likely as women to be incarcerated, and women were significantly more likely than men to plead guilty to a reduced charge, across all offense categories, whether homicide or armed robbery or extortion or simple assault. In Coramae Richey Mann's six-city study, prison terms were assigned to women in only 41.1 percent of the cases she reviewed, and the average time served was 6.4 years. By 1995, the average prison sentence for women convicted of killing their spouses was six years, a full decade less than the average sixteen and a half years for convicted wife-killers.

Even taking into account the argument that the female murderers in question were abused, coerced, or impoverished, one study found that men were 11 percent more likely to be incarcerated than women for violent crime. Noted the authors, "Judges viewed female defendants as less 'dangerous' and less culpable than their male codefendants." Kathleen Daly observed the same sentiments at work in New Haven: "Of women I could classify, half were viewed as reformable or as being more victimized than victimizing. Court officials more frequently linked victimization and criminalization in the women's social histories than in the men's, according a less blameworthy quality to some women's acts." This is true not only in the United States. In a 1987 review of London crown courts, the British scholar Hilary Allen found a tendency "toward the exoneration of the [female] offender" by judges who "concentrated on psychological states."

Clearly, chivalry justice will continue to operate as long as the justice system has a host of exonerative excuses for female behavior and a highly simplistic vocabulary of motive. "This is a masculine system," says Justice Michael Corriero of State Supreme Court, Manhattan. "When a woman enters into it, your train of thinking gets derailed. All the more acutely when it's a girl." Women are the ones in a position to argue for our own individuality and tumult, to promote ourselves as unique, some worthy of punishment, others forgiveness, to propose a deeper story about someone like Karla Homolka and why she did what she did.

Rates of rising crime by women, coupled with a mid-1990s backlash against the "abuse excuse," press the issue of how long women have left to benefit from chivalry justice, and whether it is, or ever was, in our interests. Within criminology, this has given rise to the "equality/difference debate." Should we protest leniency in honor of female equality, or let it continue, in honor of the view that women are less responsible when they transgress against their society?

Perhaps that is not the most compelling question. Perhaps what we need to ask is whether all women, by dint of their sex, should be treated and perceived as one woman: Guinevere Garcia, in her candor no different from Karla Homolka with her lies; Homolka no different in turn from Francine Hughes, and no woman as victimizer distinguished from the victims she harms.

THE PROBLEM THAT STILL HAS NO NAME

Women Who Aggress Newborns & Infants

> With regard to the public, [infanticide] causes no alarm, because it is a crime which can be committed only by mothers upon their newly born children.
>
> SIR JAMES FITZJAMES STEPHEN, eighteenth-century jurist

> The power of the mother . . . is to give or withhold survival itself.
>
> ADRIENNE RICH, twentieth-century writer

The day that the baby was found, naked, entangled in the reeds along the shore of Laurel Lake, the heat was almost unbearable. It was September, but the affluent towns of Long Island's North Fork, across Montauk Bay from the celebrity-crowded Hamptons, were doing brisk business at the ski and board shops, as local teens traversed Main Road from the salty Atlantic to the freshwater pond tucked in behind Laurel Lake Vineyards. A couple of swimmers splashing through the sandy shallows noticed Michael James Ellwood, of indeterminate age—a day, a month, it was hard to tell—no one was going to stare into a dead child's face.

The news got around pretty fast, bouncing through Peconic, Mattituck, Cutchogue, and Greenport as people stopped in at The Cider Mill, Wayhouse Antiques, and McDonald's, until eventually it reached Michael's mother, who was hanging out at her friend Cheryl's house. Amy Ellwood, the eighteen-year-old, college-bound daughter of two local teachers, summer employee of Dave Allen's Tent and Party Services, was shocked. Not by the news itself—she knew where she'd disposed of her son on the day of his birth—but by the fact that people she didn't know, adults in suits with somber faces, were making inquiries. She hadn't anticipated an investigation. "I couldn't imagine," she later explained, "why the police were involved."

Amy Ellwood, of English rose complexion and long blond hair, inhabited a corner of the universe so tidy and safe that she might have been Betty, denizen of Riverdale in the Archie comics. Hers was a world of trim, white sidewalks shaded by apple and elm trees, a community both prosperous and placid: a world in which the teen still reigns supreme. Parents are benevolent but unobtrusive, providing their kids with cars, kisses, and spiffy clothes—not negligent parents, just confident ones, who smile over the good report cards issued by Mattituck-Cutchogue High School, which itself could have been in Riverdale, with its red-brick facade, white-pillared entrance, and glossy green lawns.

So it was that for several months in 1989, Amy Ellwood went about the earnest tasks of doing homework, getting good grades, co-editing the school literary journal, and attending the German club, all the while growing progressively rounder with child, and not one adult—her parents, her gym teacher, wives who work part-time at the A & P mall, where she hung out—remarked on her condition. Under the circumstances, the idea that she was now a suspect in a criminal investigation came as a hair-raising surprise.

Ellwood's bemusement is evident on September 12, 1989, in a videotaped statement taken by the Suffolk County district attorney's office after her friend Cheryl tipped off the police about who the Laurel Lake baby's mother might be. Assistant District Attorney Randall Hinrichs interrogates Amy politely. She responds in kind; neither is remotely overheated. They could be going through a theft complaint. Amy peers upward at Hinrichs through her bangs, a poised young woman whose expression suggests she's just found herself on Mars and is trying to avoid sudden movements lest she aggravate the aliens.

Her story, as it unfurls through this interview and at her subsequent trial, began in August 1988, when she met nineteen-year-old

Chris Wilshusen. He was a maverick, a pretty cool guy who had recently been expelled from the high school where Amy's father served as principal. That lent their romance a Romeo and Juliet quality; it had to be kept secret from her family. They began dating, she said, "four days before my seventeenth birthday"—the sort of detail so treasured by young women in love they consider it rightfully theirs to insist upon, a date to celebrate as an "anniversary," whereas the right to insist upon birth control is neither owned nor remembered.

Amy's revelation came on New Year's Eve, at a party cluttered with beer and wine coolers and most of her girlfriends, a group who dubbed themselves "The Circle of Women." But it was a boy to whom she turned. Randy Sigurdson was in the kitchen when Amy came in, crying. She'd just had a fight with Chris, and she blurted out the news. "It was after midnight," he told the jury at Amy's trial, "and I don't remember [what] led to it, but we were just talking and she said that she had a couple of problems and that she was pregnant." Randy was sympathetic. But this wasn't the era of the Scarlet Letter, when pregnancy out of wedlock was catastrophic, leading to social ostracism; nor even a time when immediate marriage was called for lest the girl slip away in shame to a special home. "I said there's lots of things you can do, there's adoption, or abortion."

Amy Ellwood was intelligent, aware, she knew what her options were. But they were such unexpected options to confront. "You see, when I was studying biology," she would testify, weary and defensive, "I was in tenth grade. I wasn't exactly planning on having a baby. It wasn't like I was learning the stuff for my own use." Yet she understood that her decision had a deadline, less than three months to opt for "termination," and a few months after that, the body announcing itself, and then a baby, bawling and clinging, changing her life forever.

For a time, she convinced herself that she wasn't pregnant after all. Then, toward the end of February, when Amy's parents went on a holiday cruise, her friend Dawn Swiatocha spent the week sleeping over at her house. One night, they decided to drive to the drugstore and pick up a home pregnancy test. The timing was strikingly teenaged, like filching from the liquor cabinet or smoking a joint in the kitchen and raiding the fridge, things to do when parents are away: making illicit runs at grown-up vice. The test was positive, and that abruptly changed the mood. "I asked her if she was going to have an abortion," Dawn said, "and she wasn't sure." Mostly, she didn't want to think about it. "I did not want to believe I was pregnant," Amy testified.

Nevertheless, she discussed it with Chris. His response was typical of young men in these times: to become awkwardly solemn, respectful of a woman's "right to choose," tell you they'll stand by you, help you with the money, drive you to the clinic, whatever. They won't break up with you, they promise, they ask if you're okay, they even evince shy pleasure at the fact that you've conceived their child. But they don't offer to marry you, and you don't expect them to, and they don't stake a claim to the baby, and you wouldn't expect that, either. At some point, after this is all over, the odds are very good that they'll vanish from your life. Not because you spawned an incipient family together and lost it, and the relationship was strained by the trauma, but because love itself is disposable.

For the post–Sexual Revolution generation, raised on a rhetoric that celebrated sexual freedom but had no memory of what the revolution was for, there are no links between intimacy and commitment, pregnancy and childbirth, sex and the beginning of a bright, constructive love. AIDS may have made them more fearful, ushering in a fad of celibacy, but it hasn't taught them how to caretake their hearts. For Ellwood, the decision to have her child or not had to be made in a vacuum. "We talked about, I guess, the decision we had to make," she said at trial, "and at that point the most sensible thing to do was to get an abortion." But "sensible" was pure abstraction. "It didn't feel like the right thing for me to do. Just the fact that it was Chris's and my baby and I—I couldn't do it."

Without being able to articulate what she'd found, Ellwood held on. She held on the way that a child, discovering something of uncertain value, a beautiful shell on the beach, carries it in the palm of her hand until, unable to grasp any further purpose for it, she lets it fall to the sand. "At the very beginning, after I decided that I wasn't

going to get the abortion, it still didn't seem real that I was pregnant." She quit smoking, for about three weeks, then resumed, perhaps because to quit was to acknowledge the baby. "Later on, when I
started to gain weight, I realized that it wasn't going away and it was
real and I was pregnant."

There is a late-June high school graduation photograph of Ellwood, smiling through a bouquet of flowers on the steps of the
school, surrounded by family and school chums. She is about seven
months pregnant, blooming outward from her gown, her smooth,
pale face still baby-round. In July, after observing her in a bathing
suit, Amy's parents gingerly asked her to take "a test." Instead, she
took off for several days with Chris. "My parents and I were pretty
close," she would later say, defending them against insinuations
about the "frightened seventeen-year-old girl" who conceals a pregnancy from parents to evade their wrath. "They just, they basically let
me make my own decisions and they trusted me. They felt I was
responsible, [but] I never really had any problems that I would have
to go to them with." This, as the first problem, was far too disastrous
to confess. Ellwood's father said, "We goofed, that's true, we knew
she was pregnant . . . but we were scared if we pushed it she would
end up on the road with her boyfriend." Plus, her mother, Patricia,
added, "We thought there was more time. . . . We're both trained
educators. But that doesn't make us experts."

Left to their own devices and running out of time, Chris and Amy
began tossing around ideas. "I was going to go down to North Carolina to a friend of his. There's a house down there. And I was going to
put the baby up for adoption. . . . I kept putting it off. I just—I didn't
want to deal with it, and I just figured I would do it someday." As the
summer progressed, her friends grew increasingly worried. "In
August, we were in my car," Dawn Swiatocha told the jury, "and I said
that it was getting kind of close to, you know, her pregnancy being
over, and I asked what she was going to do, and she discussed—said
that she had talked to someone about adoption—that she had
spoken to a lady and the lady was going to take care of everything."

But at 3:30 in the morning on September 8, when Amy sat up in
her Raggedy Ann sheets, awoken by contractions, and began to pace

back and forth between her bedroom and the bathroom, there wasn't any lady to take care of everything. "I knew I was in labor," she said. But when her mother knocked on the bathroom door around six—"Amy, are you all right?"—Amy said, "I'm fine." She wasn't. "I was scared." But she'd made a decision. The baby was going to go away now. The problem was going to end. This was not going to be a live birth, it was going to be a miscarriage; that happens, doesn't it, and isn't the mother's fault, is it?

The video camera rolls in the Suffolk County district attorney's office. A pack of cigarettes, a cup of coffee, and a tin foil ashtray have been placed before Ellwood, but she touches none of them, not even to fidget. Instead, she leans forward, shoulders slightly slouched, resting her elbows on the table, and interlocks her fine-boned hands. She is concentrating hard, watchful and compliant. Because Randall Hinrichs has asked her, she says, "My water broke around five, five-thirty." He keeps asking, and she keeps answering, detail by detail. "I went back into the bathroom, into the shower . . . uh, that's when I started giving birth . . . my brother Brian probably left around six and my parents left around seven or seven-fifteen. . . . it [came out] around six-thirty, seven. . . . I pulled on the umbilical cord and pulled out the afterbirth, I heard it make a noise, twice, I saw one of its legs jerk . . . I put a towel around the baby and I picked it up out of the bathtub and I put it into a bucket, I added another towel around it and I brought it into my room . . . I fell asleep."

At some point in this account, the ADA needs to clarify an issue: Was Amy Ellwood intending to be a good mother, but didn't know enough, when she wrapped her boy in towels and placed him in a bucket?

"I just decided I could—"

"You thought you could—"

Their words overlap.

"Yeah—"

"I don't want to put words in your mouth—"

"Get away with it." She fixes him with a grim half-smile and nods.

"Get rid of the baby right after it was born?"

"Yeah." She adds, "Well, that's not what I planned all along. You know, I wanted to tell my parents eventually, but I never, I never could."

"And you decided you weren't going to help the baby once it was born?"

"I didn't know what I was thinking. I just, I thought my parents wouldn't find out that way."

On September 12, the Suffolk County district attorney's office charged Ellwood with one count of murder in the second degree. A Grand Jury then reduced the charge to manslaughter.

In 1988, more than four thousand teenagers between the ages of ten and nineteen became pregnant in Suffolk County. Some had abortions, others gave their newborns up for adoption, others kept them. A handful, as Amy Ellwood did in 1989, gave birth to them and gave them back to God. A colleague of Ellwood's father watched his daughter, Loretta Campbell, plead innocent in Hempstead to charges of second-degree manslaughter for smothering a boy she'd given birth to on January 1, 1991, at a friend's house in affluent Hewlett and leaving him in a garbage bag. Two weeks earlier, a C. W. Post College sophomore had been charged with first-degree manslaughter for gagging her baby with toilet paper and dumping him in a dorm hallway garbage can. Then there was a twenty-one-year-old Uniondale woman who pled guilty to first-degree manslaughter for killing her newborn boy, and a twenty-year-old Brentwood woman who threw her baby out a window, and an East Northport woman who left her infant to drown in a tub. Other babies in Suffolk County were found by the police but never connected to those who destroyed them. Still others were probably never found.

Across the country, according to the National Center on Health Statistics, the killing of infant children climbed 55 percent between 1985 and 1988, until it was several times the rate at which adult women were murdered. Nearly half of the child maltreatment fatalities between 1985 and 1992 in the United States involved infants up to a year old. According to data compiled by the World Health Organization, infanticide was (as recently as the mid-1970s) as common as or more common than the killing of adults in most of the industrialized nations, from Canada to Austria to Japan. In the

United States, more infant boys are killed than girls. The gender of the perpetrator varies. An American one-year-old is as likely to be attacked by a woman as a man, while the vast majority of murdered newborns are victims of women. A wide consensus exists within the community of academicians who try to track neonaticide that many "neonates are discarded but not found, making the overall rate . . . considerably higher than the data suggest."

Ever alert to the possibilities of a new trend, the media turned their short attention span to this issue in the early part of the decade. In April 1991, for example, the *Saint Louis Post Dispatch* ran a story headlined "Infanticide Increasing, Experts Fear." The story cited more than a dozen cases in Missouri and southern Illinois in the previous five years and commented, "Authorities have no idea how many have gone undetected." The cases reported by the *Dispatch* echoed those in Long Island—babies born in dorm rooms and disposed of in trash cans. A forensic psychiatrist at the Menninger Clinic told the newspaper, "Most of the women who kill their newborns are quite young, single, uneducated and desperate. The child is obviously a burden to them, and they get rid of the burden the only way they can think of, by killing it."

Amy Ellwood's parents retained for her a lawyer, Eric Naiburg, who told the media that he planned to launch an "unwed mother syndrome defense." He explained that women who deny their pregnancy and neglect their newborns suffer mental derangement caused by being young and single. "In the mind of a frightened seventeen-year-old," Naiburg said, "the realization of pregnancy is not like flicking on a switch." Amy was troubled, he explained, because her parents didn't approve of her boyfriend. "She tried to please her parents a lot." Her father thought of her as his "good little girl." The suggestion of a wrathful father lurking behind the scene added a frisson of drama.

What Ellwood did on the day that her son lived and died was as follows: "I went and got garbage bags from my garage so I could put the baby in them. Then I . . . got a Styrofoam cooler and put another garbage bag inside of it and then I put the other garbage bag inside of that one. I put the cooler in the hatch back of my car. Then I took a shower, and I washed my sheets. Then I went to my friend Cheryl's house. I told her that I had a miscarriage and that I'd been to the hospital the night before. We went to 7-Eleven and got something to drink and then we went back to her house and watched TV for a while. She wanted to go swimming so we went down to Laurel Lake. . . . We only stayed there for about a half hour. Then we went and she got ice cream and then I went and dropped her off and then I went home."

Having driven around all afternoon with a dead or dying infant in the car, Amy decided to call Chris. "I told him the same thing that I'd told Cheryl because I didn't want them to know, you know. He asked if I was okay and he asked why they didn't make me stay in the hospital." A couple of hours later, she met him at the A & P parking lot. "[Then] he went to Greenport to one of his friends' house, and I went to Riverhead with my friend Cheryl." Emotion momentarily flushes into Ellwood's voice, triggered, seemingly, by the memory of Chris going off with his friends—the revelation that the intimate links are, indeed, so eroded that a man makes no connection to the child he's just lost and cannot rearrange his social schedule to console the mother, any more than she could connect with the child or reveal his fate to the man.

The parents went their separate ways along Main Road, leaving their son behind in a two-dollar cooler in Amy's parked Toyota.

Around 10:00 P.M., Ellwood returned from Riverhead, where she'd been hanging out with friends at The Circle, a traffic roundabout with a rock in the middle. She picked up her car, drove around for about ten minutes, and made her way through darkness to the lake. "I parked my car and, uh, I shut my lights off and I opened the back and I took the cooler out and . . . I waded into the water and I dumped the cooler." Later, in her defense, the pastor at Amy Ellwood's family church wrote a letter to her judge describing what she'd done in the lake as "a baptism."

At the end of his interrogation, ADA Hinrichs holds up a police photo of a dead infant for the video camera to zoom carefully in upon. Across the bottom, written in Ellwood's flowery hand: "This is the baby I gave birth to." She will not look at her son.

·   ·   ·

Long Island Newsday ran an editorial at the time of Ellwood's trial that was sympathetic to her refusal to face what she'd done: "Almost everyone practices denial at one time or another. We may put off calling the plumber in hope that the leak will go away; or avoid breast self-examination because we don't want to find cancer. . . . Amy Ellwood is troubled, not malicious." The view is shared by Suffolk County detective lieutenant John Gierasch, who investigates the babies abandoned in his county. "I think it's a matter of, it's like having a simple problem, your car doesn't work, and you're not a car person, so you just let it go, and the next thing you know you're broken down on the side of the road. You're procrastinating, you just defer and defer and pretty soon you have a mess on your hands. They must make some half-assed attempt to determine that they are pregnant, just to confirm in their own minds, so it's not like they're denying that they're pregnant to themselves. They're denying it to the world. They're just not going to deal with it, which maybe young females are more inclined to do than other people. I don't know if you can call that aggression. But if you shove toilet paper down its throat because it's crying to shut it up, that crosses another line, that's aggression. I mean Ellwood just wrapped it up, put it in a bag and disposed of it; there was no overt homicidal act."

The community perspective on Ellwood's act of neonaticide raises some important questions about who is in denial here. Our myths about maternal grace—under pressure, pure as nature—are so deeply ingrained that infanticide is the one crime to be all but ignored in discussions of violence. Murdered infants show up on the evening news with surprising frequency. But to most of us, they aren't reflective, somehow, of female aggression. We only prick up our ears to what, as French historian Michel Foucault once said, is "In The Truth." Another young offender on a shooting spree? Look at what's going on with kids today! Another woman raped in Central Park! A new serial murderer! It is as if the killing of newborns and infants fails to compute. As a result, every time a new case compels our attention, we are left to grasp at a few clichés, to point fingers and to invent syndromes, as the moral ground shifts beneath our feet.

When women like Amy Ellwood commit neonaticide, they tend

not to be considered women, exactly. They are "young" and "un-wed." They are "uneducated." They can't think what else to do with newborn children except stuff them in Dumpsters—they're dumb. In other words, they are not mothers in a culturally understood and celebrated way. Mothers are strong, long-suffering, altruistic, and resourceful. Mothers are never callous; they are not indifferent. Ell-wood seemed to understand this distinction and to play to it when she testified in her own defense, on March 5, 1991. She brought tears to the eyes of Suffolk County Court jurors when she told them that she thought she had miscarried, thought her baby was prema-ture and stillborn when it arrived. She knew nothing of biology. She had imagined that her baby "had gills in the back of its neck and that's how it breathed in the fluid." Had she known that her son was alive, she told the jury, when he made his plaintive sounds and kicked his feet, "I would have picked the baby up and loved it like any mother would."

Ellwood was guessing what any mother would have done. She was guessing, though she knew differently from her own experience, that "any mother" loves her baby at the instant of its birth. References to maternal instinct are so commonplace in our culture that most of us assume there's some basis for the belief that women instinctively bond with babies and small children in a manner that is inherent to our sex. Is motherhood instinctive? If we are to speak of instinct, which is to say preconscious impulses governed by the limbic brain, we cannot look to the animal kingdom for an axiom about maternal behavior. Most mammals are instinctively protective but selectively so. Animals will foster, reject, or devour their young depending upon circumstances, and females of several species are actively hostile to the young of rival females. But we *shouldn't* speak of instinct, because women cannot be simplified that way. To say so debases the interplay of our psychological, moral, and intellectual faculties.

There has nevertheless been a marked tendency within medical literature to extrapolate from animal behavior to human mothers. In 1964, for example, animal behaviorists observed that goats reject their offspring, butting them away, if they are separated after birth for even five minutes. In short order, it was cautioned that women might have the same response. This idea was developed by other scientists, in other laboratories and barnyards, and in 1974, the notion was broadcast that mothers went through a biologically "sensitive" period, immediately after birth, when they had to have skin-to-skin contact with their infants or they wouldn't bond. This in turn gave rise to a host of articles in nursing and medical journals, as well as the popular media, about how a baby had to be brought to the mother as soon as possible in the hospital, lest the critical period lapse and she butt the baby off her bed.

Ideas about instinctual maternal attachment also come from studies of infant bonding needs, which actually show that the identity of a primary caretaker is irrelevant to the infant, so long as care is consistent and empathic. If a mother dies in childbirth, a child is not developmentally thwarted if a father or stepmother or nanny takes the infant into his or her care. With disconcerting frequency, however, the findings on infant bonding get reversed in medical literature so that the instinctual attachment needs of a baby are portrayed as the instinctual responses of the mother. At the same time, the term "primary caretaker" mysteriously disappears and is replaced by the word "mother," so that attachment and bonding remain exclusive to the experience of women.

What is really going on here is that science is reinforcing the transcendent sentiment of a unique mother-child bond, an ideal that has waxed and waned throughout history, regaining currency in the eighteenth and nineteenth centuries, when a division of labor between the sexes intensified in the shift from an agrarian to an industrial society. When men were forced into the factories and mines, women came to symbolize the nurturant safety of the home and took on attributes of softness and sentimentality they hadn't possessed before. As labor divisions grew starker, so did the character attributes of gender.

Idealizing women into a tender-hearted class of perfect mothers does not lead them to behave that way. Dr. Stuart Asch, a psychiatrist and analyst at New York Hospital, began his career in the 1950s by serving as a liaison to the obstetrics ward, counseling pregnant women. The women confided their anxieties to him: that pregnancy made them ungainly, robbing them of their beauty; that their husbands wouldn't take them out to dinner anymore; that, some-times, they had "crazy thoughts," like wishing their baby was dead. "I started to wonder why so many women were saying this," Asch recalls. This was the fifties, after all; women were ascending to the summit of their identity as mothers in the months leading up to birth. What could possibly make them so disconsolate? Asch also wondered what would happen to the women he spoke with after the babies were born. Would they still have "crazy thoughts"?

Tracking the women he felt were at risk over a period of years, Asch found a high incidence of Sudden Infant Death Syndrome among their children. He published his suspicions of infanticide in a medical journal. The article marked the beginning and the end of his research. "The SIDS people got women to write me terrible let-ters, awful letters. What kind of a man was I to suggest that a woman could kill her child?" Asch wasn't willing to venture into the arena. "I dropped my work." Very few doctors or academics have proved any more willing than Asch was to challenge the maternal ideal.

The sentimental vision of Mother in the nineteenth century has persisted well into the twentieth, left intact by feminists when so many other so-called female attributes have been radically chal-lenged. Indeed, the maternal ideal lies at the very heart of feminist resistance to the possibility of female aggression. Thus when femi-nists have pondered infanticide at all, they have tended to construe it as a masculine conspiracy to make good women do bad things. Of Ellwood, Greenport, Long Island, resident Deb Winsor wrote to Long Island's *Suffolk Times*: "I find the verdict to be another sad and pathetic indictment of our legal system as it addresses women's reproductive rights. . . . Once again our system reinforces that men have the option of abdicating their reproductive responsibility after conception." A letter to *Newsday* from Shirley Abbott Tomkievicz read: "Many of us seem to view female sexuality as a punishable offense. . . . Why wasn't [the father] on trial for manslaughter as well? Is this 1991 or 1691?"

"Under Christianity," Adrienne Rich wrote in 1975, "infanticide was forbidden as a policy but it continued nonetheless to be prac-ticed as an individual act, in which women, raped or seduced and then branded with their 'sin,' and under pain of torture or execution, have in guilt, self-loathing and blind desperation done away with the newborns they had carried in their bodies." Of course, history is rich with evidence that married women freely loved and made love to their husbands, and took freely chosen lovers, and did not treat the offspring of those unions well. Thirty-three percent of the infanticides in France during the eighteenth century were committed by securely married middle- and upper-class women. Infant abandonment and killing were rather rampant among the aristocratic women of Greece and Rome. In all these cases, there were abundant servants to whom such offspring could be farmed; in very few instances had the mothers been tortured or executed.

Infanticide has been committed throughout human history for a multiplicity of reasons—personal, political, superstitious, and strategic. Whether or not a culture supports the perpetrators of infanticide, it is, like other forms of violence, highly mutable. In many cultures, offspring weren't considered to be fully human until they reached a certain age, one or two, sometimes three years old. Perhaps the most common cause of violence against infants arose from the need to space children in the absence of birth control. The Japanese word for infanticide means "weeding," as in the thinning of rice saplings. Today, in some of the poorest communities in the world, infanticide as birth control takes a passive-aggressive form: babies are given birth to, then simply not fed. Cultures have also engaged in crude forms of eugenics, turning against twins, against girls, against deformities—as some societies continue to do, now, through selective abortion. Infants have been killed, as well, during famine, or in the midst of war, or as an offering in ritual sacrifice.

Stepparents have often posed a particular threat to infants and small children, primarily, it seems, for sociopolitical reasons—the desire to preserve their own bloodline when resources (food and inheritable land) were scarce. Hence the origin of wicked stepmother figures in fairy tales. The monstrous relations of Snow White and Cinderella were dreamed up by their tellers as cautionary figures—not of the inherent evil of women but of the perils of being a stepchild. Some scholars argue that human beings, like other mammals, have an instinctive hostility to genetically unrelated offspring. The psychologists Margo Wilson and Martin Daly point out that in the United States a preschool-age stepchild is one hundred times more likely than a biological child to fall victim to familial homicide. In 1996, a twenty-three-year-old C. W. Post College psychology student was arrested for paying three thousand dollars to an undercover police officer to smother her boyfriend's toddler, born to another woman. To the evolutionary psychologist, this woman was acting on an ancient, preconscious drive to promote her own DNA. She was jealous, but her jealousy had magnificent instinctual cause.

Infanticides that convey the deepest mythic resonance are acts of Medea-like revenge against the patriarch, in which a mother harms or kills her children to strike at the father. Medea is a figure of Greek legend who was abandoned by her husband, Jason, who claimed to love her still but said he needed to marry a princess so that he might realize his dream to be king. Medea, like her grandmother, Tyro, avenged herself for this insult and betrayal by destroying Jason's two beloved sons. A modern name for this, typically implying mental illness, surfaced in the 1990s: "divorce-related malicious mother syndrome." In 1994, Maria Montalvo, a nurse in Union Beach, New Jersey, drove her son and daughter to her ex-husband's home. She doused the car in gasoline, rang the doorbell, and, when he stood upon the threshold, set the car ablaze. While it is extremely rare in North America to see such retaliation taken to the extreme of filicide, the destruction of children as an act of revenge or rebellion has its place in history. Psychologist Shari Thurer has suggested that a woman's resentment of her status as a second-class citizen related to high infanticide rates among Greek aristocrats. Historian Ann Jones describes widespread infanticide in colonial America as a "revolutionary" act in a "patriarchal society," committed by women who resented being punished for sex.

Historically, it has been difficult to isolate individual female motive from cultural practice and belief. Personal impulses in the murder of infants merge, as Brandt Steele notes, "almost imperceptibly into other forms of infanticide that relate to economic, moral, religious, political, or military causes." In the twentieth century, no explicit cultural support for this deed exists, and as a result, it ought to be easier for us to see the nuanced diversity in female experience that inspires the crime. But if this is increasingly true for child homicide and fatal child abuse, we are still prone to sweeping and reductive generalizations where infanticide is concerned. According to Donna Stewart, a physician and the head of the Women's Health department at Toronto General Hospital, "Women who commit infanticide run a wide spectrum, from those in denial, who were concealing their pregnancy and concealed its consequence, to highly impulsive women who, in a fit of rage, shake their baby to death, to manic-depressive women, to those who are suffering from classical depression who wind up killing their babies *and* themselves." They are women from all classes, all races, all shades of fortitude, sanity, love. "We need," Stewart notes, "to broaden our categories, recognize the individuality of women, so that we can confront risk on a case-by-case basis."

Research on maternal aggression is stunningly scant. Most of it is lumped into a single category of madness, linked directly to female hormones. "Postpartum depression," also known as "new mother syndrome," has been advanced for well over a century to explain why good women, culturally celebrated mothers, would turn inexplicably violent. About half of all women who give birth do experience a hormonal shift within three to eight days that makes them disconsolate, weepy, or irritable. Sometimes called the "baby blues," this passing storm is loosely comparable to how one feels in early pregnancy or premenstrually. It isn't a springboard for serious aggression. It comes, it goes. The body resolves itself. About one in five hundred women, however, get more unhinged when they have a baby, to the point of becoming suicidal or homicidal. Some enter a frightening realm of the mind known as postpartum psychosis. They become delusional, they hallucinate, their babies fall from bridges, are suffocated, drown. Within the medical community, there are those who insist that postpartum psychosis is purely hormonal, that if women are treated with hormone supplements while still in the hospital after giving birth, they'll remain grounded and content in their new maternal role. Internationally, the most prominent advocates of this view are members of the Marce Society, a research organization devoted to isolating the biological underpinnings of postpartum disorders. The logic implicit within this view is that hormonal insanity is something to which all women are automatically susceptible as soon as they get wheeled out of the delivery room.

In England, support for hormones as the cause of *all* maternal aggression against infants is enshrined in the law. In 1922, parliament introduced the Infanticide Act, which reduced the crime automatically from murder to manslaughter on the basis of insanity if a mother "had not fully recovered from the effect of giving birth to such child, but by reason thereof the balance of her mind was then disturbed." The point of the Infanticide Act was not that British doctors had suddenly discovered a link between postpartum hormones and violent behavior. To this day that link hasn't been categorically established. The point was to rid the courts of the necessity of imposing murder sentences, since juries had been refusing to convict women when the penalty was execution. For instance, following five thousand coroner's inquests into child deaths held annually in Britain in the mid-nineteenth century, only thirty-nine convictions for child murder resulted, and none of those women were executed. Similarly, in Canada, when a mandatory death penalty applied to the murder of children, "courts regularly returned 'not guilty' verdicts in the face of overwhelming evidence to the contrary."

In 1938, Britain revised its infanticide statute, extending the age of victims from "newly born" to "under the age of 12 months." To justify this extension, the revised statute cited "the effect of lactation" on a woman's mind. It was decided, in effect, that breastfeeding could drive women mad. The experts who proposed the revision to the courts privately believed that social and psychological factors were more critical than biology. Studies consistently show, for example, that preexisting histories of depression and life stress are a common denominator in women with postpartum mental disorders. But psychiatrist J. H. Morton defended the diagnosis of "lactational insanity" as being acceptable to conservative judges and barristers. It was never proposed that the Infanticide Act forgive mothers for killing older children, spouses or others, even while said to be suffering from the same insanity.

Adopting the discreet position of British psychiatrists, the American Psychiatric Association views childbirth as simply a trigger for a variety of psychiatric conditions. The APA bible, the Diagnostic and Statistical Manual of Mental Disorders (DSM-IV), has no listing for postpartum psychosis but cites "postpartum onset" for certain mental illnesses, such as bipolar disorder and clinical depression. In pre–World War II Britain, psychiatrists believed that "exhaustion psychosis" due to sleep deprivation was more operative as a risk factor for mothers than hormonal change. Recognized in both England and the United States, exhaustion psychosis refers, essentially, to being so tired that one can't navigate the shoals of reality anymore. Anyone who has gone without sleep for a long period of time knows what it's like. Truckers, doctor-trainees, nurses, soldiers, and new parents can all describe the experience of being so exhausted that they get delusional, disoriented, extremely emotional. Mundane annoyances can trigger weird, wild rages and crying jags. Pushed to the brink, people in this condition temporarily lose their grip. Some hallucinate. When sleep deprivation combines with the constant demands of a baby, a lack of support, and insecurity or resentment about parenting, a normally well-balanced person can come perilously close to violence. This is not true just of biological mothers. Fathers and adoptive mothers have been documented with postpartum onset exhaustion psychosis.

Kate R., an upbeat, happily married woman in her thirties with some money in the bank and lots of solid family around her, gave birth to her first baby in 1992 and fell into the special hell of infant colic. She recalls the precipitous crash downward from her elation as an expectant mother: "When I was pregnant, it was wonderful. The sex was great, people were terrific, they smiled at me on the street, they helped me out. Then you give birth and doors slam on the stroller." Add colic: "After Claire was born, when we were still in the hospital, I could hear her crying down the hall. No one else's baby was crying. And she wouldn't stop, it just wouldn't stop. The nurses would say, 'Maybe it's your milk.' They'd have to bring her to me so often to try to calm her . . . they'd give me these looks. From the word 'go' even the hospital society was telling me, 'This isn't cool.' "

Kate sits in her New York living room, cross-legged, cradling a cup of tea. Claire is out in Central Park with her father, who was attentively present through the nightmare, right away giving Kate a leg up to sanity that some mothers don't have. "I can see how sleep deprivation is a torture, how it's used all over the world. At one point I didn't wash my hair for ten days, because washing your hair takes six minutes, and that was six minutes to sleep. It was scary, because I could *not* relieve her pain, and I felt it was something I was doing wrong. My exasperation and exhaustion turned to fury in the middle of the night. Motherhood wasn't what I wanted it to be. It wasn't my ideal." Beset with conflicting emotions, unhinged by exhaustion, Kate felt turned upside down. "So you lose it, you lose it. You feel like you're not going to be able to cut it, that you're not going to be a good mother. . . . I would *never* have hurt my daughter, but I can see that, in the worst way, it's reasonable to think of smothering the baby, just making it stop."

Kate had a loving and supportive extended family, who took Claire off her hands for hours at a time. But what if she'd had none? What if she were isolated, and the expectation of perfection was that much more intense? What if her personality was that much more impulsive or volatile? What if, biochemically, her brain were more vulnerable to psychosis? What if she'd grown up in a violent family, so that lashing out in a sleepless frenzy didn't seem all that crazy? These are factors that add their force to individual women's responses, becoming trigger mechanisms for fatal abuse.

Kathleen Householder, of Rippon, West Virginia, smashed a rock over the head of her two-week-old daughter to make her stop "fussing." Eighteen-year-old Josephine Mesa, of San Diego, battered her two-month-old baby with a toilet plunger. Sheryl Lynn Massip, of Orange County, California, had no sleep for six weeks, took her colicky baby outside, put him on the road, and ran over him with her car. Had these women been treated with "hormone supplements," as the advocates of postpartum psychosis suggest, would they have been any less tired? Less isolated, ambivalent, impulsive, or stressed? Interestingly, one of the strongest advocates of the hormonal basis of postpartum disorders, Katherine Dalton, notes in her 1989 book

Depression After Childbirth that depression and psychosis were less severe in the early part of this century, when mothers were permitted to stay in the hospital for up to fourteen days, surrounded by supportive staff who gave them help and let them rest.

Another cause of postpartum psychosis may be manic-depression, or "bi-polar disorder." As early as the 1930s, a handful of American psychiatrists came to see, in the life histories of women who experienced psychotic breaks, such as hallucinating that their baby was the devil, an underlying bipolar disorder, with swings downward into depression and upward into mania. Both psychologically and physically, childbirth could trigger an intense bipolar swing, far more dramatic than anything the woman had experienced before. In a manic psychotic state, a woman might kill her baby optimistically, as in the belief that the child will ascend straight to heaven and become an angel. Verlyn Harris, of northern California, slit her baby boy's throat in imitation of Abraham's sacrifice: "I thought that I would be seen as having God's favor," she explained. Angela Thompson of Sacramento drowned her nine-month-old son in his bath, hallucinating that he was Satan and her husband was Christ. "I believed . . . in order to expunge the world of the devil that I had to do this tremendous act of faith and drown my baby," who would then be resurrected by her husband/Jesus. She added: "It was happening to me because of biochemical changes that were occurring in my body because I was weaning my baby at the time." Thompson was borrowing from the vocabulary of motive, from the notion that biological mothering makes you crazy. Incidentally, she also described herself, at the time of the crime, as being "on a manic high."

When bipolar mothers suffer depressive psychotic breaks, feelings of nihilism and despair darken into intensely negative delusions. A baby who, for healthy mothers, might merely pose a threat becomes for these mothers a dragon who must be slain. In the 1970s, Dr. Stuart Asch saw the movie *Rosemary's Baby*, in which a woman gradually realizes that the fetus she is carrying is not human but demonic. It struck him as an interesting depiction of depressive psychosis. The key, he says, is the specificity of Rosemary's psychotic obsession with the baby within her, the idea that this child is the devil. "Women who are depressed, postpartum," he says, "are conceiving of their children as the bad part of themselves, because children are an *extension* of themselves. By killing them, they get the rottenness out. It's not hormonal at all." His is a psychoanalytic perspective. Others, in this bright new era of Prozac, might argue that the affliction is mainly biochemical. Whatever its cause, manic-depression can be screened for, with high-risk mothers kept in the hospital in the weeks after the birth to ensure the infant's safety. But virtually no hospital in North America will do this. According to both Dr. Asch and Dr. Stewart, it is a form of cultural heresy to suggest that mothers aren't naturally good. Suspicion of harm interferes with our faith in the maternal ideal. "Mothers are supposed to be *blissful*," says Stewart.

Over the years, Stuart Asch has received hundreds of letters, some anonymous, all from American women who've killed their babies. They tell the same tale, of reaching out to relatives, pastors, doctors, only to be told, "It's just the baby blues, you'll be fine." "The obstetrician would tell their husbands to go buy them a box of candy. One woman wrote to me saying that she had gone to her minister in desperation. He told her to be a good Christian. That afternoon she killed her child." In another letter, the woman described smothering her baby, then discovering that her doctor had listed it as SIDS before she'd even had a chance to confess. Sheryl Massip tried for two weeks, before she ran over her son, to get doctors' attention, even trying to admit her son back into the hospital, where he would be safe from her. With the trend among health maintenance organizations toward overnight stays for mothers who give birth, the women that Asch was able to observe rather carefully in 1950s maternity wards would no longer even attract attention.

Women who suffer from postpartum depression fall into a different group from those with exhaustion psychosis or manic-depression. They don't lose touch with reality. They find themselves, instead, overwhelmed by its implications. "Pregnancy and the transition to motherhood arouse many psychologic stresses," note Dr. Stewart and C. E. Robinson in a recent article. "A woman must come to terms with changes in her body image, her relationships with her husband and parents, her responsibilities as well as society's perception of her role. Jealousy and hostility toward the infant and fear of losing her identity are common feelings as she makes the adjustment." Stewart and Robinson cite the example of a professional woman who gave birth to twins. "She had long-standing marital problems and was ambivalent about having children. After leaving the hospital, she became increasingly depressed and anxious." One month later, the woman was rehospitalized, given antidepressants, and treated in psychotherapy. While she was able to work through "her relationship with her husband and mother, her fears of losing her career and becoming trapped and dependent," she never did bond with her babies.

Queen Victoria apparently succumbed to severe depression after the birth of the Prince of Wales. Being a queen, she was able to sit listlessly about under a dark cloud without changing diapers. Not so most women. Infant and child neglect are probably the most common results of severe maternal depression, far more widespread than infanticide and far more problematic for the culture as a whole. With child abuse, a parent actively attacks the child, but in neglect, as psychologist Brandt Steele notes, "The parent may decide it is a hopeless task, the infant is beyond help, too worthless and unrewarding to bother with; there is no longer any point in caring for it or about it, and the picture of neglect ensues. In general, neglecting caretakers, mostly mothers, tend to be more depressed, listless, hopeless, and more isolated, with their aggression more deeply submerged."

For Paula Sims, of southwestern Illinois, there was no support from a hospital, no intervention with antidepressants or psychotherapy. She lived penned in in a remote rural home. Over the course of a few years, Sims gave birth to two baby daughters. In each case, after a few months alone in her hauntingly empty home with her baby, popping tranquilizers, pacing, she drowned her daughters in their baby bath tub. Not directly: She didn't hold them under the water; she wasn't *murdering* them. She just went downstairs, poured herself a drink, and lingered in the living room, blown away by what she knew she was doing—which was letting each baby slide

downward beneath the water's tepid surface. Sims managed to persuade her community and her husband that the first daughter had
been kidnapped. The second time a baby "vanished" with a "masked
intruder" from her house, the police wouldn't buy it. The found her
daughter buried in the woods behind her home, and Sims was
charged with murder. For duping her community, she received a life
sentence. Having said nothing at her trial, Sims later phoned a journalist from prison and tried to explain for the first time what had
happened. It was hard to articulate. It was like a compulsion, which
began with what Dr. Stuart Asch might call "crazy thoughts." Images
of her daughters dead and gone. "I was like I gotta do this. I gotta do
it. I cannot handle things. I'm a failure. . . . It just seemed like a dead
end. I thought this was a way out, to end it."

Paula Sims did not speak to anyone about what had happened
until she came across some literature on postpartum psychosis in
prison and felt maybe that was what had happened to her. She had
found her vocabulary of motive, and maybe she was right, as the
Marce Society would argue. Or maybe it is just simpler to believe that
she'd been insane, that she hadn't taken action in order to wrest
herself free of a stifling life.

Around the time of Susan Smith's trial for drowning her two small
boys in a South Carolina lake, CNN's "Talk Back Live" broadcast an
hour-long show on infanticide. Smith did not commit infanticide,
insofar as her older son was beyond the age bracket defining the
crime. But she proved a springboard for an audience discussion that
focused mainly on cases like Paula Sims's. CNN's Susan Rook urged
the lifting of women like Sims out of social isolation, and accepting
that not all women want to be mothers. The audience was supportive
of this view, but they asked: Why don't these mothers give the babies
to women who are waiting to adopt one? Why, instead of destroying
them, don't they offer them as gifts to someone else? In fact, in several cultures, the extended family is alive and well and takes over
where individuals must leave off, so that often aunts and uncles and
grandparents raise children. In North America, on the whole, isolation is a much more dominant feature of family life. Perhaps women
can't concede their collapse as mothers when no one is around to

intervene. But a more complex set of psychological factors is also at work in some cases. If a child can thrive without his or her mother, the mother perceives herself as an abject failure when held up against the maternal ideal, a self-concept that becomes intolerable. When, in the late 1980s, Asch testified at the multiple murder trial of New Yorker Anne Green, who'd killed two of her infants and tried to kill a third, he was asked on the stand, "Would you let this woman baby-sit your children?" "Yes," he said, "they're *my* children, they're not her children."

Murder-suicides are the direct consequence of a mother who perceives herself to have failed. She has much in common with the father who gets fired from his job or can't break an alcohol addiction and comes home to kill his family and himself. A mother who takes her children with her into a garage and lets the carbon monoxide flow is doing so in much the same spirit.

As with spousal homicide, however, fathers are *more* likely to engage in murder-suicides than mothers, whereas mothers are more likely to borrow suicidal intent as an explanation after the fact. Lieutenant Gierasch can recall only one murder-suicide in Suffolk County, in which a policeman's wife killed herself and her child. Of eighty-eight infanticidal women in a 1988 study by Martin Daly and Margo Wilson, only two killed themselves. Significantly, of all English women admitted to London's Broadmoor Hospital between 1919 and 1969 for having committed infanticide, 49 percent had *attempted* or *threatened* suicide at the time of the offense.

Scholars sometimes describe infanticide as suicide by proxy and argue that it is altruistically motivated, meaning that the woman is not being possessive and selfish in taking children with her or sending them off to death on their own but believes she is tenderly protecting them from hardship. "It may seem paradoxical," a British psychiatrist and the first to lay out this view wrote at the turn of the century, "but it is not vice that leads to the death of the infant, rather is it morbid and mistaken maternal solicitude." Nearly one hundred years later, this idea swirled around the death penalty case of Guinevere Garcia in Illinois, when Bianca Jagger and others told the Board of Review why she shouldn't be executed. Garcia's drunken smothering of her daughter was attributed to her "fear that her uncle would gain custody of the girl and molest her." The rather clear implication of describing this sort of murder as "mistaken maternal solicitude" is that women are well-meaning but dumb. They don't think logically. Death is a "mistaken" act of nurturance. By contrast, when a sample of men convicted of infanticide were surveyed in Brixton Prison in Great Britain, those who offered altruistic motivations were scoffed at. Wrote their interviewer: "The statement 'that it was best for the children' . . . is an expression of the fact that the perpetrator himself thought that the infanticide was the best way out—that is to say, the act was egosyntonic." It served his purposes, not the children's. Whether altruism is, truly, at the heart of some infanticides is a matter for research and debate, as is the question of why female suicidal intent rarely turns into suicide in fact. The closest anyone has come through imaginative power to describing altruistic infanticide is Toni Morrison, in her novel *Beloved*, about an escaped slave, Sethe, who slits her baby daughter's throat so that she will never be enslaved. This was not uncommon in the antebellum South, and Morrison reportedly based her novel on a real case. Even here, though, "altruism" is a somewhat misleading word. As the writer Jennifer Uglow points out, "Sethe could not have killed her child unless she thought she owned her."

In 1989, Lifetime Television ran a documentary called "Postpartum: Beyond the Blues," narrated by Susan Sarandon. The objective was to expose "the insensitivity of the U.S. court system to mothers who are more victim than victimizer." The problem with the court system, however, is not that people can't see women as victims—precisely the opposite was true in Amy Ellwood's case. The problem is that the response to the crime is so philosophically incoherent and laden with sentiment that the jurisprudence is ambivalent, uncertain of itself. On CNN's "Talk Back Live" show, the psychologist Patricia Singleton informed the audience that "when a woman is incarcerated for this crime, she generally is punished more severely than a man." In truth, it only tends to be women who *dupe* the public into pitying them for a lost or kidnapped baby who receive severe punishment when the truth comes out, as happened to Susan Smith and Paula Sims. Most women aren't incarcerated for infanticide. Of those who are even convicted, about two thirds avoid prison, and the rest receive an average sentence of seven years. In England between 1982 and 1989, fewer than 10 percent of mothers convicted of manslaughter for killing their children (at any age) were imprisoned; only two of the mothers who'd committed infanticide were. British fathers were more likely to be charged with murder than manslaughter. Over half of the fathers convicted of manslaughter went to jail. Three times as many mothers as fathers are deemed to be mentally ill for killing their children.

We seem to permit a maternal sphere of influence over our youngest citizens, which recedes as children grow and enter the public domain. A woman who is acquitted of infanticide will not so easily escape censure for killing a child. Our collective sense of what is aggressive, of what we deem to be acceptable or unacceptable violence, is reflected in the comments of Suffolk County's Lieutenant Gierasch: "To me, when girls have babies without anyone else effectively knowing—I don't view it as aggression in the classic sense. My feelings aren't so strong, personally, with respect to that. But young toddlers, children, if they're the victims of outright homicide, is about as outrageous as I deal with." The child, as opposed to the baby, is the most cherished of all potential victims in our society. This is why a postpartum mother may not, in her "hormonally induced" psychosis, attack an older child and still be considered "more victim than victimizer."

Juries frequently cry when delivering verdicts in infanticide cases—as they did at Amy Ellwood's trial—regardless whether their decision is innocence or guilt. According to Phillip Resnick, a professor of psychiatry at Case Western Reserve University in Cleveland, juries are sympathetic in infanticide cases because "they view the mothers as having lost their most valuable possession already, in terms of the infant." It is curious that Resnick should say "possession." If children are regarded as citizens worthy of our protection, infants are perceived, on some level, as mere extensions of women—owned by them, as Uglow observed of Sethe.

Suffolk County Court Judge Stuart Namm, known in legal circles on Long Island as a progressive who generally sympathizes with the poor and downtrodden before him, was not at all sympathetic to Amy Ellwood. He sensed a moral vacuum at the heart of the trial, an absence of cultural wisdom to sustain the overwhelming support for his defendant. If, at one time in history, cultures openly proclaimed their indifference to their newborn members, this wasn't the time. A long-faced, gray-haired judge with thick, dark glasses, Namm gazed at Ellwood as she leaned into the protective arm of her lawyer. "This, Amy, was no miscarriage," he began, urging her to give up the satis-fying lie she'd told herself. "It was no abortion. It was no baptism. This was purely and simply an act of selfish and reckless man-slaughter." He turned his attention to her supporters, including Long Island's most tireless victims' rights advocate, who'd broken ranks in this instance to embrace Ellwood. "All of you believe that you are the real victims," Namm said. "Well, I'm sorry. But I don't agree." He lectured Ellwood's parents for failing to intervene when they knew she was pregnant. He criticized her lawyer for promising the "unwed mother syndrome" defense, which never materialized. He chastised the district attorney's office for trying to plea-bargain down to probation, and he expressed anger at the Probation Depart-ment for offering a sixteen-page personal evaluation of Ellwood with extensive psychological analysis, which Namm had not requested.

Judge Namm didn't see any evidence that Michael James Ellwood had been valued. Sentiments about motherhood and young woman-hood had together usurped a respect for the child. "It is my firm belief," he told Ellwood, "that you have yet to come to grips with the tragedy." No one, he said, "can callously take someone else's life and walk away with a slap on the wrist." He sentenced her to two and a half to seven and a half years in prison. Eric Naiburg appealed, and a New York State appellate judge permitted Ellwood to postpone prison until February 8, 1995, so that she could go to college.

What would happen if we took the British route, and enshrined in law a homogeneous view of women as biologically prone to mad-ness—as, by definition, insane to attack their own flesh and blood? As of 1993, only eighteen criminal cases in the United States involved a formal postpartum psychosis insanity defense, although women have been afforded this presumption less officially for years. Of all perpetrators who avoided prosecution for infant murder in Dade County, Florida, between 1956 and 1986 on a presumption of insanity, 83 percent were women. The British legal system invented postpartum insanity as we now understand it, much the same way that battered woman syndrome was tailored for U.S. courts—to accommodate a collective sense that women should be treated lightly for certain crimes. With what result? An enlightened view of women's lives? Postpartum psychosis was widely used in the nineteenth century in England as a reason why women shouldn't vote. British criminologist Nigel Walker calls the laws that govern infanticide in his nation "myth-making by legislation."

Infanticide, like any act of violence, is profoundly idiosyncratic. We can label it this way and that, make generalizations, but ultimately the truth is too personal. In North America, we are still in a position to draw distinctions between one woman and the next, between those who are psychotic and those who are sane, those whose stresses are insurmountable and those who choose not to surmount them. "You are," Judge Namm told Ellwood, "an intelligent, overindulged and privileged child of two educated, upper-middle-class parents, not some lonely, undereducated, underprivileged, abandoned teenage mother alone somewhere in a dirty room." Whether or not one agrees with Namm's judgment, his quest was honorable: to balance within the jurisprudence the social reality of women against the right of small children to live, to be valued.

MEDEA IN HER MODERN GUISE

The Use of Children as Pawns

The ideal mother has no interests of her own.

ALICE BALIN, psychoanalyst, 1974

Powerless women have always used mothering as a channel—narrow but deep—for their own human will to power.

ADRIENNE RICH, 1975

When the paramedics arrived, the child had been dead for some time. A delicate girl, four months old, with bright clowns on her sleeper and a wisp of blond hair, she lay on the living room floor of her parents' apartment among the unwrapped Christmas gifts. The room filled with a sting of winter air and the clamor of panic as adults rushed in and tripped over each other, shouting and muttering, reaching down to Tami Lynne to blow breath into her small blue mouth. It was December 20, 1985, nearly two in the morning in the manufacturing town of Schenectady, New York, twenty miles north of Albany.

Night sinks deeply in Schenectady in winter. The roads are poorly lit; they wind past shuttered houses and run-down malls. An ambulance siren keens through the somnolent quiet. Forty-two-year-old Marybeth Tinning was familiar with the sound of that siren. Over the years she had rushed her children to the emergency room at Saint Clare Hospital many times. Marybeth and her husband, Joe, were strong people, robust, rarely ill. But their children . . .

The Tinnings' neighbor Cynthia Walter lingered with them in the hospital waiting room, stunned with fatigue, high on adrenaline, until the last thread of hope had unraveled and snapped. She didn't want to let go of Tami Lynne, couldn't believe the girl had simply "stopped breathing," wouldn't see her Christmas presents, would be covered with earth like a stone. She was grief-struck, like a mother, and although she didn't know it, she was not the first to feel that hollow sorrow on the Tinnings' behalf. She was, in fact, the last in a long line of wrenched souls—neighbors, relatives, friends, the withdrawn and devastated father—to watch Tinning children die.

Marybeth Tinning, an expansive, handsome woman with too-bright eyes, began a round of announcing phone calls at 8:00 A.M. It was presumed that Tami Lynne had succumbed to sudden infant death syndrome. She called her sister-in-law, who sank to the floor. She called a friend who worked in a children's clothing shop and requested a bonnet to match Tami Lynne's Christmas dress, which would be her funeral attire. Then she and Joe went home, and she set to work packing up her daughter's clothes and toys in boxes. Two days later, the funeral, and the mother standing above her infant's grave, citing a prayer in a whisper: "Now I lay me down to sleep, I pray the Lord my soul to keep. If I should die before I wake, I pray the Lord my soul to take."

There were many troubled mourners at the funeral of Tami Lynne Tinning that morning two days before Christmas. People there who felt more than grief, who felt the leaden weight of realized dread. They knew this would happen, they should have done something, they didn't. Now they were watching the last rites administered to the ninth dead Tinning child. This time, the Schenectady child abuse hotline flashed with calls. For the first time, the police department got involved. It would take investigators several weeks, but they would gradually assemble enough information to provide a grim retrospective on the maternal career of this ostensibly ordinary American housewife.

Over the course of fourteen years, police suspected, she had deliberately harmed, hospitalized, and murdered eight of her nine children, ranging in age from one week to five years. On February 18,

1986, Tinning confessed to the New York State police to killing three of her children. Ultimately there would be enough forensic evidence to convict her for the murder of Tami Lynne.

In psychiatric parlance, Marybeth Tinning seems to have had Munchausen syndrome by proxy. The phrase describes a condition that is a spin-off from Munchausen syndrome, in which a person self-inflicts injuries or invents symptoms in an unceasing quest for attention from family and doctors. Unlike the expressive self-destruction of angry women, Munchausen syndrome is "instrumental" aggression, meaning that it's calculated, strategic—a deliberate and manipulative deception. In Munchausen syndrome by proxy, a person inflicts injuries on someone else—specifically, a child.

MSBP is almost exclusively the province of women who find themselves in maternal roles, either as biological or adoptive mothers or as babysitters or caretakers. They are very often nurses or are married to doctors. They have an expert grasp of medicine and a keen sense of medicine's power. They know that if they do certain things, or administer particular drugs, they can elicit seizures, respiratory arrest, or stomach problems that will enable them to rush their children to hospitals, enacting a dramatic last-minute rescue on a brightly lit stage. The psychiatrists Herbert Schreier and Judith Libow describe MSBP as "a 'career' pursued by ostensibly wonderful mothers who repeatedly offer their children's bodies to entice and simultaneously control their powerful, professional victims." Their victims—the targets of their power plays—are doctors. Their children are pawns. Although some of them kill their children (the death rate ranges from 10 to 30 percent), most keep them alive through careful dosing, tossing them with stunning cruelty into constant states of peril.

In 1991, Schreier and Libow sent out questionnaires about MSBP to all 870 pediatric neurologists in the United States. Of the 190 responses they got back, 107 doctors reported 89 confirmed cases and 198 suspected cases. Pediatric gastroenterologists responding to the same questionnaire reported 267 cases of the syndrome. Though there is still no accurate tally in the United States of how common this phenomenon is (estimates run to about 500 new cases a year) "we can safely say that the disorder is far from rare, and that it is frequently missed." In 1995, the FBI issued a report on MSBP to police investigators, citing "a growing list of cases" being brought to their attention by medical personnel. "This disorder represents a substantial challenge to the criminal justice system," the report cautioned. MSBP women are such effective liars that police officers have to pursue their suspicions with a firm handle on the complexity of the suspect.

Marybeth Tinning began this strange dance in 1972, when she had her labor induced to make, of her third child, "a Christmas baby." Newborn Jennifer died (naturally) of meningitis within days, and Tinning seems to have become abruptly fed up with the point of children, as if they no longer served a purpose. She was enraged by Jennifer's dying, then depressed, and finally overwhelmed by the sympathy and adulation she received as a grieving mother. The funeral, some who attended remembered years later, seemed in an odd way to cheer her up. Events unfurled from there with lightning speed. Within a matter of weeks, Tinning burst through the doors of Saint Clare's emergency room with Joe Jr. in her arms, the toddler gasping for breath as his mother screamed for help. Joe was admitted and recovered immediately. He went home. A few days later he was back. This time, the oxygen deprivation had gone on too long. By daybreak he was dead.

Two months went by, another funeral, and at the end of February, Tinning arrived at the emergency room with five-year-old Barbara in convulsions. The little girl was having seizures, bucking and writhing. She, too, was stabilized by hospital specialists. She, too, went home to recover and came back in the same state. By March, she, too, was dead. Marybeth Tinning had discovered in the ambulance siren her song, a triumphant cry to the world: I command your attention. I give life, and save it, and take it away.

The gap between what we assume of all mothers and what some of them actually feel was the space that Marybeth Tinning passed through. If Amy Ellwood committed her crime because her pregnancy had lost its meaning, Tinning suffocated her infant daughter because power was more important to her than love; ego gratification more compelling than toil. She was a predator. Had she been a man, she might have been a particularly ruthless entrepreneur, an organized criminal, a serial rapist. But she was a woman, and she located her well-spring of power in maternity. Not in the mundane, thankless mothering that most endure invisibly, without admiration, as our children flourish and grow. Tinning was drawn to the currency of motherhood, to the cultural prestige of pregnancy, the public admiration of a newborn, and the vast communal sympathy surrounding loss. Asked why she continued to get pregnant, given the alleged gene of death that seemed repeatedly to strike her, she replied: "Because I'm a woman, and that's what women are supposed to do."

When did people begin to suspect that something was amiss? Not after these first three children died; at that point, everyone was struck by the tragedy. How could a mother lose so much, so fast, and keep her wits about her? People pitied and admired Marybeth, which inspired her to do it again. A fourth child lived and died. Then a fifth. A sixth. Several nurses at Saint Clare were suspicious and called the child abuse hotline at various times, to no avail; Tinning's pediatricians were stalwart in their support of her. As the sorrow of a mother is presumed, so is her tender protectiveness. The death of a healthy child must, by cultural dictate, be proclaimed a natural mystery. If a pattern emerges wherein nature strikes one family more times than the odds would allow, then suspicions are quickly quelled by the interplay in our culture between two icons: the saintly mother and godly doctor. Munchausen syndrome by proxy thrives in the context of medical arrogance, where doctors cannot admit to the failure of their expertise. They cannot admit to being mystified. They cannot say "I don't know."

Although there was never a clear cause of death in Marybeth Tinning's children, the pathologists who examined each child resisted writing "Cause of Death: Unknown" on the death certificates. Barbara and Joseph and Timothy and Nathan and Michael and Mary Frances and Jonathan and Tami Lynne were listed, variously, as victims of SIDS, pneumonia, and Reye's syndrome. In retrospect, it was apparent that none of these labels fit. What the children had in common when they died was signs of asphyxiation. They were smothered. Had the pathologists and pediatricians involved been less pre-occupied with science, they might have thrown up their hands and so opened the door to an investigation. Still, one wonders if any serious investigating would have taken place. The culturally celebrated mother at the center of tragedy is one of our most potent symbols.

The name Munchausen syndrome by proxy was coined in 1977, around the same time as battered woman syndrome. The label is hugely misleading, insofar as it implies a treatable illness from which someone suffers, presumably without control, without the ability to make moral and rational choices. Many MSBP mothers suffered as children from neglect or abuse, but by the time they are adults, they are no more treatable than a serial killer like Paul Bernardo. Indeed, the psychiatrists Schreier and Libow contend that MSBP "may be a gender related form of psychopathy." In a moral context, we might simply call it evil. The term psychopath was introduced in the late nineteenth century but is best described in a 1941 book called *The Mask of Sanity*, by American psychiatrist Hervey Cleckley. As Cleckley defined it, psychopathy covers a cast of characters whom we traditionally understand to be men and might recognize in a villain such as Bluebeard: people without conscience, who, in the clinical phrasing, lack "empathy" for and "insight" into other human beings. They are perfectly sane individuals, Cleckley argued, except for their inability to love. They are hollow.

Since Cleckley, various scholars have narrowed in on the telltale traits of the psychopath. Among the most consistent behaviors are pathological lying, short attention span, grandiosity, manipulativeness, recklessness, remorselessness, and an absence of fear. According to biocriminologists, psychopaths are physically incapable of getting nervous. They don't experience the physiological arousal that goes with fear and anxiety, such as racing blood and sweaty palms. When people talk about "cold-blooded criminals," they are intuitively describing a very real biological phenomenon. They may be referring to a lack of compassion, but they are also picking up on the lack of *reaction*. Psychopaths will as calmly murder a child as eat their supper. In fact, it is often remarked upon in accounts of serial killers that after the crime, they forget all about it and sit down to dine.

Dr. Robert Hare, of the University of British Columbia, has been analyzing psychopathic speech patterns, using functional magnetic resonance imaging scans to monitor brain wave activity. Theorizing that a vital link is missing between emotion and language in the neural structure of their brains, he shows psychopaths words, like "wood" or "hat" or "love" or "death," to see if their brain waves distinguish emotionally resonant words from neutral ones. Most of us react differently to "love" than to "wood." The psychopath does not.

"What is love?" a psychiatrist at the Penetanguishine Mental Health Center in Ontario asks a psychopath in a videotaped interview done in the 1980s.

"Having someone put dinner on the table," the young man guesses.

"What is trust?"

This gives pause. "It's just a word," he replies, after mulling it over. "It doesn't mean anything."

The psychiatrist J. Reid Meloy compares the structure of the psychopath's brain to a reptile's. A cold-blooded animal like an alligator has a fixed set of instincts, "such as home site selection, establishment and defense of territories, hunting, feeding, mating, competition, dominance, aggression." What a reptile doesn't have "is a parental response to its offspring." The analogy reveals why it's so difficult for people to picture women as psychopathic predators. All women are presumed to have a parental response, even if it's an anguished response or a crazy one. Even if a woman grows wild and furious with her child, that, at least, is engagement. But what if the child has no ability to affect her at all? That child is invisible, annihilated. The most painful cases of child abuse to read about are the ones in which a child was simply ignored. Nothing can be so threatening to one's remembered childhood ego as the idea of maternal indifference. Yet neglect, not just by psychopaths, is one of the most common forms of maternal aggression. "Neglect is continual," argues Dr. Mindy Rosenberg, a child psychologist in Oakland, California; "it's pervasive, it's chronic, it's insidious. And it's far more common than abuse." The Swiss psychoanalyst Alice Miller has defined neglect as "soul murder." Often, neglect is expressive of sublimated rage or depression, but it can also be instrumental. The starved, discarded child in the closet frequently has well cared-for siblings. The mother is using this one child for some other purpose: to punish the father, perhaps, or to disavow an aspect of herself. At any rate, her obliteration of the child is careful, considered, and pro-longed. And so horrifying, we can barely even conceptualize it, which goes some way to explaining why the psychopathic mother is a type found virtually nowhere, in either literature or medicine.

What would a psychopathic mother look like? How would she talk and act? Meloy points out that psychopaths "share with the reptilian [brain] an inability to socialize in a consciously affectionate and genuinely expressive manner." Because they cannot feel affectional emotions, only boredom, exhilaration, and rage, psychopaths be-come mimics of human behavior in order to fit in. This is what Cleckley meant in his title by "mask of sanity." Through careful observation, psychopaths learn to appear to be loving, principled, and kind. They are predators in disguise. When Schreier and Libow describe Munchausen syndrome by proxy as "a form of mothering imposture," they could be describing the mask that is donned by a female psychopath. If these women resemble anyone, if they summon any particular stereotype, it is that of the culturally cele-brated mother.

There is a photo of Marybeth Tinning, taken perhaps in 1970, with her eldest daughter Barbara, who looks to be about four years old. The girl wears a perfectly pressed dress tied in the back with a bow. Her hair has been brushed until it gleams. Mother Marybeth sports an expression of cheerful concentration as she shows Barbara how to work a toy. Her own dark hair falls to the shoulder, then bounces with an insouciant flip, like Mary Tyler Moore's in "The Dick Van Dyke Show." Barbara would live for roughly one more year.

As if auditioning for parts in a play, Marybeth Tinning pursued roles that she identified with femininity and nurturance: She was the president of a girl's club in her high school called Future Home-makers of America. She was a mother, nursing assistant, school bus driver, and volunteer ambulance attendant. One year, she got a job as a waitress and seemed to imitate the idea of waitress, painting

on her eyebrows and dying her hair. She also engaged in a full repertoire of feminine self-denigrations, displaying tears, a chin cocked
downward, a hope for approval. Yet, alone with Joe, she had a violent
temper, once kicking her foot through their TV.

The same duality surfaced in her mothering. A telling detail in
the short life of Tami Lynne was that she was always beautifully
attired, according to the family, but the doctors who examined her
on the night that she died found severe, untended diaper rash. "In
Marybeth's mind," writes the journalist Joyce Egginton, "a baby was
an extension of herself, and when the infant was admired it was she
who received the compliments." But what others didn't see need not
be done. Tinning showered her babies with store-wrapped gifts but
often left their bottles out on the counter for a day or two, until the
milk grew sour. When attention wandered from her, she upstaged
other people's events. She announced her eighth pregnancy, for
example, at a christening party for her seven-year-old niece, effectively usurping the mood by casting a pall over everyone's day. Even
her murder trial, an event of justice sought for her children, became
an opportunity for self-promotion. Tinning was delighted by the
media. "You could paper the walls with all my photographs," she
bragged to a staffer in the courthouse cafeteria, according to Joyce
Egginton.

Some cultures invoke the belief that if you photograph a person,
you steal their soul. According to J. Reid Meloy, the relationship of
the psychopath to those around her is somewhat akin to the process
of a body in search of a soul. People become "projective containers,"
alternately idealized and devalued to sustain the fragile structure of
the psychopath's "grandiose self." Even in death, Tinning's children
were mirrors, reflecting back a confirmation of her own importance.
Tinning's behavior at her trial was reminiscent of that of an Oregon
woman named Diane Downs, whose three children got in the way (as
she saw it) of her infatuation with a married man. Having showily lav-
ished attention on them throughout their young lives, she now
unhesitatingly shot them—at close range with a Colt .45—in an act
of premeditated mayhem that was made to look like a carjacking.
One of her children survived and eventually summoned the courage

to tell investigators what happened, which led to Downs's arrest. In 1983, Downs appeared at her murder trial pregnant and smiling serenely, having conceived a new child on a one-night stand so that she could project an aura of maternal grace to her jury. Like Tinning, she didn't understand that her femininity had lost its currency the night she fired her gun.

Eventually, female psychopaths unmask themselves this way. They reveal a fundamental failure to get the point about love or mothering. Even so, it takes much longer for people to see the mask slip on a woman than on a man. Marybeth Tinning confounded observers because she seemed so genuinely torn up by her losses. Emotion in predators often trips us up because we don't expect them to be able to show it. "I've seen psychopaths cry like a baby," says Dr. Bill Tillier, a forensic psychologist in Edmonton, Alberta. "But it's the focus of the emotion you have to look for. Their emotion is flowing through an egocentric filter." They cry in self-pity, not grief. If the difference is only remotely evident in men (Paul Bernardo sobbed hysterically the night Tammy Homolka died), it is extremely obscure in women because it plays so directly into feminine stereotypes. The people around Marybeth Tinning saw her as "childlike," "needy," "craving affection," "insecure." Add to this their preconceptions about motherhood, and a lack of suspicion turns into outright protectiveness. Even when she gave her confession, the state police investigator, William Barnes, led her to answer questions that he hoped would win her forgiveness at trial, "doing his best to elicit a confession . . . which might be the basis of a plea of temporary insanity."

The idea that Tinning was temporarily insane on eight different occasions (some suggest she had postpartum psychosis) was somewhat belied by her attempt to kill Joe, after an argument over money, which she spent copiously and recklessly. In the spring of 1974, according to Joyce Egginton, she appears to have poisoned her husband with seventy capsules of phenobarbital, a drug her nephew took to prevent seizures. Far from being suspected of attempted murder, she won pity for the fact that her husband "had tried to commit suicide"—a scenario that Joe didn't oppose because he couldn't remember what happened. Tinning came close to being charged with arson when, at her insistence, Joe bought and renovated a trailer that she decided she didn't want, at which point it mysteriously burned to the ground.

Over the years between 1972 and 1985, Tinning hinted to people that she might harm their children—or may have killed her own. She placed these warnings in the mouths of third parties, as if commenting on unfounded accusations against her. Her favorite book was *Where Are the Children?* by Mary Higgins Clark, in which the heroine is falsely accused of killing her children and n. 'st keep on the run from police sirens, fugitive-style. Joyce Egginton interprets these dark insinuations to be her cry for help. But do people who want help indulge in multiple murder as a means to that end? Psychopaths don't want help, they want power. One suspects, instead, that Tinning was flexing her muscle—boasting, as nearly as she could without getting caught, of her magnificent accomplishment. What could ever be so potent as to kill?

When Medea used her children as pawns in her war with Jason, she became one of the last figures in Western culture to mirror the truth that women can be strategically aggressive toward children, that their violence isn't always personal, private, or impulsive, that sometimes it is expressly political—a means of making a public statement, furthering an ambition, punishing a man. Greek and Roman mythology is fairly plain on this point, with an abundance of wrathful godesses and heroines who imperil children in pursuit of some other goal. The fate of the child is irrelevant to the mother. The child is a vehicle for her own empowerment. Yet if all this was quite explicit in early Western mythology, it has since disappeared. Apart from the wicked stepmother, who is not biologically related to the child, one searches literature in vain for an archetype of instrumental maternal aggression.

Perhaps one reason for the absence is that maternal aggression isn't always physically explicit; the injury is less visible than Medea's slaughter of her sons. Instead, it takes the form of pushing or forcing children to behave a certain way. Sons throughout history have been pushed into wars and other conflicts by their mothers, for the sake of her honor or aggrandizement, only to lose their limbs or their lives. In her book about the history of motherhood, Shari Thurer comments that "the Roman mother's use of her own sons toward the attainment of power was elevated to a high art." The same could be said of several other epochs and cultures. Adrienne Rich understood this in terms of sublimation of forbidden emotion: "A woman whose rage is under wraps may well foster a masculine aggressiveness in her son." But less purely emotional motives come into play as well. Women use children to express their will to power.

One of the most influential explanations for crime in the twentieth century is anomie theory, which holds that criminality is a response to frustrated ambition. Men who hope to achieve success will turn to crime if no other route is available. At the same time, anomie theory has been used to explain why women *do not* commit crime: Since their ambitions are to marry and raise children, "extremely accessible" goals, they are less likely to be frustrated in their aspirations. Applied this way, anomie theory becomes the economic version of the psychological theory of relationalism— women's point of reference is the family and the home; therefore, they are less inclined to be antisocial and destructive. Both theories miss the point. Social and economic arrangements do not, in themselves, erase a woman's will to power. What they do is shape her concept of empowerment and redirect her efforts.

Is there a connection between the ambitious woman who endangers the life of her child to enhance her own prestige and the MSBP mother? It's important to make the distinction between two bids for power: One aims for vicarious access to the masculine world, such as the mother who pushes her son into war, politics, or sport because she cannot pursue power directly. The other bid is to project feminine power into the masculine world—to remind men, as it were, that women have control over life and death itself. This was Medea's strategy, and it is the far more fearsome of the two, for the power is more potent and the tactic more ruthless. Unconscious of her mythic ancestress and, perhaps, of her own motive, a woman like Marybeth Tinning promotes herself in much the same way. Working within the conventional boundaries of femininity, a psychopathic woman who is searching for an arena in which to aggrandize herself may well be attracted to the grandiosity of the medical establishment because it has become the locus of power and prestige for the traditional maternal role.

The rise of MSBP coincides with the ascendance of medical control over motherhood and the rise of so-called scientific mothering. Before this century, women largely raised their children through a combination of experience, common sense, and collective wisdom. By the time Marybeth Tinning joined the Future Homemakers of America in high school, male doctors' influence was paramount. Women were responsible for children, but they were not in control. Motherhood was a career, for which they had to train, in perpetual apprenticeship to doctors.

The anthropologist Rima Apple has unearthed magazine advertisements from the twenties, thirties, and forties that encapsulate the paradox. In one ad, dating from 1938, a woman is portrayed at a table flipping through an expert's child-rearing text. She is telling her daughter, "I wish I'd had this manual when you were born!" Beneath the tableau runs the caption: "Add science to love and be a 'perfect mother.'" Apple cites an advice columnist who tells her women readers, "Ideal motherhood, you see, is the work not of instinct, but of enlightened knowledge conscientiously acquired and carefully digested. If maternity is an instinct, motherhood is a profession."

Psychopathic women might be attracted to the concept of scientific mothering because of its assumption that maternal behavior isn't instinctive but is, instead, something they could train for. They might also calculate its power-play potential: If maternity in the guise of medical knowledge is prestigious, they can appropriate that knowledge and empower themselves in a male world. They can win, all at once, the adulation of the feminine and the power of the masculine, usurping both control and prestige. There is an intriguing overlap in the behavior of mothers with Munchausen syndrome by proxy and nurses who commit multiple homicides and are known, euphemistically, as angels of death: Both pursue acts of feminine nurturance, a role that, if disconnected from true or spontaneous compassion, has the *appearance* of compassion, and more than that, the prospect of heroism—the potential for the caregiver to be adored and respected for the rescue of life itself.

Take a tour of a hospital pediatrics ward, and you begin to see the discrepancy in status between nurses and mothers, on the one hand, and doctors, on the other. So it seemed one afternoon at The Hospital for Sick Children, in downtown Toronto, which had its own brush with an angel of death. Sick Kids, as it's known, is a light, airy, plant-filled oasis for ill and wounded children from around the world. Their dramatic tales often get newspaper play: the South Asian Siamese twins who were successfully separated; the Ghanaian boy who recovered from a rare cancer. On 7D, the general pediatrics ward, the doctors make their early morning rounds through the white corridors, pushing a computer on a trolley past posters of Babar and Winnie-the-Pooh. They are accompanied by two junior residents, an intern, and a visiting doctor from Poland. Everyone is well dressed beneath their white coats, young urban professionals whose identical stethoscopes mark them as members of the medical elite.

Every few feet, the group pauses to discuss the patients whose names they see slotted into plates beside each doorway. One doctor pulls up the relevant file on her computer, and the group debates diagnoses. Could five-year-old Brian indeed have cystic fibrosis, as "Chest" insists? A second doctor feels the child also suffers "clinical malnutrition." Were the liver biopsy results back from G.I.? The junior resident notes that Brian hasn't been "tolerating his feeds." The first doctor worries about that, tapping at her keyboard, "We need him to be optimized for his operation."

As the highly clinical medical scrum goes on, nurses in sweatpants and running shoes squeeze by with muttered "excuse me's" to get into the patients' rooms. They carry Monopoly boards and teddy bears, bottles of juice, packs of crayons. They sit the children on their knees, cradle them in their arms, and, when the children vomit or soil themselves, the nurses roll up their sleeves and clean it all away. The contrast is striking: Authority and respect is on the doctor's side, toil and sentiment on the nurse's. It runs parallel to the division of esteem in the traditional home.

In 1979, the Hospital for Sick Children was plunged into crisis.

Twenty babies died in a handful of months, apparently from overdoses of a heart medicine called Dioxogin. For a time, code blues were sounding almost every day. Ultimately, a nurse was charged, but was released for lack of evidence; the deaths were never solved.

In 1981, officials at Bexar County Hospital in San Antonio, Texas, telephoned the Hospital for Sick Children for advice when a large numbers of children in *their* ICU began perishing unexpectedly as well. Usually, the pediatrics unit had two or three code blue resuscitations in a month. In August of 1981, they had nine; in September, thirteen. The children were hemorrhaging internally or dying of cardiac arrest. Without exception, the dramatic emergencies took place on a shift under the supervision of a nurse named Genene Jones, who appeared to be flourishing in her role at the center of crisis.

The parallels of character between Jones and Tinning are striking. Genene Jones was a "charming and manipulative" liar, who, like Marybeth Tinning, "told colorful stories about her life and exaggerated illnesses to her friends and children." In Jones's first two years as a pediatric nurse, she proved unreliable and arrogant, making several serious nursing errors, showing up for her shift drunk, swanning dramatically off to Bexar County's outpatient clinic and emergency room a total of thirty times for mysterious ailments, and presiding with operatic flair over the children on the unit. At one point, presumably for thrills, she announced to a mother and father that their child had died when he hadn't.

Everything about Genene Jones's behavior should have sounded alarms when the code blues sprang up on her shift, but at the same time, it seemed implausible that a woman who so clearly relished the rescue of children could be causing them harm. Eventually, hospital administrators agreed that Jones was too strong a suspect to ignore. Doubtless armed with words of caution from the Hospital for Sick Children in Toronto about pegging the wrong person, Bexar County fired all of the nurses in the ICU rather than risk litigation for firing Genene Jones alone. Within weeks, she'd moved to a private pediatrics clinic in a small town, hired by one of Bexar County's former residents, who was apparently unaware of, or who dismissed as un-

founded, suspicions about her conduct. In less than a month, four
little patients went into respiratory arrest, exactly the type of code
blue that had occurred at the hospital. Then a girl who was tagging
along with her mother to the doctor's office suddenly developed
breathing difficulties after sitting on Jones's lap alone in the waiting room. The doctor sent the girl to San Antonio for investigation, and on the trip, accompanied solely by Jones, she had a heart
attack and died.

The parents took out an ad in the local paper thanking the doctor
and her nurse, Genene Jones. The local medical community
responded differently. They forced the head of the clinic to investigate her nurse. The doctor found vials of Anectine, a drug that
causes muscle paralysis and respiratory arrest, and Jones was charged
with two counts of murder. Shortly after her conviction, a Texas
Department of Corrections official wrote to the Bexar County Hospital District to ask if there was any problem with inmate Jones being
assigned to the hospital dispensary.

Mothering, whether in the home or on the hospital floor, is a
much more common route to power for psychopathic women than
is commerce or sex. That route should be clear. That it's so veiled is
less a comment on the cunning of the women themselves than on
the prejudices of our culture. As Schreier and Libow wrote about
MSBP, "That we have so much difficulty seeing these mothers as cha-
rades says as much about our wishes and needs as it does about the
women themselves."

In recent years, academics have tried to uncover MSBP rates by
tracking cases of confirmed abuse or death in children and then
researching the fates of their sisters and brothers. Dr. Roy Meadow, a
professor of pediatrics at St. James University Hospital, Leeds, England, who coined the phrase Munchausen syndrome by proxy,
reported in 1990 that of twenty-seven children who had been suffocated by their mothers, he'd found eighteen siblings who had died
"suddenly and unexpectedly in early life." Three similar studies
found high rates of unexplained sibling demise. Chicago, which has
one of the highest unexpected infant death rates in the world, was

the subject of a 1985 study by the Committee to Prevent Child Abuse. Twenty-two percent of the crib deaths recorded in a two-year period, the committee found, "were related to suspected child abuse and neglect." Though not all of the suspicious Chicago cases were the result of Munchausen syndrome by proxy, the data reveal how easy it is to harm children, and particularly babies, without falling under suspicion.

According to Dr. John Emery, testifying at Marybeth Tinning's trial, the term sudden infant death syndrome was coined at the turn of the century in the state of Washington. "As deaths due to what you might call classic disease such as pneumonia disappeared," Emery explained, "relatively larger numbers of children died unexpectedly . . . at home instead of at hospital." Without any obvious or medically understood cause of death, parents became suspects in neglect, either for "sleeping on top of them, or being drunk or disorderly." A group of Seattle doctors "said let us, as it were, invent a term which could be used to describe babies that are found unexpectedly dead, and we will say that this is a natural cause of death so these parents shall not be harassed. Eventually they called it sudden infant death syndrome, and this had a very fine effect."

As with postpartum psychosis, SIDS is not always the wrong conclusion to draw, insofar as there quite clearly are breathing and metabolic disorders in some infants that cause sudden death. In some cases, the problem may be a subtle neurological malformation affecting respiratory control; in others, a respiratory infection. Smoking during pregnancy increases the risk of SIDS. So does premature birth. Babies are also vulnerable to suffocation when lying facedown on bunched bed clothes, because they don't have the strength to lift their faces. The peak risk age is between two and four months, with 90 percent of SIDS deaths taking place before six months. Natural infant deaths are not a fiction. SIDS itself is not necessarily a misnomer. The problem is that it's become a catch-all explanation, used when autopsies show no clear cause of death. Coroners tend to apply the label indiscriminately. In 1995, two babies in the Boston area who suffocated in battery-operated cradles were listed as SIDS cases without death scene investigations. Another eight babies died before any connection was made to the design of the cradle.

Death by smothering is virtually indistinguishable from SIDS at autopsy. If medical examiners don't seek out clues at the death scene, as they do for all suspicious adult deaths, then it's not difficult to see how infanticides by smothering are overlooked. Police investigators and academics guess that 10 to 20 percent of the six thousand to eight thousand SIDS cases reported each year in the United States conceal accidental or deliberate suffocation. "I remember handling all the deaths, and you'd get a lot of crib deaths," recalls detective Leroy Orozco. "We had one where one gal's baby died, then several months later, another one. We thought, this gal could suffocate her kids and we'd never *know* it."

Karisa Santiago, of Yonkers, New York, was charged with murdering her five-month-old daughter, Maria Lisa Ruiz, in 1994 after two of her other children died of SIDS—Mildred, eight months, on March 25, 1994, and Benjamin, two and a half, on November 18. Although the New York City Medical Examiner had found Benjamin's death "suspicious" because of bruises on his nostrils, not to mention the fact that he was too old to be dying of SIDS, his case was listed as SIDS due to "insufficient evidence." Only when Maria died were the earlier two cases reopened. Karisa Santiago pled guilty to one count of manslaughter in November 1995. "The only way you can prove [smothering]," according to Dr. J. M. DiMaio, a coroner in San Antonio, Texas, "is to show a pattern of behavior."

DiMaio worked on the case of Martha Woods, which set a precedent for introducing patterns of behavior in infanticide in 1973. Woods was the wife of an army officer who had harmed nine children and caused seven to die (only three were her own) over twenty-three years. In each case, she rushed the baby or toddler to the hospital in a state of oxygen deprivation, doctors performed extensive tests, found nothing wrong, the child recovered and after repeated episodes, finally died. In one instance, a doctor cited the cause of death as "status lymphaticus," a condition that doesn't exist. In another, a physician cited the cause of death suggested to him by Martha Woods rather than performing an autopsy. Woods eluded detection from 1946 to 1973, in part because she and her husband were moving around. Marybeth Tinning, on the other hand, was not moving around. She stayed in one place in full view of her community. "A lot of doctors," notes Dr. DiMaio, "are very naive about these cases. . . . they think that all mothers care about their children and find it very hard to believe that some mothers don't."

One such doctor seems to have been Alfred Steinschneider. In 1972, the pediatrician published an article in *Pediatrics* magazine announcing that multiple deaths in one family probably had a genetic or inheritable component—the gene of death that Joe Tinning thought he and Marybeth were carrying. SIDS, the doctor claimed, ran in families. Twenty-two years later, Dr. Steinschneider's case study for this article, a New York State housewife named Waneta Hoyt, confessed to smothering all five of her children.

In the meantime, however, Steinschneider's article was widely influential, preventing coroners and doctors across North America from entertaining suspicions when multiple babies perished in a family. After a Chicago woman named Deborah Gedzius lost her fifth child, a healthy two-year-old, to mysterious causes in 1979, her husband requested an investigation. Their pediatrician, Dr. Eugene Diamond, phoned Steinschneider, confirmed that SIDS ran in families, ruled that all five toddlers had died naturally (in spite of the fact that they were well beyond the SIDS age bracket), and published his own journal article about it. Then a sixth child died, and Deborah Gedzius's husband, who in grief and disgust was planning to divorce her, was shot in the head while he slept. Gedzius collected one hundred thousand dollars in life insurance. She wasn't charged with the crime. Nor would the attorney general's office prosecute her in connection with the deaths of her six children. Their reasoning? They'd heard expert testimony at a preliminary hearing (which determines whether there is sufficient cause to go ahead with a criminal charge) that was based on Steinschneider's article.

If Marybeth Tinning was able to get away with murder for so long, the SIDS-in-families theory was certainly one of the culprits. It wasn't the only one, of course. The child welfare system failed the Tinning children by repeatedly erasing its records of abuse calls, creating for itself a continuous tabula rasa about her behavior. Given the virtually invisible nature of certain forms of female-perpetrated abuse, the mistake is perhaps unsurprising.

When Marybeth Tinning began to kill, infanticide and child abuse had not yet come to the fore of American social politics. By the time she was arrested, questions about how citizens treated their children were urgently being posed. Reports of child abuse increased 50 percent nationwide between 1986 and 1992, with a total of 1,160,400 children confirmed as abused by investigators—a 10 percent increase over 1991 alone. In terms of fatal child abuse, a 1993 Department of Justice report, "Murder in Families," states that mothers were more likely than fathers to be the perpetrators of child homicide. Smaller samples by scholars show conflicting results, concerning nonfatal abuse, with men found to be more responsible for "shaken baby syndrome," while mothers more commonly commit general assaults—or vice versa, depending on the research. Women appear to be more responsible for the severe physical abuse of American children, with sons being more frequent targets than daughters. Female involvement in sexual abuse, virtually ignored in the discourse, is more common than previously believed. A number of new studies have focused on female child molestors, though the incidence rate remains controversial—ranging upward to 25 percent of all cases.

There is a marked tendency to preface the admission that women abuse children with a reminder that they spend more time with them. This is akin to insisting that men are more violent in war only because they are the ones to be drafted. It is hardly an *explanation*. We obscure the role of women in child abuse and neglect because it doesn't fit well with current rhetoric on violence. "Women are linked more intimately into networks of interpersonal ties, and their moral decisions are more influenced by an ethic of caring that inhibits criminal activities that hurt others," noted two crime scholars in 1993, echoing the thinking first elucidated by Harvard psychologist Carol Gilligan. Crime runs contrary to "the values of womanhood." Anyone who has been physically or sexually assaulted by her mother or a female caretaker knows that this truism has too many exceptions to hold.

There are compelling reasons to resist an *exclusive* emphasis on maternal child abuse. Freud began a long tradition of blaming everything that went wrong in human development on Mom. But what is vitally important about acknowledging female contributions to family violence is that mothers can act as powerful forces of socialization, either teaching a child through the trauma she inflicts how to behave in the wider world, or compelling that child, who is damaged, to wreak destruction in turn. Alice Miller has traced the links between child abuse and violence particularly eloquently. "When a person cannot talk about the cruelty endured as a child," she writes, "then he or she must *demonstrate* cruelty." Miller cites the case of an eleven-year-old Newcastle girl named Mary Bell, who strangled two small boys, aged three and four, and left their small bodies amidst litter in a junkyard. Her mother had given birth to her at seventeen and immediately rejected her, shouting "Take it away" when the baby was brought to her in the hospital. Several times she left her small girl in adoption offices, simply walking out. The child was returned to her repeatedly, and ultimately she tried to kill her. Strikingly young, Mary Bell began to kill in turn. "A child who has been mistreated at such an early age," Miller wrote, "must be able to tell in some way or another about the wrong that has been done her, about the murder perpetrated on *her*."

A recent study of rapists and child molestors found that fully 62 percent of them had been sexually abused when they were young, by female caretakers as well as male. Studies of wife-assaulters frequently reveal a majority who were abused as children—as often, if not more often, by mothers than fathers. Research on the relation between child abuse or neglect and female criminality shows that twice as many girls who were mistreated were later arrested for adult crime. Men and women who were abused themselves are far more likely to fatally assault or neglect their own children. It is not that bad men are the fault of evil women, but to separate one sex from the other as virtuous or blameworthy is to follow a false trail in understanding the causes of violence. If a man learned physical or sexual violence from his mother, how useful is it for us to blame it on his maleness, to educate him about not being sexist, to decry "violence against women," as if women weren't contributors to the trajectory of his rage? If we are to understand his crimes, we might just as well understand his models. "Only the last murder," writes Alice Miller, "the final act in a very long chain of events, is punishable by the court." The first, the neglect or abuse of the child, goes unremarked, and "spreads over the world like a plague."

If the formation of the child—morally, emotionally, and socially— is a more plausible cause of violent behavior than testosterone, say, or patriarchy, how much weight should we lend a child's abuse in our perception of the adult offender? It depends on the point of the perception: prevention or justice. Where prevention is concerned, we must obviously assign it a lot of weight. Justice is more problematic. Maltreatment teaches, but it does not decree. Millions of battered children grow up to be compassionate adults, and if their relationships are difficult, they have nevertheless chosen to *try* to construct for themselves loving and ethical lives. Abuse interacts with a number of other factors, both external to the growing child and intrinsic to her personality, which complicate cause and effect. In describing MSBP mothers as once-neglected children who are "hurting for love," Schreier and Libow assign to these women a childlike innocence that the criminal justice system cannot, as a matter of principle, concede. Childhood is no longer the sum of who adult offenders are. The court could no more exonerate Marybeth Tinning than the court in Canada could acquit Paul Bernardo. Their deeds may have been only the last in a long chain of events, as Miller says, but they *must* be punishable. Otherwise, the chain extends, unbroken, through a long line of harmed and harming souls.

BALANCING THE DOMESTIC EQUATION

When Women Assault Their Spouses or Lovers

We must not keep to ourselves the shameful secrets of
men.

ANN JONES, *NEXT TIME, SHE'LL BE DEAD*, 1993

Why are we, as a culture, loath to expose the responsibility
of women in domestic abuse?

JUDITH SHEVRIN, clinical psychologist, 1994

Before his life fell to ruins, Peter Swann inhabited a world that felt
good to him, purposeful and clear. As he entered his thirties he had
solid work as a municipal engineer and was raising his seven-year-old
daughter, Grace, in a house perched high on the grassy bluffs of
Lake Ontario, east of the city of Toronto. From that untroubled vista
he could pursue his love of the natural world, taking Grace up onto
the roof on clear summer nights to show her the stars through his
telescope, riding their mountain bikes through the sprawling ravines
of Toronto's Metro Zoo. He filled the house with small wonders—an
aquarium full of rare fish, a collection of rocks. Sometimes he'd dig
out the treasure of his mother's phonograph, to teach Grace what
snatches of old songs he knew.

Peter had always wanted to be a teacher, preferably of science. In
the manner we associate with men, he felt most comfortable con-
necting to others through the learning of facts and the doing of
things. Social politics intimidated him. Interior landscapes mystified.
A little shy, emotionally awkward, he wasn't one to navigate the swift
headwaters of intimacy with anything approaching skill.

As Grace approached puberty, with all its attendant moods, he began to look for a relationship, hoping to find a woman who might act as a mother figure to her. Her own mother had vanished, not long after the Catholic Children's Aid charged her with abuse and transferred custody to Peter. He had been immensely relieved to have Grace back. Her upbringing was his mission. He had been given up for adoption as an infant. His daughter would stay with her own flesh and blood. "Mr. Swann," a counselor wrote some years later, "presents as a mature, warm and caring father."

In 1989, a mutual friend introduced Peter to a thirty-year-old clothing store manager named Dana, whose marriage was on the rocks. Dana was a bright and charming woman, and if her temper seemed extreme, Peter reasonably attributed that to her frustrations with her husband, who was something of a boor. "They fought all the time," he remembers. "She used to beat him up on the couch. Hit him in the face. He thought it was a joke. The rest of us . . ." Peter makes a face of consternation. "But I felt, I'm not like him, so it won't be like that for us. I'm more easygoing, not the same personality."

Once Peter and Dana got involved, their relationship deepened quickly. Within months she'd moved into his home on the bluffs, continuing to work in retail, a job that she loved and was good at. They appeared to be a well-adjusted couple: two professionals raising a child. Three full and busy lives. There was only one, very private problem. Dana's temper, which Peter had attributed to her anger at her first husband, didn't go away. Far from calming her down, his more peaceable (and avoidant) temperament seemed to fuel her. "She'd start making an anthill into a molehill into a mountain," he says. Then he abruptly switches to the present tense, as if he's returned to that place in their kitchen, or his basement office, where something he said or did tripped an invisible wire. "She comes home from work, comes downstairs, and starts screaming at me, kicking holes in the walls. I don't know what to do. What's bugging her now? Somethin' at work, or what? I cleaned the kitchen, I paid the bills . . . It's goin' through my mind, and I'm just sitting there stymied, you know? I just don't know what to do. How do I calm her down? It just didn't work. Wham, bam. I'm getting hit."

Peter should have seen, he adamantly tells himself, that Dana's violent outbursts would continue, that his disinclination to respond with crude jokes and counterpunches, as her ex-husband had, would serve him no better in checking a fury that was essentially impersonal, an unresolved maelstrom of emotions from childhood. But Peter was stunned by her anger. He tried to appease her. "I became more passive." Whatever wound Dana up to the point of violence, he would simply refrain from; it wasn't worth it. "Our honeymoon was the only time we got along. It was like passing through an empty space, and then, Bang! Back into the hard stuff again." The list of nixed activities grew longer. He didn't go off on his bike rides with Grace; he didn't go out with his friends by himself; he didn't go out with his friends at all. Eventually, he didn't even wander out of sight in the supermarket, lest it start another fight he couldn't win.

"She couldn't compromise," he explains. "It was her way or no way. She controlled me, hit me, controlled me, hit me. Any excuse would do. She told me I was no good, that I drank too much, my family's no good, I'm useless. She'd throw metal address books at my head, ashtrays. Oh, bruises, right?" He lights another cigarette and rubs his forehead, his embarrassment rising. "I go to work, and guys say: What happened? 'Oh, I fell down,' whatever. Later I told them. They said, 'Get out of it.' " He flicks his cigarette ash, missing the ashtray, then wanders over to pick up his pet guinea pig. "I tried to get out, but I didn't . . . I just didn't know how. We've got a town house, my daughter's there, between us we're making fifty-two grand a year. I started giving her the paychecks. I had to ask her for a pack of cigarettes. 'Please?' you know, like a dog. I didn't realize it, I was stupid, okay? I'm a wuss, okay? It's hard to say it. It's hard for a man to say that."

But Swann has to say that now, because Grace is gone. So is his job, his house, his telescope, everything he owned, even the phonograph, and Swann is sleeping in a boardinghouse with the guinea pig as his sole family. One night in that paltry place, he fumbles with the screw-top of an unrefrigerated bottle of wine, pours another splash into a coffee mug, and stammers out the simpleness of what he'd hoped: "A family is supposed to be a family. You know? We all get along." He waves his hand feebly, his voice weepy, his words slurred.

"I want to be responsible for my daughter. Is something wrong with that, did I do something wrong?" What Peter Swann did was to meet and marry a female batterer, a woman who was angry, controlling, abusive, and manipulative, and who ultimately walked away with everything in his life, including his thirteen-year-old daughter.

Husband abusers aren't supposed to exist, but they do.

The idea that domestic violence refers exclusively to wife abuse or to violence against women is so deeply ingrained in Western consciousness that it is impossible to grapple with Peter Swann's story without first unraveling some potent conventional wisdom. Most of us believe that masculine power is the fountainhead of private, as well as public, violence. Spouse assault is what *men* do to *women*, women from all walks of life, getting punched in the face by the dark fist of patriarchy. Even if we concede that women batter their children, we cannot take it a step further and picture them battering men. We might learn that a man's nose was broken, that he lost his job, that he was emotionally devastated, but we still think to ourselves: He's a man. He could have hit back. He could have hit *harder.*

On the whole, men do indeed have a more powerful left hook. The problem is that the dynamic of domestic violence is not analogous to two differently weighted boxers in a ring. There are relational strategies and psychological issues at work in an intimate relationship that negate the fact of physical strength. At the heart of the matter lies human will. Which partner—by dint of temperament, personality, life history—has the will to harm the other? By now it should be clear that such a will is not the exclusive province of men. If it were, we wouldn't have the news coming out of North America's gay community that violence by women against women in personal relationships occurs with a frequency approaching violence in heterosexual relationships—with the smaller, more conventionally feminine partner often being the one who strikes.

A great source of skepticism for people confronting the concept of husband assault is the absence of visible injury. Few abused men or lesbians emerge from their relationships resembling Hedda Nussbaum, the New Yorker whose common-law husband, Joel Steinberg, was prosecuted in 1988 for the beating death of their adopted daughter, Lisa. When Hedda Nussbaum testified, her appallingly broken face, with its cauliflower ear and boxer nose, was so vividly captured by television cameras that she quickly became the iconographic figure of the battered woman. Every time an activist proclaimed that one in four American women were assaulted by their partners, the image of Nussbaum sprang to mind.

In reality, victims like Hedda Nussbaum dwell at the extreme end of a continuum of violence in marital and dating relationships, in which about 4 percent of women are that severely injured. The majority of couples embroiled in intimate power struggles engage in a spectrum of violent acts, which women are statistically as likely as men to initiate: the slaps across the face, the glass suddenly hurled, the bite, the fierce pinch, the waved gun, the kick to the stomach, the knee to the groin. Add the invisible wave of violence that washes over American households in an acid bath of words, the children used as pawns, the destruction of property, the enlistment of community as a means of control, and all this paints a much more complex picture of domestic violence than that summoned by one woman's face in a heartbreaking trial.

That we have not been able to get at this complexity, in terms of the range of behavior, its causes, and its victims, has everything to do with how the issue evolved in the popular mind to begin with. Spousal assault was once a silent crime. The violence was private, like child assault. What people did behind closed doors was the business neither of their neighbors nor of the state. The first radical alteration of this paradigm came about in the early 1970s, through the work of Second Wave feminists. Because they were concentrating on the problems of women—transforming what were once considered personal issues into political concerns—they exposed the female victims of domestic assault. The subject made headlines with the publication of *Battered Wives* by the journalist Del Martin in 1976, one year after Susan Brownmiller opened the door on rape with her landmark book *Against Our Will.*

The first order of business, for many feminists like Martin, was to remove the stigma attached to battered women. Prior to *Battered*

Wives, the few investigations that had been made into battery had been conducted by court-appointed male psychiatrists who were asked to assess male assailants for trial. Since the assailants refused to concede any problem, the psychiatrists refocused their attention on the wives who'd been assaulted and, in the grand tradition of pathologizing female behavior, came up with a host of victim-blaming labels: "masochists," "castrators," "flirts." From the outset of claiming this issue for women, it was critical to clear battered women of blame. As this mission gained momentum, with more and more women testifying about their experiences to feminists and journalists, the need to shield victims from blame gained currency. To pose the question "Why did she stay?" quickly became unacceptable. It emerged that there were a number of reasons why women stayed— for the sake of their children, or because of financial dependency, or because, even if they left, their husbands would track them down. Most people accepted such reasons as credible, as evidenced most recently by the funds allotted in 1994 by the United States federal Violence Against Women Act. Male approval of spousal assault has dropped 50 percent in this period, from 20 percent of men thinking it's acceptable to strike your wife to 10.

Soon after the first battered women found safe haven in the feminist movement, research began to reveal that violence in the home actually claimed victims of both sexes. The most significant data came from a survey published in 1980 by three highly respected family violence scholars in New Hampshire, Murray Straus, Richard Gelles, and Suzanne Steinmetz. Their random survey of 3,218 American homes uncovered that severe abuse was committed equally by men and women. Minor, but recurring, violence was also on a par, with 11.6 percent of women and 12 percent of men reporting that they hit, slapped, or kicked their partners.

At this point, people working on the subject of family violence had a choice. They could expand the field to include male victims— establishing that abused men were not the same men who were abusing, and vice versa for women—or they could do what they did: devote an extraordinary amount of energy to shouting male victims down. For feminists, the idea that men could be victimized was nonsensical. It didn't square with their fundamental analysis of wife assault—that it was an extension of male political, economic, and ideological dominance over women. If women were so clearly subjugated in the public domain, through rape, sexual harassment, job discrimination, and so on, how could there be a different reality behind closed doors? Activists anticipated, moreover, that the New Hampshire data might be used to devalue female victims, in the manner of male lawyers, judges, and politicians saying, "See? She does it too"; case dismissed.

As a result, critics rushed to accuse Straus and Gelles, who were the primary authors, of shoddy research. They argued that their measurement tools were "patriarchal" and that they hadn't explored the context of the violence: If women were equally abusive, it was only in self-defense. None could assert this as fact; nor did they criticize the lack of context for assaults against women. On the contrary, the Straus/Gelles survey method (called the conflict tactics scale) was quickly adopted as a tool for research into violence against women. But Straus and Gelles, put on the defensive, reworked their survey questions and sampled several thousand households again. Their findings, published in 1985, were virtually identical, with the additional discovery that women initiated the aggression as often as men. About a quarter of the relationships had an exclusively violent male, another quarter had an exclusively violent female, and the rest were mutually aggressive.

Once again, there was a flurry of protest and scrutiny. Scholars set out to prove that male self-esteem was less damaged by abuse, that men took their wives' violence less seriously, and that injury had to be measured in terms of harm rather than intentions. A woman with a broken jaw could not be compared to a man like Peter Swann, who only got an ashtray to the head. In truth, both sides were guilty of using a male-centered measure of harm, in that neither was looking at the damage women could cause through indirect aggression. Moreover, Straus and Gelles, as well as subsequent scholars, have found that men often do, in fact, sustain comparable levels of injury. A 1995 study of young American military couples, arguably the most patriarchal of all, found that 47 percent of the husbands and wives had bruised, battered, and wounded each other to exactly the same degree. The argument about harm versus intention has been confounded in recent years, at any rate, by the addition of "mental" and "emotional" abuse to the lexicon of female victimization. A spate of new books on the self-help market argue that verbal abuse damages women as badly as physical blows. Picking up on this theme, California has added new provisions to its prisoner clemency policy, allowing women to apply for release for killing their mates due to "emotional" abuse. Since nobody can sensibly argue that women aren't capable of extremely artful and wounding verbal attacks (studies find high degrees of female verbal hostility in violent marriages), the whole question of "harm" gets turned on its head.

Nevertheless, battered women's supporters are so invested in a gender dichotomy that some have even stooped to attacking male victim researchers on a personal level. After Suzanne Steinmetz proposed the battered husband syndrome in an article published in 1978 in *Victimology*, a speech she was asked by the ACLU to give was canceled because the organization received a bomb threat. Steinmetz also received so many threatening phone calls at home that she had to get an unlisted number. Thirteen years later, in 1991, the chairwoman of a Canadian panel on violence against women, Pat Marshall, when asked if she was familiar with the Straus/Gelles studies, replied that she was familiar with Murray Straus as a man and insinuated that he abused his wife. Marshall repeated these comments so frequently that Straus had to write to the Canadian minister responsible for the status of women to request a public apology. He received one. His wife, the pawn in this pretty maneuver, did not.

Accompanying the resistance to statistics on men has been a tendency to suppress data altogether. A 1978 survey conducted by the Kentucky Commission on Violence Against Women uncovered that 38 percent of the assaults in the state were committed by women, but that finding wasn't included when the survey was released. (The information was discovered some years later by scholars.) In Detroit, a tally of emergency medical admissions due to domestic violence was widely reported by activists as evidence of injuries to women. No one told the media that 38 percent of the admissions were men. In

Canada, the federal government allotted $250,000 to a research project on comparative rates of violence in dating relationships. The lead researcher, Carleton University sociologist Walter DeKeseredy, released his data on women, generating a wave of violence against women headlines and conveying the impression that Canadian college campuses were bastions of violent misogyny. DeKeseredy didn't mention in his report that he had collected evidence of dating violence against men. If his data, which he intends to publish in 1997, reflect most other studies on dating violence, the rates will be equal. Physical aggression by young women in premarital romance is among the best documented.

"The battered husband syndrome is a backlash," DeKeseredy said in a 1994 telephone interview. "Men are using this information to keep women out of shelters." In fact, men are not using the information for anything, because academics with a particular political agenda are keeping it to themselves.

Under the circumstances, it is not surprising that those who stumble across evidence of battered men and battered lesbians do so quite by accident. A Winnipeg social scientist named Reena Sommer conducted a citywide survey on alcoholism for the University of Manitoba in 1989. Out of curiosity, she included six questions about domestic violence, interested specifically in violence against women. Some years later, she went back to her data and looked at the rates she'd collected on violence against men. To her astonishment, she found that 39.1 percent of the women in her survey had responded that they had committed acts of violence against their spouses at some point in their relationships, with 16.2 percent of those acts defined as severe. Sommer went back to her original list, found the telephone numbers, called up her respondents, and interviewed 737 of them. Ninety percent of the women who'd reported being abusive told her that they hadn't struck in self-defense. They had been furious or jealous, or they were high, or frustrated. Rational or irrational, impulsive or controlling, they had hit, kicked, thrown, and bitten. Fourteen percent of the men went to the hospital.

In Columbus, Ohio, two young sociologists, Laura Potts and Mary Reiter, were working in a "misdemeanor intake program" in the city attorney's office, criminal division, trying to settle minor charges through mediation, without bringing individuals to trial. Although nothing they'd read as feminists prepared them to expect it, they kept encountering men who'd been assaulted by women. One was an ailing, seventy-five-year-old man whose much younger wife had smashed him over the head with a porcelain vase. Another was a man attempting to break up with his girlfriend who got slashed in the temple with a screwdriver. In a third case, a man leaving his home to avoid an argument with his wife was chased down the street and stabbed in the back. "What we were seeing in reality," Potts told a meeting of the American Society of Criminology in 1994, "was a far greater use of [violence by women] than what we saw in the literature."

In Seattle, a therapist named Michael Thomas encountered the same gap between his schooling and his on-the-job experience. "My initial work was with a child abuse agency," he says. "When you start listening to the children's stories, you start to realize that there's an awful lot more violence by women than any of us had been trained to expect." Moving into private practice, Thomas began meeting "men who'd been sexually abused, often by their mothers." Within that distressing realm he heard his first accounts of husband abuse, for it is often men who witnessed or experienced violence in childhood who permit themselves to be assaulted as adults. As one battered husband who'd been abused in his boyhood explained: "We have not had control, as men, so we're not familiar with it and we're quite willing to give it over."

One mild October afternoon in Toronto, Steve Easton sat on the front porch of his small, ramshackle wooden house. A small gray cat, "rescued from an abusive home," peered warily out the window, perched on a pile of Easton's homemade fliers about the Easton Alliance for the Prevention of Family Violence, which runs support groups for both battered men and women. It's hard to know what to expect from a self-proclaimed "abused man"—someone touchy-feely, fragile and bohemian, plying his visitor with herbal tea. But Steve Easton, who is twenty-nine, resembles one of the college-age guys in a Budweiser beer commercial. He is clean-cut and well built, with blow-dried hair and a Gap-style dress shirt.

Easton wasn't remotely interested in the issue of domestic violence until he fell in love at the age of twenty-two, and fell deeper, into a traumatically volatile romance. His partner, an exotically beautiful woman from upstate New York, had seen her mother abuse her father. Ursula approached her lover the same way. She called him "cock-sucker" and "prick." She chose what clothes he could wear to work, arguing that certain ties or shirts would attract his female colleagues. If he disregarded her choices, he came home to find his wardrobe burned to ashes. She insisted, as Dana had to Peter, that he couldn't go out with his friends. If he did, she locked him out of the house for the night. He wasn't permitted to read the *Toronto Sun*, because the tabloid carries daily photos of a woman in a bikini—the "Sunshine Girl"—and that was evidence that he lusted after other women. When she started a fight, she would follow him from room to room in their house, keeping him up all night: "I'm not *finished* with you!" Exhausted, he came late to work too many times and got fired. Ursula punched him, hurled bottles and books at his head, and shoved him through the glass pane of their dining room window. But it wasn't until the day he hit her back that Easton resolved to leave her.

Against the counsel of friends and family, Easton returned to the relationship again and again before he gathered the emotional resources to end it. When he went to collect his things a final time, several friends escorted him for protection, at his request. Stigmatized, homeless, unemployed, he went in search of counseling. One organization, Education Wife Assault, handed him a pamphlet entitled "Why Husband Abuse Is a Red Herring." Other shelters and family service organizations responded similarly, reflecting the views of prominent Toronto columnist Michele Landsberg, who wrote, "The next time a men's advocate starts moaning about 'husband-battering,' question his material and suspect his motives. He sure isn't operating from a basis of reality—and he probably knows it."

In desperation, Easton finally called his local city hall councilman, wondering if there were organizations *anywhere* that counseled battered men. He was told no, but that the councilman actually got quite a few calls from men asking that. "This is my number," Easton said. "If any more men call you, tell them to get in touch with me." He also placed an ad in the local community paper, to which men like Peter Swann, starved for validation, responded at once. "When I read Steve's ad," Peter says, "I thought we'd been with the same woman."

Since it began, in 1993, The Easton Alliance—which is perpetually broke, and run out of the home Easton shares with his fiancée, Holly—has received between three and ten calls a day, one thousand to four thousand calls each year, from men who are enmeshed in violent relationships they cannot get out of. The reasons are as multifarious as they are for battered women: the men are afraid for their children; they are unemployed, or working class, and can't afford new housing. Some men love their wives and don't want to leave them, just want them to stop; others are too depressed to get out, or they've taken cover in booze and don't have the wits anymore; some think they can take it and can't. None of these reasons should be surprising, given that men can be broken-down souls, that they can care passionately about their children, that patriarchy may control the economy, but millions of individual males are flat broke. Yet as Easton discovered when he founded his group, the politics that once proclaimed family violence to be a private affair now proclaim it a woman's affair. There is no longer room—if there ever was—for men to be victims themselves.

By the late 1980s, activists and scholars within the battered women's movement had grown markedly more militant about the inherent distinctions between men and women. In 1984, for instance, it was still acceptable for a sociologist like Mildred Pagelow to speculate about the differences among women rather than between women and men. She suggested that a strong commitment to traditional beliefs—the husband as master, the bond as sacred—might be an important factor in why some women stayed in violent marriages. But as the female survivor culture swept onto the scene with its mantra of victimhood, scholarship that focused on interpersonal dynamics eddied into backwaters, and more simplistic dogma coursed into the mainstream. It became fashionable to compare battered women to hostages who are kidnapped and terrorized into identifying with their captors. The bottom line was that it could happen to any woman. No one was safe, no one could prevent herself from becoming Hedda Nussbaum.

Critics decried this thinking as a dangerous assault on women's agency. "It perpetuates the specious notion that women are doomed to be the victims of the abnormal psychology of love at all costs," Susan Brownmiller wrote in an editorial in *The New York Times*. Brownmiller was referring specifically to Nussbaum, who garnered sympathy from most people but also stirred up unease, because she wasn't a trapped, dependent wife who couldn't escape the clutches of her patriarch. She was a well-educated book editor. She *came* from somewhere, was fully intact, equipped with resources and a will to make her own choices. She chose, month by month, to stay with a man who belittled and bullied her, until finally she really did have no choice and was ruined. What was the crucial turning point? What happened along the way? What could other women learn from her experience?

Documenting the Nussbaum case, journalist Ann Jones did not entertain these questions. She went into great, indignant detail about Joel Steinberg's cocaine addiction but failed to mention Nussbaum's own cocaine use or her abuse and neglect of her children. Considering the extreme collapse of Nussbaum's life, any violence or addiction she fell prey to was hardly shocking. But it was no longer permissible to depict women as fallible humans, prone to flights of rage and dissolution. By the 1990s, battered women's advocates had transformed their shield-the-victim strategy into a kind of whitewash campaign. Women weren't merely normal human beings who didn't deserve to be pathologized for the hell they'd gone through, which was the position Del Martin began with in the 1970s. Now they were to be seen as moral innocents, purer of motive than the male in every way. Hollywood cottoned on to this zeitgeist by casting doe-eyed Julia Roberts in the 1992 film *Sleeping with the Enemy*: not angry, just trembling, in flight from a Patriarch. Endless numbers of TV movies now employ this theme in their woman-in-jeapordy plots.

If women were inherently blameless, it followed with mounting conviction that men were inherently blameworthy, to the point where any investigation of their motives was denounced as providing them with "an excuse." Childhood abuse wasn't relevant, because it was an excuse. So were individual pathologies, marital dynamics, personal circumstances—until the whole field of inquiry was blocked. Women's roles couldn't be analyzed because that was sexist. Men's behavior couldn't be analyzed because they didn't deserve "the excuse." The damage this vision of men and women did to family violence research was profound. Any attempt to disentangle the dynamics of cycles of violence with a respect for human complexity was condemned as a sexist conspiracy. "The search for causation [is] a wild-goose chase," wrote sociologist Ellen Wilson, "because [wife abuse] is concerned with wider issues to do with the control of women by men." In Canada, the final report of a multimillion-dollar government panel on violence against women, which canvassed experts from across the nation for several years, concluded in 1993: "If [a man] abuses his wife, it is because he has the privilege and the means to do so." Ten million dollars to cough up a cliché. In the United States, the situation was no better. Those who advise policy makers had their view summed up in *Ms.* magazine's 1994 special issue on wife beating: "Researchers are now beginning to examine the batterers," wrote Ann Jones. "It's the same old crap. Nobody wants to admit that men do this because they like to."

What began as a nuanced discussion of one of the most volatile arenas of human relating had been reduced to a bigoted creed. Men are evil. Women are good. Domestic violence is wife beating, and any man who finds himself at the receiving end of a woman's fist is a liar or a freak.

No agency will grant them space or funds, so Easton's group congregates where they can. One very cold night in November, they meet in the children's nursery of an empty community center. A dozen men sit scrunched up in a circle among brightly colored posters of giraffes and bears. In unison, their voices solemn and halting, they recite something Steve Easton wrote to begin each meeting, based on the letters in the word "Solutions." S is for Safety: "I will accept responsibility for my own personal safety. I will no longer allow myself to become involved in situations which will cause me emotional and physical pain. I will be diligent on my own behalf." They go through the letters, vowing to be Open-minded, Loving, Understanding, Trusting, Independent, Open-hearted, good at Negotiation, and willing (not embarassed, as men) to accept Support.

A man named Charles is the meeting convener tonight, but he's shy about it, tentative. He's in his mid-thirties, a tall, gaunt man who has lost his hair. Except for a softness around his mouth and in his blue eyes, he looks rather skeletal. He cries a lot, apologizing to the group with an embarassed wave of the hand. He's supposed to be following an agenda, but his words keep straying to his three-year-old daughter, Susy: how he had her for Thanksgiving, taught her to finger paint, how good she was; she drew a big "S" for Susy. He misses her. The other men listen in silence. They've learned their function here is to let each other be sad, fucked up, afraid.

Next to Charles sits Ruben. Older, perhaps in his fifties, he is alert and bespectacled, with a briefcase by his chair. No longer in the thick of his own predicament, he acts more as a counselor. Beside Ruben is Dave, a bulky biker type in a leather jacket. His physical presence is so strong (and so incongruous, beneath a cheerful string of alphabet letters) that it's hard to envision him as victim. When he speaks, his gruff voice is anxious and rambling, his experience so chaotic that he can't tell it straight, sum it up, and it's clear he's a big, broken child. Life as a fractious sequence of injuries and anger, abused as a boy, roughed up on the street, his wife drunkly belligerent, his sons two small wrecks he can't repair, he himself losing his temper with them. They've got to stop the fighting, he and Candi. She's gotta stop with the booze. "Jesus Christ, I come home and Greg's runnin' around on the *street*, he's two years *old*, and she's passed out in the bedroom for Christ fuckin' sake." Dave's lost control, he never had it, he needs it now. Can the others help?

Asking for help is the hardest part. These men are mostly working class. Their identities are coded by masculine scripts. Among their buddies and colleagues, they have everything to lose by admitting they need protection from the blows of a woman, that they can't stop the spiral of raised voices, too much booze, jealousy, insults, shattering glass. "For men," says the sociologist Murray Straus, "[abuse] is a double whammy. Like women, they don't want people to know that their partner is treating them badly, but there's the additional shame of feeling that a 'real man' ought to be able to 'handle his woman.'"

As far back as the Middle Ages, men whose wives beat them were ridiculed by their fellows, paraded through the village streets backward on a mule. Now, they're taunted with the phrases "pussy-whipped" and "henpecked." They know to keep their mouths shut. Murray Straus once appeared on the "Sally Jessy Raphael" show with two men who'd been severely assaulted by their wives. On the way in from the airport in a limousine, the segment producer reviewed what questions Sally wanted to ask one of the men, a fellow who'd flown up from Tennessee. His wife had stabbed him several times and smashed his nose with a brass crucifix, a totem he was now carrying in his hands as if to ward off the further assault of TV. "We'll start by asking you to recount the last time you were beaten," said the producer, and the man interrupted her in a state of high alarm. "She never beat me!" he protested. The producer stared at him, astonished. "She *stabbed* me," he corrected. "I ain't going on the show if you say she beat me." Puzzling the exchange over later, Straus realized why this distinction was so important: "to him, 'beaten' meant that she had subjugated him, gained dominance over him, and he couldn't accept that."

How internalized that feeling is for men—whether they actively want to see themselves as dominant or it's something they realize that other men expect of them—depends on the individual. Steve Easton didn't want to dominate Ursula. He saw himself as her healer. Peter Swann was willing to let Dana be the strong one, as long as they could get along without fuss. "These men are appeasers," says the therapist Michael Thomas, referring to the battered husbands he counsels in Seattle. "They always back down to keep things calm, to keep the conflict from escalating. In my experience, the women [in these particular marriages] have a lot of problems with anger control. They are much more likely to throw things, they're more likely to hit or kick when he's not looking or asleep or driving. He doesn't hit back because, number one, he's conditioned to believe that you never hit a woman. Two, he's afraid of losing his kids. Three, [our society] doesn't think of violence as mutual—it's always 'him' doing it to 'her.' So if he hits back, the attention shifts to him and he knows that he'll be up against the wall." By the time the men have reached Easton's group, they've thrown up a white flag and surrendered the masculine visage: they are no longer "under control, cool under pressure, masters of their own domain." They are children in tears in a nursery.

Labeling goes a long way to explaining why domestic violence is such a cloudy picture where men are concerned. Consider the memories of Andrea, a Philadelphia lawyer whose mother is alcoholic. Throughout Andrea's childhood, her mother berated, slapped, and kicked Andrea's father in the evenings, when he came home from work. It never occurred to Andrea that her mother was abusive, because that was a label for men. Her mother was simply "a drunk." Other women are "unstable" or "shrewish." In comic strips, they throw frying pans, like the wife in "Andy Capp." The ambiguity and trivialization of female-perpetrated abuse inhibits battered men from voicing need, but it also causes women to underestimate their impact, to see that what they're doing is abusive. "I try to get these men to give her feedback when she's hurting them," says Michael Thomas, "rather than provoking her into lashing out more. The problem is that many of these women have no sense at all that they've hurt their partners." Why would they? What information is there, out in their culture, to suggest that men are vulnerable? Female approval of husband assault remains as high now as it was twenty years ago: Twenty-three percent of women believe that "slapping the cad" is just fine.

In 1993, the writer Ann Jones angrily cast aspersions on people who would dare to use such a nongender-specific phrase as "domestic violence": "I suspect," she indignantly penned, "that some academic researcher coined the term, dismayed by the fact that all those beaten wives were *women*." It must be equally dismaying to those in Jones's camp that some of those beaten women are gay.

On a political level, violence within this strongly feminist community has indeed generated anguish. When the sociologist Claire Renzetti surveyed one hundred battered lesbians, she discovered that four of them couldn't go to their local shelter for protection because their abusers worked there. Another woman told Renzetti that she and her partner were going to attend a national conference together on violence against women, but because she was covered in bruises, including the dark swell of a black eye, they decided that only her partner would go. Other lesbians, like battered men, are turned away from shelters for heterosexual women. "When shelter workers or advocates meet a situation that appears to defy their own understanding, the battered lesbian herself is seen as the problem," notes psychologist Nancy Hammond.

Barbara Hart, a counselor in Pennsylvania who was a member of the National Task Force on Violence Against Women, wrote in 1986: "[The revelation of gay violence] is painful. It challenges our dream of a lesbian Utopia. It contradicts our belief in the inherent non-violence of women." There were compelling reasons to be circumspect. The homophobia lesbians face would be further fueled by images of them as nasty, butch-dyke brawlers. It would reinforce the worst stereotypes of gay women, and no one wanted to see it happen. Lesbians seem to have been roundly abandoned on this point by their straight sisters. Feminists who refuse to admit that heterosexual women can also be violent leave the gay community by itself out on a limb, vulnerable to further slander by self-appointed keepers of public morals. There is a long tradition in our culture of depicting aggressive or criminal women as sexually perverse. That link can only be fortified if feminists refuse to concede straight women's violence, forcing lesbians to appear as the only ones who abuse.

In a *Ms.* magazine special issue on wife beating published in 1994, lesbian violence was discreetly confined to one column, with a feeble attempt to distinguish it from what men do. "The tactics may look the same on the outside," the magazine quoted Valerie Coleman, a southern California psychologist who works with battered lesbians, as saying. "But, for the most part, heterosexual men feel they have a right—in the global sense—to abuse their partners, which lesbians do not." How this is a meaningful distinction, given that both groups throw punches, is never made clear. Lauria Chesley, a therapist who works with abusive women, notes that global entitlement or lack thereof has little effect on the substance of gay violence. The women she counsels often use the same rationalizations for what they've done that men use. "They'll say: 'She knows I don't like it when she does that,' or 'I warned her.' " Coming from women, these justifications reveal how explanations are culled after the fact from a vocabulary of motive, rationales that anyone—male or female, gay or straight—may reach for to explain what is otherwise mystifying.

That men have used a patriarchal vocabulary to account for themselves doesn't mean that patriarchy *causes* their violence, any more than being patriarchs prevents them from being victimized. Studies of male batterers have failed to confirm that these men are more conservative or sexist about marriage than nonviolent men. To the contrary, some of the highest rates of violence are found in the least orthodox partnerships—dating or cohabiting lovers.

A look at the gay community's tumult reveals that relationship violence cannot be understood in terms of male social and economic power. In many abusive gay partnerships, it is the women with the higher earning power and self-esteem who get assaulted. In her survey of women who identified themselves as victims of abuse, Claire Renzetti found an important distinction between what might be described as "strength" and what we tend to describe as "power." On the whole, the women who got abused tended to be more independent and self-sufficient, less jealous, and had higher incomes. Socially and economically, they were the ones with the "power." At the same time, the gay women being abused saw themselves as the strong ones, possessing not only the economic power of self-sufficiency but the emotional power of stability, of basic strength. As a result, they considered themselves to be the anchor for their insecure, volatile partner: "Many expressed worry over what their partner would do without them," Renzetti noted. Therapist Lenore Walker has made a similar observation of battered women in heterosexual relationships: "Many . . . believe that they are the sole support for the batterer's emotional stability and sanity." If he is the financial pillar, she is the emotional one, and so the house stands. That insight resonates in a comment that Hedda Nussbaum made at Joel Steinberg's trial: "He was a little boy and I was his one-eyed teddy bear." It also resonates in the experiences of men like Peter Swann and Steve Easton, who saw themselves as anchors for their lovers. In this sense, the masculine idea of "taking it on the chin" appears to be a value that's internalized by both sexes, to varying degrees, with those who perceive themselves as the stronger partner more susceptible to its currency than those who appear more powerful politically or economically to the outside world. It becomes an important clue to understanding why economically self-sufficient men and women stay in abusive relationships. They aren't kidnapped like hostages, or shocked like monkeys. They are making a decision that they can *stand* it, that they have the fortitude, the endurance to go the rounds. Quite often, they miscalculate. They lose their bearings and fall.

In *Naming the Violence: Speaking Out About Lesbian Battering*, more than a dozen women agreed to come forward for the U.S. National Coalition Against Domestic Violence, Lesbian Task Force, and write about their own experiences. Arlene Istar, of Albany, New York, described her two-year relationship with a woman who had "intense displays of rage." At first, "threats of violence" were accompanied by much pleading and cajoling. Her lover would insist that Istar was at fault for not being understanding. "[S]he explained that I was not respecting her honesty and vulnerability. She convinced me I was being rigid." Istar was "expected to take care of her, and the kids, and the house, before I attended to my own needs." Over time, Istar "was hit and slapped, often till I was black and blue. I was picked up and thrown against walls. . . . I was physically thrown out of the house in the snow with no shoes or coat. I had black eyes and fractured fingers. She destroyed things I loved. She would trap me, not letting me leave the room or the house or the car until the outburst was over." Like Peter Swann and Steve Easton, Arlene Istar thought she could "heal" her lover, that she could ride out the early storm and, through her patience, impose some calm. "In the beginning, I ran from the room when she hit me. It was to be our pattern, her yelling, my yelling, her hitting, and my running." After a while, however, Istar

refused to run anymore. "I began to fight back. . . . I became so accli-
mated to living with violence that the only way I saw to get out was to
fight my way out."

In retrospect, Istar wrote, what troubled her was that she didn't
see herself as the battered woman she'd read of in books. "I want you
to know that I am an assertive and powerful womon [sic]. . . . Most
lesbians I know who have been battered impress me with their presence and strength. None of them fit my stereotype." In the arena of
family violence, stereotypes abound. The only figure for which there
is no prevailing image is the heterosexual violent woman.

Research on the motives and feelings of abusive heterosexual
women is scant, for the obvious reason that they aren't supposed to
exist. Like abusive men, however, the available studies show them to
be a widely heterogeneous group who defy simple labels. Some are
alcoholics, others addicted to drugs, still others perfectly sober.
Some (perhaps 25 percent) have "personality disorders," such as psychopathy. Some are immature and impulsive, others depressed,
others dramatically damaged by childhood. The styles of violence
also differ, from spontaneous gestures of frustration to years-long
campaigns of manipulation and control.

Perhaps the most well-documented cause of domestic violence for
both men and women is the "intergenerational transmission of violence." The female abuser is repeating the style of communication
she learned as a girl. She saw her mother beat her father, or she and
her siblings were beaten themselves. "Violence is a learned behavior," says Debbie DeGale, who runs an anger management course for
women at the Elizabeth Fry Society in Winnipeg. "Women, as well as
men, have witnessed or experienced it in their childhoods." Family
patterning is a force so powerful that it transcends gender conditioning. A woman may lack models for aggression in the public
arena yet still find them in her home. Children who are beaten by
their fathers tend to grow up to become victims, whether they are
boys or girls. Children who are beaten by their mothers, on the
other hand, are more likely to become victimizers. One theory about
why this would be is that men act as authority figures in children's
lives, breeding in them habits of submission that last a lifetime.

Women are teaching figures. They are most likely to show their children how to communicate emotionally.

The effects of child abuse, depending upon the sex of the parent, explains how a man who was abused as a child can tolerate abuse from his female partner. "About eighty percent of the men coming through the program," says Steve Easton, "were also abused as children. And so were their wives. We're picking each other." Soon after he fell in love with her, Easton began to see that Ursula was insecure about him because love had always come packaged for her in the sour wrapping of insults and fists. Her mother, Annie, had beaten both her and her brother. When Ursula grew up, she fought her mother back. Several times, Easton watched Annie and Ursula in the hallway of his apartment building, swinging at each other, yelling, "You cunt!" and "You bitch!" while he sat there, tense and quiet in the kitchen.

A person's experience of childhood abuse or abandonment may have been so horrific that she experiences her emotional vulnerability as virtually life-threatening. To need and to trust, she recalls, is to hurt like no other pain. Women who feel this way are perhaps more likely to use violence instrumentally. They need to control and diminish their mates in order to feel safe with them, to convince themselves that they are not the weaker of the pair. "Domination begins with the attempt to deny dependency," notes the psychoanalyst Jessica Benjamin. "The primary consequence of the inability to reconcile dependence with independence . . . is the transformation of need for the other into domination of him." I love you, therefore you terrify me, so I must strike you down.

Thus the beloved is not allowed to go out with friends, or wear certain clothes, or read certain newspapers, or spend time exclusively with children, or simply walk around looking upbeat, because betrayal lurks behind all of these gestures. If the beloved can be controlled absolutely, it will be safe to love.

One interesting finding from the annals of psychology is that male batterers score high on tests for anxiety, low self-esteem, and neuroticism. Men generally bring to adult life more trouble with the concept of dependency, and more inclination to thwart it, purely on the level of gender identity. Claire Renzetti speculates that lesbians are more uncomfortable with the notion of feminine dependency than heterosexual women are. "She who is dependent is likely to feel weak and ashamed, since dependency is associated with a destructive, culturally proscribed female role." Since feelings of dependency ranked high among the emotional traits of abusive lesbians in Renzetti's survey, it may be that, like male abusers, they experience their vulnerability as a threat to their identity, as well as their psyche, and try to vanquish that dependency by controlling their partner and empowering themselves through violence.

Mutual abuse makes up about half of all domestic violence scenarios, although only recently have scholars focused on the role of women in provoking and perpetuating conflict. In a 1990 study of one hundred mutually combative couples in Austin, Texas, William Stacey and his colleagues found that both sexes engaged in taunts, insults, and threats, hitting and shoving, destroying household property, preventing each other from seeing friends, and stalking or closely monitoring with suspicions of infidelity. Couples' violence "ultimately results from partners' personal insecurities," the researchers concluded, "and lack of trust in their separate relationships." Judith Shevrin and James Sniechowski have described the dynamic as a "dance of mutual destructiveness," in which both partners "need each other to perpetuate personal and collective dramas of victimization and lovelessness." Clinical social worker Eve Lipchik, of ICF Consultants, in Milwaukee, Wisconsin, who treats couples engaging in mutual abuse, cites the example of a young African-American couple who, during a six-year marriage, "had spent most of their time drinking heavily and fighting violently, aided and abetted by their extended families, who fanned each partner's jealousy." Through couple therapy, Lipchik got them to give up drinking, think about more peaceful ways to solve conflict, and "not allow themselves to be manipulated into fighting."

"Hitting is just one part of the overall dynamic," says Michael Thomas. "There's a huge amount of psychological warfare going on. A husband may stonewall [emotionally], so out of frustration the woman's violence escalates." Stacey and his colleagues cite the case of William and Carrie: "William locked her out of the house. She destroyed $700 worth of his leather clothes, carved an X on the top of his car, and threatened to stab him." Or the reverse scenario unfolds, with the woman as provocateur and the man retaliating. Ninety-two percent of the women studied in Austin admitted to "name-calling, belittling, or insulting" their partners, with much of the taunting "aimed at the men's resources or abilities as providers and childrearers"; 72 percent of the women withdrew emotionally as a form of punishment; 46 percent threatened to use violence.

Police officers frequently encounter the messy and confusing mutuality of violence. According to former patrol officer R. Kim Rossmo, now at Simon Fraser University in Vancouver, domestic violence calls are extremely difficult to mediate; officers have to interpret a set of interpersonal dynamics that have little to do with rote gender divisions. "You can't count on anyone to tell you the truth, not your victim, not your suspect. The phone call [to 911] may be for the express purpose of getting back at him, or the call may be to just put out the fire and she doesn't want it to go to court. Sometimes you get there and she will deny that anything's happened, even though you think that it's happened, or sometimes she's complaining about him but she's equally at fault, or sometimes she's actually commited a criminal offense and he hasn't."

Society demands that these situations be portrayed in black and white. But reality inevitably throws us back into a gray zone. In 1988, Annette Green, of West Palm Beach, Florida, shot her lover, Ivonne Julio, after a stormy eleven-year relationship in which the violence—which Julio started—grew more and more reciprocal. At her murder trial, Green mounted a battered woman syndrome defense, citing several instances in which she'd been attacked physically by Julio. But her two adopted daughters testified that she'd once held a gun to Julio's head, and friends came in to say they'd seen her kick Julio at a party. On the night Julio died, she was hiding in a closet. Green chased her down, cornered her, and pulled the trigger. Who was the victim? Who the abuser? Who was the man, and who the woman?

The same question arises in the case of Mae Favell and Ernie Pelly of Northern Ontario, for whom alcoholism and family violence patterning proved a marital Molotov cocktail. In 1985, Favell accidentally knifed her lover to death when they were both drunk. Favell was well known by neighbors and relatives in her small community to be as assaultive as the more diminutive Pelly, whom people called the "Pin Cushion" for the scars and scabs that dotted his physique. Favell and Pelly also took cracks at each other with, for instance, a baseball bat. In addition, Mae Favell abused her children and, on one occasion, assaulted her elderly neighbor. Her sixteen-year relationship played out as a passionate, alcohol-fueled brawl, not unlike the union of Martha and George in Edward Albee's play *Who's Afraid of Virginia Woolf?*, except that the battle consisted in body blows instead of quips.

The couple's neighbors figured that, sooner or later, one of them was going to go down for the count. As it happened, it was Ernie, whom Mae left lying on the floor one night after stabbing him in the leg. She then staggered off in search of some music, and when she returned, having invited over the people next door, she discovered that Ernie had bled to death. The tragic mutuality in their alcoholism and aggression wasn't remotely reflected in Favell's sentencing hearing, where she was positioned as a victim of battered wife syndrome. She *was* a battered wife; there's little question. But she had a battered husband, and she killed him.

Women are seldom the victors, strictly speaking, in cases of mutual abuse, but it is irresponsible and counterproductive to promote them exclusively as the victims. For one thing, it deprives them of access to counseling. As one Austin woman whose husband had received treatment for wife assault said, "[Now] he tries to understand my side of the argument. He talks to me rather than hits me. I still hit him, however. I would like to enroll in a class in anger management, but the shelter for battered women does not help women with this problem."

Therapist Laurie Chesley notes that a lot of gay women who were abused in one relationship go on to be the abuser in the next one. The feeling that the psychoanalyst Alice Miller identified in the battered child—"I will never, ever let this happen to me again"—seems to well up in adults, too, in the aftermath of their own adult experience. The possibility that love can shatter us so many times as adults that we are changed by it, made brittle, fearful, and hateful, is central to the experience of the postwar generations. The Sexual Revolution generated a many-partnered cycle of loving, being left, and leaving, while we amassed scars to make us flinch and ghosts that come to haunt us. For those who have been physically and psychologically wounded by love, the need or desire to retaliate may carry over into the next relationship. This cycle was largely obscured in earlier generations because of the greater commitment to monogamy.

The phenomenon might be called shadowboxing. It is the ghost of a former lover you're reacting to, not the person who sits there before you now. Say a woman has a love affair in her twenties with a man who demeans her by sleeping around. She suppresses her rage because his is the stronger personality, the one in control. Years later, she finds a loving union with a faithful man, with whom she is the stronger partner. Her new lover glances at a beautiful woman or has a flirtatious exchange, and she "sees" her former beau's behavior. A terrible anger wells up in her. She lashes out. Shadowboxing seems to describe the fate of Ruben, the divorced, fifty-year-old man from Easton's support group. Ruben lives in a tiny studio apartment in Toronto's East End. It is a space decorated in a surprisingly childlike manner, with posters of dolphins and *Sesame Street* characters on the wall, brightly crocheted pillows on his bed: home sentimentally envisaged as one's childhood bedroom, a safe and trusted place. He is a handsome man, with the long-lashed dark eyes of his native Greece and a lush mouth that always hovers on the edge of a smile— uncertain, and appeasing. Ruben is the sort of man a woman might retreat to when she wants to flee from love's combative field. His presence would be reassuring but placid, a source of warmth without too much heat. Women sometimes derisively call men of this character Milquetoasts. But Ruben isn't dull; he is thoughtful and observant.

He and his future second wife met in 1983. After an exchange of smiles on a long subway ride, the two began to talk, leaving the train with each other's number pressed into a pocket, a purse. Ruben was a lonely divorcé who wanted companionship. Jenny was a former waitress who'd had it rough and was looking for a stretch of peace. "Later," says Ruben, carefully stirring a cup of instant coffee, "I found out she was from an abusive background. When she was a teenager she did an abortion on herself. She told me that her ex-husband tried to hit her. She got a divorce for that reason. When she was a waitress, a man tried to rape her. So she was coming from a lot of bad experiences with men. She had a lot of rage, a lot of rage. She used to say to me all the time that men are evil."

When they married, Jenny's stipulation was that Ruben get a vasectomy. She said she couldn't fathom having children—she was thirty-nine. Perhaps she was also so traumatized by her past that the only way she could accept Ruben was to diminish his power to violate her. "I married her in August," he says, "and three months later I had the operation. A few days after that we were sitting at home watching television and all of a sudden without any provocation she hit me on my groin. I hit the roof with pain. I had to go to the hospital to make sure there was no internal bleeding. She told me that this was an accident, and I bought that. But then she out of nowhere kicked my chair from beneath me, and this time I realized there was something wrong with the marriage.

"She became very irritable and noncommunicative and she had been a very, very good communicator [before]. She was outgoing, she used to confide in me. Now, every day she would come home and throw herself in front of the television, and watch it for hours, and sleep a lot. She was extremely depressed, no question about it. We never went anywhere, and any time we did, she used to get lost on me. I'd turn around and she'd just disappeared into the crowd. I used to spend hours looking for her."

The next instance of physical violence was connected to sex. After months of mutual solitude, with Ruben's sense of rejection simmering into anger, he entered the separate bedroom she'd taken, intending to insist that they make love: They were husband and wife. Hovering over her in the bed on his sad, desperate mission, Ruben got a vicious knee to the head. "She grabbed my head and pulled it down and hit me with her knee above my right eye. Blood started running, and she called the police. She told them, "I hit my husband." The police arrived, took me to the hospital, I received six or seven stitches. The police brought me back, but they wouldn't press charges against her. They said I could do it myself."

It was this fact—that Jenny reported her assault—that lent the impression she was shadowboxing and knew it. Ruben's presence elicited a rage in her that she must have realized had little to do with him as an individual but rather with the men that came before him. Her 911 call was a call for help on his behalf. Ruben responded to his wife's extremely indirect expression of concern by expressing his hurt and resentment in an equally indirect manner: He pressed charges. When the judge reviewed his complaint and audibly chuckled, however, Ruben was so humiliated that he dropped them.

"It was so confusing," he says. "I did not have anybody to talk to. When I told my friends about it they just didn't believe it. I started missing lots of time from my work because I was going to the hospital. Finally I confided in my boss, I told him 'My wife is beating me,' and he immediately responded, 'Well, why don't you hit her back?' " But unlike Peter Swann and Steve Easton, who both eventually did hit back—and got arrested for doing so—Ruben couldn't do it. "I don't believe in violence, I wasn't taught to be a violent person, I just don't do it."

Within the year, the physical violence abated and Jenny withdrew into a punishing silence. When he pleaded with her for discussion, she wouldn't reply. Instead, she got up and left the room. Being ignored, Ruben says, was far more harrowing than getting hit. "You're treated like nobody, like you don't exist," he says. He sighs very deeply, still stirring a now tepid cup of coffee. He couldn't move out, because it was his house, and he didn't want to ask her to leave. He wanted to reconcile. She left anyway, in spirit. Ruben, for his part, disappeared into a bottle.

"I became an alcoholic. One day I woke up in my bedroom. It was Sunday morning. I started thinking about alcohol, how I wanted to drink. I went into a rage looking for a bottle in the house, unable to understand why they were all empty because I didn't know that I'd consumed four bottles of vodka the day before. When I realized it, it really shocked me. I went back into my bedroom and I got totally undressed. I looked into the mirror and I just didn't like what I saw: a scuffed-up, liquor-beaten, watered-down man. I sat down and took a complete inventory of my life, and in every aspect the bad part was far more than the good. I realized that I had to get out, I had to figure out what it is I had going for myself."

Ruben and Jenny harbor no ill will toward each other now, he says. What is sad is that in addition to one woman's wounded spirit there is now one wounded man, and he has begun to shadowbox in turn. He doesn't lash out, because he doesn't have the temperament. But he winces and jumps. Recently, his apartment building elevator got stuck between the sixth and seventh floors. The only other passenger was a woman he didn't know. She reached for the phone, and Ruben began to tremble, panicked by the irrational conviction that she was going to phone security to say he'd attacked her. She didn't, of course. She reported the fact that the elevator was stuck.

If severe male violence is physical, bringing women like Hedda Nussbaum to the brink of death, it might be said that the most extreme form of female-perpetrated abuse is situational. Women can operate the system to their advantage. Donning the feminine mask, they can manipulate the biases of family and community, much as Marybeth Tinning did, in order to set men up. If he tries to leave, or fight back, a fateful moment comes when she reaches for the phone, dials 911, and has him arrested on the strength of her word: "Officer, he hit me." The tactic is reminiscent of well-to-do late-nineteenth-century American men having their wives committed to insane asylums—for a week or forever—solely on the basis of their say-so. Since women had been stereotyped as fragile and prone to hysteria, it was possible to persuade authorities of their insanity. A century later, a confluence of social forces has created a parallel opportunity, but with the sexes reversed: Men can be committed to prison on the strength of stereotypes about *them*.

With mounting pressure on North American police forces to disavow misogynistic attitudes and take the word of a woman over a man, female psychopaths and other hard-core female abusers have an extremely effective means to up the ante and win the game. It isn't what abusive men do, the robbing of breath, but it is as surely the ruin of a life. The most common theme among abused men is their tales not of physical anguish but of dispossession—losing custody of children due to accusations of physical and sexual abuse, and having criminal records that permanently shatter their integrity as loving men and decent human beings.

Andrea, the woman who never thought of her mother as an abuser, just a drunk, remembers when her mother flew into a tantrum because her exhausted husband refused to go out and buy her a bottle of gin. She called the police and claimed that he'd pushed her down the stairs. The investigating officer, a woman, saw the situation for what it was and declined to press charges. In the 1990s, that officer's response would be held up as evidence of indifference to women, which is why several North American jurisdictions have now implemented mandatory arrest policies in domestic violence cases, overriding individual police discretion. Prosecutors may now also override the discretion of the complainant, ignoring her desire to recant or drop charges.

"I got arrested twice," says Peter Swann, pacing his boardinghouse room and completing his tale of how Dana undid him. "I did sixty days and two years' probation. It was very unpleasant and scary, and I was wondering, what the hell did I do, what did I do to *deserve* this? The first time it happened, I spent one night in jail. Then I went to stay at a co-worker's. Dana found out where I was, she called around, and she asked me to come home. Well, she had my daughter, so, yeah, I went back. The second time she got me arrested, I was still on probation. She nailed me two days before my last meeting [with the probation officer]. I was going to go camping that weekend, everything was packed. She had a fit. The gear went flying. Thrown out in the backyard. 'You're not going camping.' You can tell when she starts. The look on her face. She's building up the pressure like a volcano." But Dana didn't explode the way a man of her ilk might, by beating Peter senseless, because she couldn't. What she could do was destroy his property and pick up the phone.

On the strength of his first conviction, he was easily convicted again, and on the strength of that, Dana won custody of Grace. A new boyfriend came to live with her in their house. Having spent all his money fighting the custody battle, Peter had no resources left with which to fight for his household possessions. He fell into a downward spiral of poverty, alcohol, and self-recrimination. Having lost his job, he fell behind on his child support payments, and got branded, on top of all the other labels, a deadbeat dad.

Dinnertime has come and gone without dinner. Peter's landlady taps on his door and invites herself in, a plump woman in her sixties clad in a bright blue housecoat, to offer a plate of chocolate doughnuts. She listens to his meandering soliloquy for a moment, then interrupts. "You mustn't blame yourself, dear," she says, and she has clearly said it before. She turns to the visitor: "I was in that kind of situation myself. My husband was a very respectable banker. He beat me black and blue." Settling herself in the room's one chair, she offers her observations of Dana, and her Scottish accent lends a proper, even disapproving, air, though her face is relaxed and quick to smile. "She's a spiteful woman, she is. The time I remember most it was Pete's birthday, and Dana promised faithfully she'd bring Grace at four o'clock so Pete could take her to dinner. Well, hours and hours and hours later, he said to me, 'She's not coming, will you come and have a drink with me?' So we did. Dana showed up, finally, at midnight, which is a disgusting time to bring a child over. She came in, took one look at the glass in his hand, and said, 'She's not staying here, you're drunk,' and off they went! I mean, that was a set-up."

Maybe it was, but who would believe it? Take one look at Hedda Nussbaum and understand perfectly what she's been through. But a stumbling, inarticulate, alcoholic, twice-convicted deadbeat dad? Where would you even begin? "Peter's not perfect, he's not a perfect man," says his landlady, "he's not a perfect husband, but he doesn't deserve the punishment he's getting. He doesn't deserve this."

No person, male or female, gay or straight, complicit or not, deserves to wind up in the vortex of violence. But how will we find a way out if what we want is the simplest answer? Trying to make a neat and pretty package of relational discord is as impossible as bottling love. No two people live it the same. The one decent thing we can do in our rush to categorize, simplify, and hurl blame is to stop for a moment and recognize, as Ruben says, "the human face of pain."

WOMAN AS PREDATOR

Methods of the Multiple Murderess

There is no female Mozart because there is no female Jack
the Ripper.

CAMILLE PAGLIA, SEXUAL PERSONAE

This is my ambition: to have killed more people, more
helpless people, than any man or woman has ever killed.

JANE TOPPAN, convicted of poisoning nearly one hundred
patients in a Connecticut nursing home shortly after Jack
the Ripper killed five prostitutes in London

When Alvaro Montoya vanished without a trace from Sacramento,
California, in the summer of 1988, no one put up posters, begged
for information, or broadcast his fate on TV. The only person who
noticed, in fact, was one of Montoya's fellow tenants in a "board and
care" home for the indigent and elderly in the leafy, gently rundown
neighborhood known as Alkalai Flats. The home, at 1426 F Street,
was run by a vigorous do-gooder named Dorothea Puente, who was
widely admired in the city for her work with the poor. In the mid-
1980s, she refurbished the pretty, Victorian-era house and divided it
into eight tidy bedrooms, reserving the second floor for herself.
Then she called on the Seventh-Day Adventist Church, of which she
was a member, to send her people in need of care. When her tenants
arrived, she briskly set about supervising their medicine, managing
their social security benefits, and mending, as best she could, the tat-
tered fabric of their lives.

Alvaro Montoya, known as Bert, lived in a small room off the communal kitchen. He was a cheerful, round-bellied fellow in his fifties,

who originally hailed from Central America. Nobody knew exactly where, but the trouble with asking was that Montoya heard voices in his head and generally preferred their company to anyone else's. He puttered about on his own, for the most part, mild-mannered and content, knocking back a beer or two at Joe's Corner down on Sixteenth Street, smoking a cigar in the sunshine on the gabled front porch, or watching TV in the chintz-curtained parlor.

Down the corridor from Montoya was sixty-eight-year-old John Sharp, Puente's most self-sufficient tenant. A tall, wiry Kansan, Sharp turned up at 1426 F Street in the fall of 1987, after landing in the hospital with a herniated disk and then being unable to afford a private clinic in which to recuperate. When he recovered, he decided to stay. He loved the rent—one hundred fifty dollars a month—the place was comfortable, as charming as a country bed and breakfast, and Mrs. Puente was an excellent cook: "swordfish, steak, salads, porkchops . . ."

Sharp could usually be found in his room, flipping through novels and history books, absorbed, quiet, reclining in an easy chair, resting from his early morning shift as a cook at a nearby diner. He wasn't especially curious about his housemates and had never said more than "hello" to Bert Montoya, receiving a friendly mumble in reply. But he did notice that the little fellow went "poof!" one day, just disappeared. One minute sitting in the living room, the next not there, and no discussion.

It was true, of course, that tenants came and went at Mrs. Puente's. But something wasn't quite right about the way they were leaving that summer. They weren't struggling out the front door with their bags, complaining about a sore back, helped by a hovering relative or church volunteer. Montoya left the same way Ben Fink, the drunk who lived upstairs, had. One night in July, Sharp heard the squeak of Ben's mattress springs over his head, an old man sinking into a drunken sleep, and then he never saw him again, not the next morning, or ever.

People were vanishing.

The next person to notice that Bert Montoya had disappeared was his social worker, Elizabeth Valentine, who paid one of her occasional visits to F Street on a hot September morning. Valentine worked long hours for the Volunteers of America, scouring malls for downtrodden souls. She was in her late twenties, lanky and loose, with long, brown hair, and a uniform of Levi's jeans. Together with her VOA partner and childhood friend Judy Moise, Valentine was a native of Sacramento, raised in the liberal ferment of California in the 1960s, streetwise but idealistic. "I believed that all people were inherently good," she says, "and that that good would rise to the surface. Give a person enough love, enough attention, a higher quality of life . . ." They would flourish and reform.

Although forty years younger than Dorothea Puente, the young social workers felt she shared their values, possessed that same combination of resilience and optimism. And in the person of Alvaro Montoya, they had a shared project. "Bert," says Valentine, with rueful affection, "had a very gentle presence." Neither irascible nor self-destructive, he conversed with his voices as if a whole family of siblings and friends lived inside his head. If he couldn't be persuaded to part with them through antipsychotic medication—and he could not—then at least he could be kept safe, clean, and cared-for.

When Moise and Valentine found a room for him with Dorothea in the fall of 1987, they watched with pleased relief as the older woman took charge. Puente chatted with him in his native Spanish, which endeared her to him at once, and she wasn't afraid of his psychosis, which made her endearing twice over. Within weeks, she had tackled his psoriasis—intractable for years—and persuaded him to wear new shoes. "He *looked* better," says Valentine. "That's what we went on."

Now she must reach back beyond the intervening years and permit herself to recall the trust she felt. "I can walk into the kitchen and smell all the wonderful food Dorothea would cook every day. Sitting in her living room in nice, comfortable chairs, a very welcoming entrance to her home. Very homey. Cozy, and clean, and smells good, and she's smiling. She was like the quintessential grandmother. Open arms, take the people that we could not. She was there to provide hope."

Puente wasn't just sweet. She had a rare degree of fortitude, sophistication, and savvy. She more nearly resembled a diplomat than a grandmother, more Pamela Harriman than Grandma Lee. Always impeccably dressed, trailing a mist of perfume, manicured just so, she had a talent for gracious conversation, which is what had brought her to prominence in Sacramento civic life. She was a revered godmother to the Hispanic community. And in her parlor there were photos of her dancing at a late-1970s fund-raising ball with then-Governor Jerry Brown. The consummate benefactress.

When Dorothea told Valentine that she'd sent Bert to Mexico to stay on a ranch with her own extended family, the social worker was surprised but not suspicious. She and Moise only wondered about his legal status, since they'd just spent the past year hunting down his birth certificate, finally figuring out he was from Costa Rica. They were still in the process of procuring his documents, so they asked Dorothea if she'd arrange for someone from Mexico to call VOA. "We just wanted to hear a voice, probably talk to her brother, see how it was going."

A busy week passed, then another, and the women realized they still hadn't heard. A call to Puente brought apologies and reassurances. Then things took a peculiar turn. Dorothea phoned one day in October to tell them that Bert had come back from Mexico but almost immediately had been picked up by a long-lost cousin from Salt Lake City, who took him to live there. Now Moise and Valentine were concerned. They had never heard of a relative in Utah. They could imagine Bert feeling frightened, his spirit voices arguing and hissing in his head as a stranger trundled him off in a van. It bothered them. A lot.

But the real "flag," remembers Valentine, was the change in Dorothea Puente's demeanor. She was growing openly hostile to their inquiries. It was jarring. She was on their team. It didn't make sense. In early November, returning to the boardinghouse, Moise and Valentine found the older woman at the top of her landing on the porch, staring down at them in a way that they suddenly found chilling. "God," says Valentine, "I'll never forget walking up on that porch. She was *not* a happy camper. The look in her eye was very different, very cold, very direct. It was a *stare* down. That's when I began to think, 'Now, wait a minute,' and sort of a crack appeared in my image of her."

Striding past Puente into the house, the women went room to room, banging on doors, demanding to know if the tenants had seen Bert. That was when they met John Sharp. It began to emerge that the tenants at F Street knew more about Dorothea Puente than anyone had ever sought to ask them. They knew, for instance, that she kept "gallons of booze" upstairs in her pretty dining room, and Sharp saw where it went, which was down her gullet. When nobody but her needy charges were about, Dorothea Puente had a volcanic temper. "You son-of-a-*bitch,*" she'd spit, if someone made a small mistake.

Sometimes, Sharp told the social workers, in the middle of the night he had woken to harsh whispers and curses, followed by a "bumping sound ... then something rolling, crashing down the stairs." Flipping back the covers, peering out his door, he would see "a small refrigerator and some picture frames." Or, shortly after Ben Fink left, "a rug shampooer." Objects hurled with surprising strength and rage.

There was something else, just after Ben Fink left. An inexplicable odor. Sharp caught the tang in his nostrils when he passed the little room just off the kitchen. He couldn't comprehend the fact of that scent in this place, but he knew very well what it was. Sharp had worked for the Kansas City Mortuary Service. "You never," he said, "forget that smell."

"When we heard there was a smell of dead bodies, we went, *Jesus Christ!*" Valentine recalls, stretching her arms out, palms down, across the VOA boardroom table, as if flattened by the weight of the memory. "Judy and I were walking down the K Street Mall, just shaking our heads, trying to get a grip, looking at each other: 'Could this really, could this *really* be true?'" In an instant, all the hints they'd ignored for so long came together, and crushed them.

Detective John Cabrera of Sacramento Police Department Homicide met the social workers' fears by raising one bushy brown eyebrow. Their allegations were fantastical. How could he even broach the subject with Puente? "I can't just go there empty-handed," the mustachioed detective protested. "This woman is highly praised, by politicians, by ambassadors from other countries, plus our officers go by and she gives them tamales and burritos." She's an *insider*. One of the good guys.

Yet there was something about the address, 1426 F Street. He'd had some woman, a junkie named Brenda Trujillo, under arrest six months earlier. "I remember we were walking to the jail," he says now, his dark eyes wide, "and she's hostile, she's yellin: 'What about Dorothea? You guys don't do nothin' about her.'" Cabrera has adopted a falsetto, altered his gestures. In the tiny interrogation room on the fourth floor of the police department, he reenacts the drama. "'She's buryin' people in her yard. I lived there, I know, and you guys don't even care.' We said, 'All right.'" He drops his voice so it's cool, reassured. "We parked it. I kinda checked on a few things, any problems with that address"—he shrugs—"nothin'."

But here it was again: 1426 F Street. So, Cabrera says, he hit the phones and did a little more research. "It took us four days," he continues, "[but] finally I find out. She's on federal parole." Dorothea Puente, Sacramento's premier provider of care for the poor, had been convicted in 1982 of fraud, theft, and attempted murder. She had built a small fortune by posing as a home-care nurse, stupefying her patients to the point of death with drugs and robbing them, for months at a time.

For the small Sacramento social services community, for the Seventh-Day Adventist Church and the parole board and the people who lived on F Street, the world had just turned upside down.

On the morning of November 8, Dorothea Puente greeted Detective Cabrera and his partners as she once had welcomed Beth Valentine, in a spirit of perfect ease. "All I'm trying to do is read her," says Cabrera, remembering how he stood in her foyer, watching this calm, dark-eyed woman in her polka-dot dress. "I'm just watching her, feeling her out. She's probably one of the toughest encounters I've ever had. I really tried to read her, and I couldn't."

"Cabrer-a," Puente said, sounding out the detective's name as she turned to him, "Cabrer-a . . . are you Hispanic?" He said he was. They talked about that. "We kinda, kinda hit it off for a second," he remembers, a bit discomfited. "Then I simply told her, 'Look, here's the deal. We've had a complaint about a missing person, and we need to check if there's been any foul play.' She said, 'Oh, gosh, no, I've had all kinds of problems with Beth.' " Nonchalant as a busy housewife who waves in the meterman to take his reading, Dorothea Puente gave the officers the run of her house and yard. Then she went upstairs and began to drink screwdrivers in slow succession.

By the time the light left the afternoon sky, the shovels of several sweating men had grated against human bone. By the end of the weekend, eight bodies would be disinterred from shallow graves across the garden. Along with Bert Montoya, seven others came up from the earth. But Puente didn't stay for the final tally. For hours, as the dig progressed on that last day, she sat silent in her upstairs kitchen. Then she rose. She freshened up. She packed an expensive red handbag. Stiff-shouldered and prim, she marched downstairs and asked the officers if she could go to a nearby hotel bar for a cocktail to calm her nerves. So utterly nurturant and harmless did she seem that the officers nodded.

It took one of the most massive hunts in California history, not to mention the most frantic police department spin control efforts, before they reclaimed the fugitive. They found her holed up in a fleabag motel in Los Angeles. By that time, all her victims had been identified. Benjamin Fink, the alcoholic upstairs from John Sharp, and James Gallop, and Betty Palmer, and Vera Faye Martin, and Leona Carpenter, and Dorothy Miller. They were all registered as still alive by government agencies. Their checks and benefits had been posted monthly to their murderess for as long as two years.

When Dorothea Puente was unveiled as a serial murderess, newspaper headline writers dubbed her the "Arsenic and Old Lace Killer," referring to the title of a 1941 drawing-room comedy in which two sweet little old ladies poison their doddering gentlemen friends. It was hardly a moniker that captured the fear Puente's tenants felt, or the physical agony of those who died slowly before her, or the rank defilement of their bodies, shoved headless and twisted into garbage bags.

But the media had no other frame of reference for the crime. Not because there weren't other female serial killers—about 17 percent of known American serial killers are women, and at least twenty-five of them have been arrested and convicted since 1972. The tally doesn't include the team killers or the Munchausen syndrome by proxy mothers but reflects only the solo operators, preying on a sequence of more than three victims, who might be family members, acquaintances, or strangers, often a blend of the three. All of the women were local sensations in their time, freaks of nature to be gawked at and joked about. But they failed to take hold in our collective psyche as monstrous, and therefore as resonant. No female serial killer has the mythic force of the classic predator. We find it impossible to perceive them as frightening creatures. There is no Jane the Ripper.

Reviewing the nicknames given to multiple killers by media and law enforcement over the century, criminologist Eric Hickey has found that, while men are referred to as "The Ripper," "The Night Stalker," "The Strangler," or "The Slasher," women receive names that make light of their crimes—and by extension, of their victims. Comical monikers like the "Arsenic and Old Lace Killer," and "Giggling Grandma" and "Old Shoe Box Annie" are utterly undescriptive of the brutality of murder, while sexual monikers like the "Beautiful Blonde" and "Black Widow" hook almost jocularly into men's sexual fear of women. The monster is tamed in her feminine guise. As two academics wrote recently, we respond to female predators with curiosity rather than dread: "We can be fascinated without being afraid."

One of the reasons we don't fear real female predators is that they tend to be "place-specific" killers. They don't prowl. They operate in one home, hospital, or board-and-care. As such, they don't touch the chord of anxiety we feel about The Dark, about the World Out There in the shadows behind our own houses, that makes male killers such potent figures. Men who commit serial murder invariably strike us as senseless in their motive and random in their targets; their action is nothing more tangible than the impulse for destruction, pure evil in a human shell, a vision captured by the director John Carpenter with his masked killer in *Halloween*.

Women, on the other hand, seem to kill more purposively. They seem to have a reason. Dorothea Puente poisoned for money, a motive that everyone recognizes. That slots her into a different category in our minds from her monstrous male counterpart, more nearly related to organized crime or serial bank robbery, where the killing is essentially incidental.

In reality, however, gender differences in serial murder are superficial. They speak, as criminal psychologist Candice Skrapec observes, "to modus operandi, not to motive." Belea Keeney and Kathleen Heide looked at twenty-two solo female serial killers arrested in the United States between 1972 and 1992 and found enough information about fourteen of them to do an analysis. The fourteen women (nine of whom were Southerners) were estimated by law enforcement officials to have killed more than eighty-eight people and were confirmed as having killed sixty-two. Forty-three percent of their victims were "in the custodial care of the murderers." Most of the dead were relatives, but 20 percent were strangers or acquaintances. Fifty-seven percent were killed with poison, 29 percent were smothered, 11 percent were shot. The women, the authors found, were evenly divided between those with "affective goals," meaning they killed exclusively for some interior emotional purpose, and those with "instrumental goals," meaning that, like Puente, they profited from their slaughter as well. All of the women were white (as was Puente, who took her last name from a brief marriage with an Hispanic man). Thirteen were living with others at the time of the murders. Eleven were employed. Over a third of their victims had been dismembered or mutilated.

Films about male serial killers are always enacted as suspense dramas—will the cops catch him in time? Will the heroine save herself in time? The victim is invariably a brave young co-ed or, more rarely, a vulnerable young man. But the only docudrama about a female serial killer—Aileen Wuornos—is billed as a relationship drama. The tag line: "A friendship torn apart by murder." Apparently, her victims are secondary to her relationship to her best friend and lover, Tyria Moore. When the TV Wuornos goes out to work the streets, her friend worries about her safety: "Hooking is dangerous,"

Tyria says in the TV dialogue. "I don't want you to get hurt." As if Wuornos hadn't figured that out twenty years ago and adapted herself, become tough, canny, and opportunistic like the pimps and thieves with whom she moved. But the movie is set to the idealized tempo of female friendship. It is the tale of two waifs against the world, good-hearted in an inexplicably naive way—considering their life experience—who try to protect each other and fail. Tyria is nothing if not tenderly concerned. What if, for some reason, seven men in a row threatened Aileen's life? What if she were obliged to kill them all, and leave them naked in forests, and steal their belongings, even though she'd never had to shoot a john before in her entire career as a prostitute? What if the two of them were up against the strong-armed law, like Thelma and Louise? In the end, however, since this is a true story, they don't hold hands and jump into a canyon. Tyria betrays Aileen by turning state's evidence. So they are "torn apart by murder."

In purely fictional dramas about female predators, the victims are also men, who, like Wuornos's victims, are depicted as having been led astray by their own lust. Only, here the women are smooth as silk, smilingly clever in their lingerie, and the theme is sexual danger. They are Linda Fiortino in *The Last Seduction*, Sean Young in *A Kiss Before Dying*, Sharon Stone in *Basic Instinct*. All of them are gorgeous bitches, man-eaters, the kind of women that men just love to fear. Unlike *Henry: Portrait of a Serial Killer*, which considers the banality of violence, or *Rampage*, which ponders the madness of serial murder, these films beautify their villainesses and ascribe a certain responsibility to their victims, who should have known better. What we never see are the real victims of female serial killers: the very young, the very old, the disabled, and the lonely. The message is not that women brutalize the innocent, but that if men follow their dicks, they'll get into trouble. It is the theme, really, of journalist Ron Rosenbaum's cover story in the March 1995 issue of *Esquire*, entitled "In Praise of Dangerous Women." "For men," he writes, "the real attraction is the thrill of disempowerment. Think about it. Doesn't it take more nerve to give up . . . control?"

The tendency to "forget" female serial killers has been a recurrent phenomenon throughout Western history. There are countless examples of men who became legendary horror figures, while their female counterparts recede into the humdrum of ordinary crime. Many of us have heard of Bluebeard, for instance, a mythic figure based on the French Baron Gilles de Rais, officer and confidant of Joan of Arc. He was allegedly responsible for murdering scores, possibly hundreds, of children. But we have never heard of the mid-fifteenth-century Countess Elisabeth Bathory, of Hungary, who bled to death 610 peasant girls, whom she abducted and kept in her castle dungeon so that she could fill rejuvenating beauty baths with their youthful blood. Similarly, the English speaking world was riveted by Jack the Ripper, but no one has heard of Jane Toppan, and no one paid much attention to Belle Gunness, who fled Chicago in 1908 after killing forty men and four children, having transformed her lush farmland into a cemetery. No lore exists about Louise Peete, either, born in Bienville, Louisiana, in 1883, to high-society parents, a psychopath who drove all four of her husbands to suicide, shot and killed at least two other men, bludgeoned to death a woman, and had another man committed to an insane asylum so that she could take over his bank account.

Our collective amnesia about female serial killers is so pronounced that when Aileen Wuornos was arrested in 1992 and charged with the shooting deaths of seven men along I-75, she was immediately proclaimed America's first female serial killer. Only four years earlier, ten female serial killers had been arrested across the United States. Less than two years before, Dorothea Puente was convicted. And less than a decade earlier, the state of North Carolina executed Velma Barfield, who poisoned five and wrote a memoir from death row. But the media went wild over Wuornos, as if she were a new species of serpent found in the sea. Even criminologists argued that Wuornos was different. She was the first woman to use a gun, some said, and the first to prey on strangers. She was not. Thirty-nine percent of American serial murderesses have used guns, not least of whom was Peete, the last woman to be executed in California. She died at Sing-Sing in 1947, after taunting Supreme Court justices that "no gentleman would put a lady to her death."

By March 1995, the flurry of excitement over the "first" female
serial killer had swallowed itself whole once again. Retired FBI special agent Roy Hazelwood reportedly announced at a homicide conference in Calgary, Alberta, "There are no female serial killers." Not
a one. Not the dozens of women who have killed up to forty patients
in hospitals; nor the dozens more who have killed ten men, or
twenty; nor Puente and others who have preyed upon tenants. Never
mind Marybeth Tinning, or any of the mothers and angels of death.

At the heart of this remarkable denial that female predators exist
can be found a complex web of prejudices and misperceptions that
inform the semantics of the label "serial killer" itself. The FBI's
Behavioral Science Services Unit, in Quantico, Virginia, is largely
responsible for having given this particular type of homicide its
name. The coinage is in some dispute, but one man who claims to
have come up with it is retired special agent Robert Ressler, who
defined the crime in 1978 as a series of homicides perpetrated
against a sequence of more than three victims, all of whom were
strangers, with a cooling off period in between each kill. Ressler
called this type of murderer a "serial killer," to distinguish him from
a mass killer, who explodes all at once, attacking several people
simultaneously, as in the massacre of schoolchildren in Dunblane,
Scotland.

Ressler and his BSSU colleagues began collecting data on serial
murderers by interviewing convicts from around the United States
who fit the FBI definition. The objective was not to explain serial
homicide per se but to quantify the characteristics of known perpetrators—their motives, methods, and patterns of attack—in order to
draw profiles of the unknown suspects still at large. Psychological
profiling, as the technique came to be called, is strictly an investigative tool, not an inquiry into the "why" of murder, just the "how." If
85 percent of known serial killers are Caucasian males between
twenty years old and forty, the BSSU can use that data to advise local
investigators to rule out women, blacks, and elderly men (among
others) from their suspect pool. If the corpses have been arranged at
the crime scene in a particularly bizarre or seemingly ritual fashion,
then FBI probabilities would point to a mentally ill offender,

because those that they interviewed who *were* mentally ill tended to behave insanely at the crime scene. By contrast, lust killers tend to sexually assault their victims, postmortem, and sadists leave the corpse untouched. So, if it appeared that the offender were mentally ill, then the BSSU would advise local detectives to look for a thin man, because the mentally ill tend to be undernourished. If the corpse was white, then that thin man would also be white, since serial killers tend to strike within their own race. If the crime scene was particularly disorganized, the killer would tend to be young, because younger men are more impulsive and heedless. Hence: "You are looking for a thin Caucasian male in his twenties."

In the two decades since the BSSU program began, the agents have refined their profiles considerably, devising ever more specific subsets of violent serial offenders. In 1992, for instance, special agent Roy Hazelwood gave a lecture at the First International Conference on Serial and Mass Murder, in Windsor, Ontario, on the "sexual sadist," a type of killer (like Paul Bernardo) who is aroused by the fear and pain he elicits in his victims. Killing them is, in a sense, secondary. The victim must be silenced so as not to identify the killer. Hazelwood noted that at least a third of such men who'd been interviewed by the FBI owned a copy of the John Fowles novel *The Collector*, about a man who keeps a woman locked in a cellar. They were also likely to keep photographic or audio records of the crime. Many had hard-core pornography collections.

The precision of the BSSU data makes it a superb tool for narrowing the range of suspects in the real world, but only if the suspects behave within the parameters already devised. Since the FBI is principally concerned with helping homicide detectives locate a suspect *after* they have found a body, they are going to concentrate on types of killers who dump the bodies in a place they aren't connected to. From a law enforcement perspective, there's no practical application for profiling "place-specific" killers, because as soon as you find the body you have an obvious pool of suspects. Jeffrey Dahmer, for example, was the only inhabitant of his apartment. Detectives in Milwaukee encountered him simultaneously with his victims. There was no need to predict what he would be like. Consequently, Dahmer's particular psychopathology is of less concern to the FBI than that of a "roaming" killer who leaves bodies along a trail. The BSSU's mandate is to develop knowledge that can assist an ongoing investigation. One reason, then, that the FBI has decided there are "no female serial killers" is because the overwhelming majority of serial murderesses are place-specific criminals, which is not the sort of crime the FBI is called upon to investigate. Nurses who kill in hospitals, for example, may very well be preying upon a series of more than three strangers, with a cooling-off period in between, but they stay in one place.

Academics who study serial murder refer to the site of attacks as the "comfort zone," a geographic area in which the perpetrator feels familiar enough to kill, like the hunting range of an animal. The most literal example of this is the Alaska killer Robert Hansen, who abducted transient prostitutes in Anchorage and flew them up to wilderness areas well known to him, where he set them free and hunted them down. Hansen felt most comfortable (and confident he wouldn't be observed) in a hunting range he'd known all his life. When Paul Bernardo was committing serial rape before his marriage, he stalked the streets he'd known since childhood, in Scarborough. When he escalated to killing, with Karla Homolka, the venue changed. The comfort zone became their home. Women have historically felt most comfortable and masterful in their homes, and that is where they have tended to kill. The next most frequent sites are hospitals, boardinghouses, or private residences they visit as nurses or baby-sitters: all zones that women can move through without being scrutinized. A woman would not feel comfortable attacking a child in a dark alley or poisoning her husband in a red-light district. Serial killers need to build up a certain confidence before they attack, and part of that psychological process involves feeling secure in their surroundings.

The selection of place has important implications for the selection of victims and has led to an emerging concept in criminology called "routine activities theory." Serial offenders, including rapists and robbers, tend to commit their crimes along routes they already travel routinely. A rapist, for example, will not hike off into a densely wooded area he has never explored before in the hopes of chancing upon a suitable victim. It is far more likely that he will pass by the same bus stop every morning on his way to work for a month, seeing the same person or same type of person, nursing his fantasy, building up his confidence, until finally he assaults him or her. Similarly, male serial killers who troll red-light districts, bus stations, gay bars, and stretches of highway where hitchhikers can be found will already have traveled these routes, sometimes for years, before formulating the intent to commit murder.

Until recently, women have had much more constricted geographic mobility in both their routine activities routes and their comfort zones. As a result, as Rossmo, now a serial homicide theorist at Simon Fraser University, puts it, female predators are "trappers" rather than "stalkers." They "select a victim who happens to come, by design or by chance, into their comfort zone." Dorothea Puente didn't pursue Alvaro Montoya, he was delivered to her by the Sacramento social work community. Genene Jones killed babies who came into the San Antonio hospital where she worked. Aileen Wuornos murdered out on the highway, a route she routinely hitchhiked and solicited along. It was a much wider zone than is characteristic of women, and Wuornos may mark a transition for female serial killers in the upcoming decade.

Perhaps law enforcement will be more prepared for the roaming female killer, given the focus of their investigative techniques. They have certainly failed in the arena of place-specific murder. Female serial killers, according to Eric Hickey, actually average a greater number of victims than their male counterparts, even though the deaths occur right under their communities' noses. Since authorities have no framework of suspicion for multiple murder in a family or hospital, they often don't even suspect there is a killer to pursue. They have on their hands, instead, a series of abrupt natural deaths or unexplained disappearances. It is lack of suspicion, nothing more complex, that enabled a woman like Nannie Doss, of Oklahoma, to kill four husbands, two children, her mother, two of her sisters, and her nephew in the 1930s and 1940s; Marybeth Tinning to destroy her children; Genene Jones to murder an estimated forty infants and small children; and British nurse Beverly Allitt to kill at least four children in a Lincolnshire hospital.

The killers themselves sometimes profess amazement at this blindness. "I got away with the first one," marveled the young Floridian killer Christine Falling, who smothered five children entrusted to her care as a babysitter between 1980 and 1982, "because they couldn't tell what actually happened and *I* wasn't gonna tell them. If they're too stupid to figure it out for themselves then why should I tell 'em? I mean, they're doctors. I couldn't believe I was getting away with it." Similarly, Jane Toppan, the nurse in Connecticut at the turn of the century, later scorned the "stupid doctors" and "ignorant relatives" who failed to apprehend her.

If law enforcement officials have been hampered by their own prejudices in identifying women as serial killers, academics have generally failed to set them straight. In the early 1980s, an eclectic group of journalists and academics started to study serial homicide, rapidly becoming the "experts" to whom media turned whenever a new killer went on the prowl. What made the fledgling field so hot was the sudden upsurge in high-profile cases in which the killer was bafflingly *ordinary:* John Wayne Gacy, the Chicago contractor who strangled thirty-three teenaged boys and buried them beneath his suburban house; Ted Bundy, a handsome law student who killed twenty-eight young women by the time of his final arrest in Florida; and Edmund Kemper, an urbane man in northern California who, after a six-month rampage that left eleven dead, cut his mother's head off, placed it on the mantlepiece, and used it as a dart board. The question "How could they?" was made more urgent by the apparent normality of these men.

The early stages of serial homicide scholarship was highly speculative. "We had no basis for our research," recalls Eric Hickey. "We were all over the place." Not everyone agreed with the FBI definition of serial killers. Were they only predators who attacked strangers, or should one include those who killed family? Did they have to have a sexual motive, or could they profit from the crimes? The criminologist James Allan Fox theorized that most worked in pairs, although the FBI begged to differ. Nobody could agree on how many dead bodies there needed to be. While Ressler at the BSSU said three, others opted for two, others ten. Nobody could explain why contract killers, mercenaries, and mafia hit men were truly an unrelated species of criminal. What about war criminals? Or women like Marybeth Tinning? Perhaps the most gender-inclusive definition would be: men and women who kill a sequence of three or more victims, with a cooling off period in between, without external provocation or incitement.

Feminist scholars might have been the ones to raise and refine questions about women's involvement, but they didn't. Instead, they coopted the concept of serial killer into their concerns about sexual violence against women, for which purpose all serial killers had to be male. Or, as Phyllis Chesler described them in *The New York Times* in 1992, "white male drifters who hate women and are obsessed with pornography." Since sexual violence against women is viewed, by most feminists, as a political phenomenon, serial killers have come to be seen as engines of misogynistic oppression. Feminist Jane Caputi writes that serial killers act on behalf of all men as "henchmen" in the subordination of women. The serial killer is a "martyr for the patriarchal state." Phyllis Chesler contended that Aileen Wuornos was not a serial killer; furthermore, the very fact that she was in prison had to do with patriarchal oppression: "It is unlikely that Wuornos and other victims of violence against women will be fairly treated by the judicial system." Trickling down from ostensible authorities like Phyllis Chesler to other feminist writers, it has become axiomatic that "serial killer" means "man." The cultural critic Susan McWhinney notes, for instance, that "the State says [Wuornos] is a serial killer. This charge seems implausible, given that the definition of a serial killer is one who kills for sexual arousal within a specific power imbalance."

In fact, there is no consensus about the definition of "serial killer." Nor is there much consensus about causation. A large number of serial killers were abused or neglected as children, including Aileen Wuornos, Dorothea Puente, Marybeth Tinning, and, indeed, all fourteen female serial murderesses in Heide and Keeney's study. A majority appear to be psychopaths, although the women are more likely to be diagnosed by local psychiatrists as "histrionic" and "manic-depressive."

Psychoneurologists have turned their attention to the influence of brain damage on episodic or compulsive violence, particularly when the behavior is combined with a brutal childhood. The Rochester serial killer Arthur Shawcross, who went to trial in 1991, suffered from "temporal lobe malformation," the effect of which was to disinhibit his impulse control. He also had extremely erratic electroencephalograph readings, which suggested that the electrical impulses in his brain were misfiring, engendering sudden surges of rage.

Paraphilias (sexual deviances) play an important role in motivating many male killers: sadism, necrophilia, pedophilia, fetishes for blood and for body parts. These may necessitate murder, but murder in itself isn't the drive. In other words, persons with deviant sexual compulsions may not set out to kill, as such, but find themselves having to do so in order to procure what they do want. British killer Dennis Nilsen used to cover himself in white powder and fantasize that he was dead. His necrophiliac fantasies, coupled with a deep and abiding loneliness, eventually drove Nilsen (in the late 1970s) to strangle the men he met in gay bars, primarily to keep them around as his "lovers." Nilsen bathed them, propped them in chairs while he watched TV, slept with the bodies beside him in bed, and wrote them love poems. He did not murder for murder's sake.

The overwhelming majority of serial killers, both male and female, are white. Candice Skrapec views this as "a supremely significant window" through which to contemplate their behavior. Why not blacks or Hispanics or Asians? They are vulnerable to abuse as children. They read pornography. They get brain-damaged and head-injured and have sexual deviances. Their ranks can be found in every other criminal category. Is it possible that a sense of entitlement to social esteem is, somehow, a critical ingredient in the crime? Whatever the answer, the fact that a white woman is more likely to commit serial murder than a black, Asian, or Hispanic man by a factor of one hundred to one should end the feminist conversation on this crime as a specifically masculine power trip.

The makeup of the serial murderer is profoundly complex, and if the homicide experts have learned anything in the past decade of furious theorizing, it should be that all of them have a point, and none paints the full picture. Dorothea Puente's childhood illustrates the interplay of life experience, temperament, gender, and psychological drive in transforming one particular individual into a predator. She was born Dorothy Helen Gray, on January 9, 1929. Her parents followed the crops along a dusty migrant trail, five children in tow, eventually drifting to Redlands, California, where Dorothy's mother, Trudie, had her sixth child. Seventh-Day Adventists, Trudie and Dorothy's father, Jesse James Gray, taught Dorothy and her older siblings that service to others was the highest mark of social esteem. "Mother once made me promise to feel sorry for alcoholics and take care of drunks," Dorothea later said. But, by the time she was three, her mother herself was catastrophically awash in alcohol, her father, in illness and despair.

Trudie hailed from Oklahoma. Restless at sixteen, she'd married Jesse James, named for the great train robber, who had known Jesse Gray's father in Missouri. Trudie and Jesse James married for love, but their union was impulsive and ultimately ruinous. Trudie joined a bike gang and began to run with other men. When she came home, she had wild, drunken flights of rage. Her effect on her children was described at the sentencing phase of Puente's trial by Dr. Mindy Rosenberg, a child psychologist in San Francisco who'd been retained by defense attorneys to investigate factors in Puente's childhood that might serve to mitigate her sentence. Rosenberg interviewed Puente's two older sisters, Audry and Sylvia. "Audry recalls that her mother threw a frying pan at her father. Sylvia recalls that [she] threw the top of a milk can [and] gashed his forehead." She whipped Dorothea with a belt and got arrested for slashing Sylvia with a pocketknife.

Jesse James was a better parent than his wife, according to his children, but his short life was suffused with trauma. He collapsed in the trenches of the First World War, exposed to mustard gas and suffering from shell shock. When he came home, he was volatile and depressed, drinking too much and getting into knife fights in local bars. Then he contracted tuberculosis, and died from it slowly, for years. Sometimes, his humiliation and sense of doom grew so intolerable that he just wanted to kill himself, get it over with. Once, he climbed up a water tower, swinging on the ladder one-handed and waving a gun, his defiant wish for self-destruction met by the sobs of his children down below.

What love Jesse James Gray had to offer was a flame always flickering and fading, threatening to darken and die. "The children," Dr. Rosenberg testified, "describe the mother as not very affectionate, and that the father, once he became ill . . . was really unavailable to them. At one point he had been a good father, but was no longer. . . . any little bit of attention was fought over, like starving children would basically fight over a crumb."

When Puente was seven, Jesse left Trudie and fought for custody of his children. "I don't want to live with Momma," Dorothea wrote to the court. "She gets drunk . . . I can tell when my mother drinks because she gets so mean I can smell it." Custody was awarded to Trudie anyway, and she left the children alone for two- and three-day stretches, without food or explanation. Afraid of the dark, unable to reach the lamp and no one else to do it, not that night and maybe never, because Momma didn't say she would be back, just left. What would that be like for a child?

"Many years ago," wrote Dennis Nilsen, articulating, perhaps, something of what Puente felt, "I was a boy drowning in the sea. I am always drowning in the sea . . . down amongst the dead men, deep down." Like Puente, Nilsen, who was raised in poverty on the eastern coast of Scotland, experienced his early life as devastatingly unpredictable. His only bond was with his grandfather, a sailor, who would abruptly disappear for months at a time and finally perished at sea. The grandfather returned to Nilsen as a corpse in a casket when the boy was six. "Come see your granddad," the family beckoned, not explaining that the reunion would be with a man who no longer answered the child or reached for him.

Puente's parents died within a year of each other before she was ten, her mother in a motorbike accident. Like Nilsen, she wasn't prepared for this final abandonment. She was ushered into a funeral home by orphanage officials who hadn't told her what she'd find.

"Your mother's in there," they said. No one spoke of Trudie with her again. The abandonment was so profound as to be almost incomprehensible. It must have felt, as Nilsen said, like drowning. The child survives, but the heart is lost. From then on, to love is to drown.

Many male serial killers attack types of people—symbolic targets—who evoke an early source of vulnerability and terror in them. John Wayne Gacy, who had often been violently attacked and abused by his father, went after homosexual youths with a yearning that abruptly switched to savagery. Edmund Kemper had been viciously taunted and denigrated (among other things) by his mother. He worked his way through a series of young women who resembled the type that his mother had told him he'd never win. He won them by obliterating them, and then he obliterated his mother.

Some female serial killers also attack symbolic targets. When Aileen Wuornos said that she killed in self-defense, she was, indeed, defending herself against a childhood of horrendous treatment from her stepfather and other men. The men that she killed (after the first one) were no more culpable than anyone who crosses paths with a drive as ruthless as hers was to rage against remembered trauma. "In most cases," Sharon Smolick, a former counselor at Bedford Hills Correctional Facility for women in New York State, told *Psychology Today* in 1993, "women will not or cannot avenge themselves upon their attacker, but they do not remain silent and passive forever. It is often an innocent person who winds up paying with their lives." One Bedford inmate, identified as CJ, was so angry at the abuse she received as a child that she began working as a prostitute to "set [men] up." They thought they were going to have sex, but "I would beat them, pistol-whip them, and take their money." She did this twenty or so times. "Money was never the reason why I did it. I needed to rob them of their dignity first, and taking money they had was just another way of hurting them."

Puente's symbolic targets were the drunks of Sacramento, who elicited the specters of her mother and father and brought flooding back to her a fear she needed to suppress at all costs. Her own alcoholism seemed to connect her to this fear; it was the portal of memory, reminding her of a reality she had long since rewritten and disguised.

Many children are abused, of course, and don't become predators. Why do these rare few grow up to do what they do? The role of
temperament is, perhaps, another critical ingredient in determining
which maltreated child will evolve to strike out in this way. None of
Dorothea Puente's siblings became dangerous adults. They all tried
to "pretend [their early life] didn't happen," as Dorothea's daughter, whom she gave up for adoption, said at her trial. Dorothea's
eldest brother, Jim, is a Christian missionary in southern California.
Another brother, Jesse Everett, self-destructed with alcohol in the
1970s. Dorothea's sisters Audry and Sylvia managed to lead quiet
lives. A third sister, Wilma, died in a motorbike accident. Only
her youngest brother, Ray, became somewhat dangerous: He was
in prison on yet another drunk driving charge at the time of
Dorothea's trial.

"Dorothea was more extroverted," Dr. Rosenberg said at her sentencing hearing. "She was openly resentful of the kinds of things that
happened to her. Sylvia was more introverted, quiet, eager to please.
Her pain was directed more inward."

In his book *Crime and Personality*, Hans Eysenck argued that
human conscience is "a conditioned reflex." We are not born with a
sense of right and wrong. Since those concepts shift from culture to
culture, we learn the appropriate responses and determine how to
direct our base impulses accordingly. People with introverted tem-
peraments, Eysenck believed, condition "much more readily than do
extroverts." (Women as a sex, he maintained, are inherently more
conditionable. That wasn't true of Dorothea's mother, Trudie, and it
wasn't true of her.) Her need to conform was wholly secondary to
her need to be admired. "There was this overwhelming need for
attention," Dr. Rosenberg said, "to be looked upon as somebody
unique, special." The need unfurled itself, at first, in fantastical lies.
Fellow children at the orphanage learned that Dorothea was Por-
tuguese. Others were told that her mother was a pattern maker for
the stars, working for Hollywood costume designer Edith Head. As
she grew up she continued to lie about herself, telling people she
was a doctor, a former movie star, a war heroine, that she had
cancer, that she was rich. Nothing in life can matter but escape from
your own life story. So you must re-imagine the narrative. Start over.

Redeal the cards. This time, be loved and respected, adored. Hence the respectability achieved by killers like Ted Bundy, John Wayne Gacy, and Dorothea Puente. People are shocked that they could have put up such a facade. But it isn't us they were trying to fool, it was themselves.

The British journalist Colin Wilson once proposed a theory called the "right man syndrome," according to which men (he wasn't interested in women) perched their egos atop such intricately structured delusions of grandeur that, eventually, any challenge to the delusion became catastrophic, compelling them to lash out at the challenger. "Expose me for what I am and I will destroy you." The need to maintain her new identity fueled Puente's compulsion to steal, poison, and murder—to get the money to buy what she feared she would not be given, and to keep the dark specters at bay.

In her twenties and thirties, Puente was a con artist, check forger, and thief. For a time, she worked as a prostitute; then she ran a brothel, which gave her the business experience she needed to start boardinghouse operations in the 1970s. (It also gave her a rap sheet, which would later be overlooked.) By 1976 Puente began to prosper, stealing two hundred to three hundred dollars per tenant, molding herself into a wealthy and munificent citizen. She also used her feminity as a form of empowering disguise. The beautiful and sexually voluptuous youth became, with no interlude of waning, a little old lady. She deliberately forsook middle age, because that is a time in a woman's life when she loses sexual allure but hasn't yet gained public sympathy, when physique compels her to be an unadulterated self. There's little manipulative power for women in such frank presentations. So when Puente was still in her forties, she began to costume herself as a much older woman.

In a photograph taken by the Sacramento police on the day of her arrest, Puente, posed like a schoolgirl with her hands behind her back, wears a simple, sleeveless, pink polka-dot cotton dress. Solemn, demure, of fascinatingly indeterminate age, she is all at once a small girl, a beautiful woman, and, with her puffed white hair, a granny. It is her eyes that determine who she is: black eyes staring at the mug-shot camera, knowing, hard, and hateful.

In constructing their fantasy selves, serial killers seem to be attracted to the flash of politics, perhaps because they can project public personae without close scrutiny. They also often cultivate a sense of themselves as moral creatures, who can appear to do good, though this comes at no actual cost to themselves. Gacy dressed up as a clown at Chicago-area children's hospitals; Bundy volunteered on a rape crisis line; Dennis Nilsen was a fervent union activist; Christine Falling was an ideal babysitter; Genene Jones, a heroic pediatrics nurse. Some of Puente's beneficiaries were homeless, others lived in the governor's mansion. The photographs of her dancing with Jerry Brown and posing with George Deukmejian remind one of photographs of John Wayne Gacy with Rosalyn Carter and Ted Bundy with members of the Washington State GOP.

For years, these serial killers walk a hair's-width line between apparent altruism and self-aggrandizement, doing devastating damage to our conception of the tangible markers between good and evil. "That was the most chilling part for me," the social worker, Beth Valentine, says of Puente. "You know, you operate under a certain model of how this world works. And navigate yourself. And she shattered my model. She blew it to pieces. What's evil? What's good? That I would spend time with her, and I would know her, and she would tell me stories, and . . ." She pauses, chasing her confusion. "She was good and evil at the same time. She took care of them at the *same time*."

Invariably, however, when male serial killers are unmasked, those who supported them in their goodness abandon that stance and come to terms with the fact that they were duped. Not so with female killers. Many to whom Puente did good stood by her. A stream of witnesses flowed down the coast to Monterey in the winter of 1990 to tell the court of Dorothea Puente's generosity. Rosemary Arroyo was eleven when Puente took her under her wing. "I will never be able to repay you for all the things you've done for me," the now grown Arroyo wrote to the killer in jail. Another character witness was a broadcaster to whom Dorothea gave his first break by using her connections in the Hispanic media. A third was an abused woman whose divorce Puente had paid for. Her jury deliberated for twenty-four days, a California record, because at least one juror could not get past that goodness.

The marked difference in public response to male and female serial killers reflects the difference in our archetypes of gender, but it also speaks to the effect on our sensibilities of their modus operandi. The violence they do is less visible, less offensive to us, somehow. Novelist Joyce Carol Oates once characterized the mutilated victims left in the wake of male serial killers as "nightmare artworks." Insofar as there is an art, an expression, a *politics* to violence, it is assuredly evident in the methods of certain male serial killers. The Public Broadcasting Service program "Nova" toured the crime scenes of Arthur Shawcross, lingering over police photos of some of his eleven victims, swollen and disheveled, legs spread, mouths gaping. It was startling to see those pictures on TV, for identity is bound up in how we choose to present ourselves. Hair combed, mussed. Lipstick carefully applied. This is a right we reserve without thinking, and we honor it instinctively by covering the dead. Men like Shawcross mutilate their victims postmortem because they seem fully aware of this need for dignity. They desecrate their victims' bodies the way others might vandalize a temple. Violence is a language of protest.

At first glance, female serial killers do not appear to aggress this way. If they mutilate a body, it's usually for purposes of disposal, not for display. They rarely engage in sexual assault. Yet their crimes are equally expressive of their politics. The female serial killer's version of sexual defilement will either be robbery or the sabotage of intellectual and political authority, because that is how she conceives of masculine power. Aileen Wuornos robbed all the men she killed in "self-defense." Nannie Doss, Judi Buenoano, Martha Beck, Virginia McGinnis, and Louise Peete profited from insurance policies, bank account transfers, the sale of their victims' possessions. Then they flaunted, rather than concealed, the wealth they acquired. Nurses and mothers who become multiple murderers manipulate the patriarchal medical establishment, taunting and confounding the doctors who rush to rescue their victims. No less than with male killers, these women seem to be commenting contemptuously on staples of power—intellectual, financial—that society has hitherto denied them. They are vandalizing men's temples of prestige.

One of our worst inclinations is to believe that, because this violence is visually less horrifying, it is somehow more forgivable. To the degree that their victims were more likely to know and trust them, one could even argue that the opposite is true. The prosecutor at the trial of Blanche Taylor Moore, who murdered three husbands in North Carolina, observed, "Poisoning is a cloak-and-dagger kind of crime. What better cloak to wear than a cloak of appearing to be loving, appearing to be caring, and appearing to be kind?"

The men and women Dorothea Puente victimized had to know that she was killing them. But Puente was their nurse and friend. She was fine, wasn't she? Affable and committed, ordinary. They get up in the morning and she's made their breakfast, set out a little row of pills with their juice glass. Yet they keep succumbing to sudden, catastrophic illness; their energy seeps away with frightening swiftness; their mind swims. They need to be soothed, and she does that. She reassures them that they'll be all right, this woman in tender control of their lives, smiling her broad smile, *of course,* like their mother years ago, adjusting their pillows, plying them with crème de menthe or tea. They know something has gone terribly, terribly wrong. But how do they believe it? Family members say that Mrs. Puente will take care of them, and the doctors agree, and the social workers have lodged them in her home with visible pleasure. But she's poisoning them slowly to death.

The children of Dorothea Puente's first murder victim, Ruth Munro, believe their mother went through this awful recognition in the spring of 1982. At sixty-one, Munro was a vivacious woman, retired from a drug store, with four grown children. Her husband, Harold, met Dorothea in a cocktail lounge and thought she and Ruth would hit it off. They were both gregarious and inventive. They had flair. And they loved their cocktails. Ruth and Dorothea did indeed spark together. Just before Harold checked into the hospital for his final battle with cancer, Puente suggested that she and Munro go into business together as caterers. It would be fun. It would give Ruth a sense of purpose after Harold died. Not long after that, on April 11, 1982, Ruth moved in with Dorothea, to save money she would need for hospital bills and to concentrate on the new business.

In the middle of April, the many people in Sacramento who loved Ruth Munro began to watch her die. "She seemed to be not her normal self, just kind of in a fog, just looking kind of trancelike. It wasn't normal," said her son, Alan Clausen. A few days before Easter, Carmella Lombardo ran into her old pal at the hairdresser's. Munro looked awful. Lombardo was shocked. Surrounded by the chatter of hair-do instructions, this week's news, the drone of the driers, Munro confided to her friend that she thought she was dying. She was dying, she said, but she didn't know why. Her friends and family wanted, urgently, to try to find out.

But the murderess ran interference, posing as Munro's protector, dissuading her children from actually seeing their mother in person when they dropped by. When Alan Clausen did manage to see her in late April, she seemed stuporous, propped in an armchair, sipping crème de menthe with an unsteady hand. He saw her one last time after that, with Puente hovering over his shoulder. Munro was in her bedroom, perfectly still as if asleep, except that a tear ran down her cheek. Puente used a poison that paralyzed. Munro couldn't move or cry out. She could see her son, but she couldn't tell him to save her. On April 28, she was dead. The coroner found massive amounts of Tylenol, codeine, and the tranquilizer Miltown in her blood. The cause of death was ruled to be inconclusive. No one noticed that the joint bank account Munro had set up with her partner was empty.

How does one respond to a nurturant monster? What archetype do we possess for that? Detective Cabrera points to the clothes that Puente regularly donated to homeless people through the Seventh-Day Adventist Church. The people who received them were beneficiaries of Dorothea Puente's kindness. The people who'd owned them were dead by her hand. Communal complicity in female multiple murder adds a dimension of trauma in the aftermath of the crime that is generally quite distinct from male serial homicide. The victims of men are rarely handed to them on a plate. No one would willingly permit children to go off with strangers; hitchhiking is universally understood to be risky for women; no one idealizes the johns who prey upon prostitutes. But when Dorothea Puente was arrested, the community that had assisted her so ably in achieving her ends fell in upon itself in self-recrimination and guilt. Fingers were pointed. Organizations ceased working together. Friendships, including that of Judy Moise and Beth Valentine, broke up. "I retreated," says Valentine. "I really retreated. I think that we were all traumatized, and each person deals with that alone. We didn't even come together as a community to try to resolve all the security problems. We stopped communicating. I think the ombudsman, child welfare people, people less involved came in to do the cleanup."

What those people discovered was how many warning signs had been posted around the city and ignored. *Sacramento* magazine, for example, ran an article in the early 1980s, before Ruth Munro died, about Dorothea Puente's fall from grace. She had been caught skimming from her tenants in the late 1970s and served time in prison, but by the late 1980s nobody remembered the prominant benefactress brought down in scandal. Then there were the social security administrators who allowed a convicted check forger to deposit thousands of checks on behalf of their recipients. Federal parole board officials visited F Street and unaccountably failed to notice that their parolee was running another board and care operation. She had them convinced it was just her private residence. Even Detective Cabrera, who knew what he was up against, had trouble "seeing" Dorothea Puente. "She played me as much as I was trying to play her," he says. "That's what made her so dangerous, was that she fit right in like a polished nail. She moves like a shadow, she moves like smoke in the air. She was deadly because she manipulated society."

Puente capitalized on a potent blend of idealism, desperation, and prejudice that brought clients to her door and at the same time silenced them when they voiced warnings. Nobody is going to listen to someone who's mentally ill, aged, or drunk. One of the ignored whistle blowers was Joyce Peterson, a scrappy old alcoholic who hobbled into Puente's trial and testified to the callousness of which

Puente was capable when she knew the weight of community sentiment would be on her side. Puente evicted Peterson abruptly, with
virtually no notice, refused to hand over her social security check,
cashed it for herself instead, and, when Peterson tried to fight,
Puente pushed her down the stairs, called the police, and had her
hauled off to a detox center.

"We did place a resident there who thought Puente was completely mad, and wanted out," Valentine recalls, when asked about
Peterson. "It just didn't jibe with my image of Dorothea, and I
thought 'Oh, Joyce is just an angry alcoholic, she'll shoot at anything
around here.' She just painted a very different picture of Dorothea
Puente, [and] we couldn't integrate those two images." Another
person who struggled to articulate the different picture was Bert
Montoya, and that is a deep source of pain for Beth Valentine. She
remembers when Bert ran away from F Street and reached out for
help. "Bert went back to Front Street [a men's shelter], which wasn't
that unusual for people I've placed. He'd been living there for
almost nine years. That was his family, the people there cared about
him. So he went back, and one of the staff brought him back to
[Puente], and we'd go to see how he was. . . . I have to really ask
myself this question of whether he was truly happy there. A lot of the
information, to be honest, came through her. That's hard to admit. I
don't know if any of us really listened to him."

"Bert was freaked out," Cabrera says. "I really believe that he saw
something that made him very uncomfortable. But we fall into that
stereotype. 'Bert, you're imagining something. It's just your spirits.' "
That it wasn't his spirits, or Joyce Peterson's drink, or Brenda Trujillo's dope, is something that this community must live with.

"I was real naive about evil," says Valentine. "I kept it very far away
from me. I never looked it in the face, 'cause I didn't have a coping
mechanism for it. Before I went into the trial, I thought, 'I've got to
look at her.' There's just nothing more horrifying to me than that
face in this entire world. It's the beast, it's looking directly into the
beast. But I needed to do that, because for some reason in this lifetime I crossed paths with a serial killer. I mean, who crosses tracks
with a serial killer? Whose choice would it be? And that happened to

me. It's part of the fabric of my life. Whether she's evil or not, I don't know. I do know her motive is always going to be destructive. Always."

This, above all, is what we must understand about extremely violent women, as we have always understood it about men. They were once needy girls, yes. Their lives were exploited, indeed. Patriarchal oppression incited them to desperate responses, perhaps. But none of that can be relevant to our social response. They are human first, and gendered second. They will destroy you in an instant, no slower than the men.

WHAT'S LOVE GOT TO DO WITH IT?

Women as Partners in Violent Crime

Most often, [women] are merely the distaff half of a murderous couple whose brain-power is supplied by the man.

JOYCE CAROL OATES

I wasn't, you know, just one of those women who like to have a strong, domineering man. In this case it was a fantasy that just got badly out of control.

CAROL BUNDY, convicted of multiple murder, in testimony at the trial of Douglas Clark, Los Angeles, 1980

Myra Hindley was tall, aloof, older than her twenty-one years. She knew she had to get married—that was the way, after all. But she didn't fancy her suitors, until she met Ian Brady. He stood back from the world more coolly than she. A man with an air of culture, appraising life disdainfully through darkly hooded eyes. They were moving to the mundane beat of working-class Manchester, two antisocial souls fed up with the rules. Ten months in the same clerk's office and not a word between them, but Myra Hindley was watching, and Ian Brady watched her back. "Ian's taking sly looks at me at work," Hindley wrote in her journal, on August 1, 1961. It was one of many terse notations. "He loves me, he loves me not." Then an entry with an exclamation point: "Out with Ian!" Their first date, and the mad, secretive thrall of Brady and Hindley began.

They unfolded their love affair up on the moors, stretching blankets across the stone-gray earth, collars hoisted in the chill, drinking German wine. He introduced her to the Marquis de Sade and turned her on to Hitler. Within Nazi ranks she found her own heroine, Irma Grese. She began to wear short, brown military skirts: a shapely platinum blond "looker" in a uniform, lining up with her beau to see *Judgment at Nuremberg*. Up on the moors, they wove grandiose notions into the curtain they drew between themselves and the city below. Notions of power and risk, of transcending the rules. Hours spent planning bank robberies to extricate themselves from society once and for all. Joining forces, all that comes to matter is him, is her, everything else recedes in shades of gray. Freed from needing, they could invent their own codes of conduct, become Romeo and Juliet in *Lord of the Flies*, and play their own, private jokes upon the world.

The first to go was twelve-year-old John Kilbride, murdered one day after John F. Kennedy—November 23, 1963. Myra and Ian were exhilarated by the coincidence of initials. Hope perishing, at home and abroad: the world mourns J.F.K., and Manchester mourns at *their* hands. Next was ten-year-old Lesley Ann Downey, tortured and killed in Myra's bedroom on Boxing Day, the girl's screams recorded with an overlay of jingly Christmas music.

Springtime and three more children gone. Long legs stretching up from the armchair, feet on the fireplace mantel, Myra Hindley dragged on a cigarette and mused aloud to her brother-in-law, the terrified David Smith: "Ooh, that was a messy one." Cool and amused. Before them on the carpet lay the bloodied corpse of Edward Evans, 17, whom Brady had just bludgeoned with an axe. Smith had been invited unawares to observe their glorious game. Brady had wanted a new "first lieutenant." Myra was bitterly jealous. What bound her to Brady was their secret, a promise of forever. David Smith was a usurper; she argued with Ian for weeks. Never in those arguments, however, was the possibility put forward that Smith might turn them in. They were so far beyond the law at this point that they failed to grasp its moral sway on other mortals.

Smith, shaken to the core by what he'd seen, withdrew politely and immediately called the police. The police found Evans wrapped up in a parcel and arrested Ian. Myra was left behind. She was utterly shocked by the separation. She went down to the station and wouldn't leave. "Wherever he has been," she explained to detectives,

"I have been." She was bewildered that they couldn't see this. "He has never been anywhere without me."

In 1966, Myra and Ian stood trial together. They remained unmoved and wouldn't admit for years to come that they had done what they'd done. To their way of thinking, it was nobody's business. Yet the courtroom was wrenched apart by the recording of Lesley Ann Downey's screams. It was an event that traumatized Britain, as the videotapes made by Paul Bernardo and Karla Homolka would traumatize Canada thirty years later. Eventually, it emerged that Ian Brady was insane. Indeed, the evidence suggests that his schizophrenia came on at the outset of their murder spree. He believed he was receiving orders to kill from the Germans. It was Hindley who saw their killing as a means to bind them together as outlaws. So caught up was she in their private waltz that she failed to recognize Brady's madness. She also failed to grasp how Manchester felt, gazing upward to the moors. The day citizens were searching for bodies in the shifting peat, she boiled in rage when the bobbies accidentally ran over her dog, Puppet. "You're nothing but common murderers," she cried.

"In 1967 I was growing up in London, just after the trial," wrote the poet Diana Fitzgerald Bryden. "I was very young, so my understanding of the 'moors murders' was cloudy and nightmarish and full of half-truths—an atmosphere exacerbated by threats that Myra Hindley would come and get me when I was bad." Hindley sank into the British psyche as a "Medusa-faced" monster. She was evil. She was not considered, as Karla Homolka was, a coerced or battered woman. No such script existed in the early sixties. Yet both women, however they accounted for themselves, claimed a powerful hold on the imagination. A critical difference exists between how we respond to violent women when they are partners in crime and our response when they are serial killers. Unlike Puente, team offenders like Hindley, Homolka, Bonnie Parker, Patty Hearst, and the Manson girls retain our interest for decades. One reason has to do with the partnered criminal's choice of victims. Women who kill or rob with men are much more likely to go after traditionally masculine targets—our children, rather than their own, or young women and men in their prime: the people whom society cherishes most. Another reason seems to be the very fact that they act as part of a team. If we cannot conceive of women as predators and so erase from our minds the likes of Puente, we can conceive of the corrupting power of love.

In literature and myth, destructive duets are often cast as a replay of Adam and Eve, equating female ambition with the moral destruction of men. Historically, the equation reverses itself when we consider partners in crime: The woman in a criminal team is held up as love's dupe, an infatuated Bonnie simpering after glamorous Clyde. When that famous couple met their end along the Texas–Louisiana border in 1934, *The New York Times* ran the headline: "Barrow and woman slain in Louisiana trap!" Bonnie Parker wasn't even worthy of a name. In 1991, U.S. District Judge A. Andrew Hauk scheduled a hearing to determine whether an armed robber in Oakland, California, named Danielle Mast had acted under the "Svengali influence" of her boyfriend, even though the police had no evidence that he was involved in her five bank robberies. Judge Hauk reasoned that women are "soft touches" for clever men, "particularly if sex is involved." Carol Bundy, a highly intelligent and remorseless psychopath who shot prostitutes with her boyfriend Doug Clark, was "a woman who would do anything for love," according to the dust jacket on her true crime biography. Charlene Gallego "just wanted to be loved," proclaimed a headline in *Sacramento* magazine, in an article detailing her involvement in ten murders with her common-law husband, Gerald, in the late 1970s.

Is violent crime, for women, reducible to love? Are women focused so naively and narrowly on the hearts of men that they follow them to hell without reflection like dopey, affectionate dogs? The only advance made on this argument recently has been to say: No, women aren't just in love—they're coerced. Karla Homolka, according to Susan G. Cole in Toronto's *Now* magazine, was a "brutalized" victim who "chose the most humane course she could" by drugging her sister so that Tammy would at least be unconscious when Bernardo raped her. Myra Hindley, according to Lord Astor, who made a bid for her parole in 1993, is "a victim: a normal human being who has been through hell." The academic discourse has been equally reductive of women's agency. Virtually the only contributor to the case literature is the FBI's Behavioral Science Services Unit. Famous for their intricate psychological profiles of male serial killers, they offer only one category for female perpetrators: "compliant victims," by which they mean that women like Hindley and Homolka—strong-willed, charismatic, nonconformist—are really just bendable creatures, easily bullied into doing one man's bidding.

No official tally of dual perpetraters in violent crime exists, but women clearly aren't strangers to predatory teamwork. When Carol Bundy was negotiating a plea-bargain agreement in return for testimony against Doug Clark, she found herself in a jail cell next to Veronica Compton, girlfriend of a Los Angeles serial killer named Kenneth Bianchi, known as the Hillside Strangler. Compton had attempted a copycat strangling to throw the cops off Bianchi's trail. Along down the row were other partners in crime, prompting Carol to marvel in a letter, "Women like us aren't as rare as we thought." Indeed, one serial murder sample analyzed by Eric Hickey found that 38 percent involved one or more women. A random sample of recent cases gives one a sense of the scope.

Rosemary West was convicted in November 1995 in Gloucester, England, of ten murders committed with her husband, Frederick. Judith Ann Neely is on death row in Alabama for six slain victims she sexually assaulted and attacked in the early 1980s with her husband, Alvin. Charlene Gallego was sentenced to sixteen years in 1982 for the ten murders she committed in Sacramento with Gerald. Cynthia Lynn Coffman went to death row in California in 1992 for abducting and strangling two young women with her lover, James Gregory Marlow. In Lexington, Kentucky, the lovers Tina Powell and Lafonda Foster went on a twenty-four-hour rampage in 1986 that left five people shot, stabbed, burned, run over with a vehicle, and mutilated. Gwendolyn Graham and Catherine Wood, nurses and lovers at the Alpine Manor Nursing Home in Walker, Michigan, suffocated six patients in 1988. Alton Coleman and Debra Brown committed eight particularly savage murders in Illinois in 1984. Said Brown of one of their victims: "I killed the bitch and I don't give a damn. I had fun out of it."

In Florida in 1989, a two-bit hustler named Kosta Fotopoulos acted as cameraman while his girlfriend, Diedre Hunt, pumped four bullets into the body of an acquaintance, Mark Ramsey. Hunt then recruited a hit man to shoot Fotopoulos's wife, Lisa; the hit man was knocked off in turn by the couple. Hunt's "kill or be killed" defense was belied by the video evidence, which documented an eerie look of exaltation on her face.

From teenage girls engaging in robbery and assault in pairs or gangs, to lovers on a cross-country hold-up spree, to sexual assaults upon children, partnered offending is possibly the most common way for women in our society to commit public and so-called masculine violence. The extremely violent man needs no approving witness to commit aggressive acts. A woman, on the other hand, if she is not as purely psychopathic as Marybeth Tinning or Dorothea Puente, is in an entirely different position. If she wants to transgress expectations of her sex with masculine forms of aggression, she needs a kind of permission. The process is psychological, one of gaining a sense of entitlement to act out forbidden ambitions. "Learning crime," as Allison Morris points out, "includes not only techniques but also rationalizations, justifications and attitudes." Women in other societies, in Somalia and Rwanda, or Aboriginal Australia, are entitled by their culture to pick up weapons and use them. African-American women are more entitled than white women to throw punches or to get involved, as Toni Cato did, in crime-as-business. White women, however, are more likely to require mentors and co-conspirators. As often as not, they look for validation to men, usually romantic partners. A particularly compelling example of this transition through men is the case of Karla Faye Tucker, whose story has been beautifully described by the writer Beverly Lowry. Tucker was a spry Texan teenager, eyes bright, spirits quick, who lived in a suburb of Houston, where older men—biker types, Vietnam vets—escorted her to Aerosmith concerts and back to ranch-style condos. She was a tomboy, attracted to men who could teach her to fight. She was fond of vodka, drugs, and of showing any guy who chose to see that he'd met his match in her. She was small, but she had a spitfire temper, the kind that invites men to say, "You're so cute when you're angry," until they get slammed in the face. In 1983, Tucker was dating a combat veteran who'd been teaching her paramilitary maneuvers. One night, wired on speed, Karla Faye hauled on her boyfriend's hand and jumped into his Ranchero, parked in the drive. They were "overamped," her boyfriend conceded later. Karla Faye wanted to break into the house of one Jerry Lynn Dean, a guy she'd been feuding with for a couple of years. The idea she had was to steal his Harley. Or maybe not even. Maybe just check things out in a "reconnaissance mission," like soldiers under cover of night.

Creeping around in the shadowy house, Karla Faye found Jerry Dean slowly waking to strange sounds. He lay on his back, on a futon. She straddled his chest like a rodeo queen. His fear made her rush. She reached out across the floor and grabbed a pickax to hold to his throat. He began to struggle, she began to slam. Bucking and speeding on her bronco, eleven stab wounds to the chest and throat, an orgasm. "I popped a nut," she later bragged to her sister. Her sister turned her and her boyfriend, Danny Garrett, in to the police, leaving the city of Houston to struggle with a picture that didn't make sense. Tucker was possessed of a fawnlike beauty, but she refused to trade on her image. She didn't project the aura of an innocent the way Karla Homolka did. She was obviously strong, genuinely likable, candid, and willing to take responsibility. "I know I've done this thing," she said, "but I don't know what I've done." The statement was apt. No script had yet been written for a woman like Tucker. No one could remember a woman—certainly not such a pretty woman—killing without motive and being sexually aroused. What was equally perplexing was that her murdering had no connection to being battered, or coerced, or blindly loving the man she was with. Failing to find the script that might somehow exonerate her or at least mitigate her actions, Houston fell back on a stereotype of "vengeful whore." She and her boyfriend were sent to death row.

The very opposite stereotype, that of pliant virgin, came into play in Karla Homolka's case, though sex was a feature in both crimes.

Understanding how the community conceived of Homolka so archetypically wasn't difficult. The hard part was trying to get at some semblance of the truth. One had to seek the story between the lines, listening to what she didn't say, hearing from those witnesses who knew her, watching for a truer history to unfold.

On May 29, 1995, Karla Homolka's mother, Dorothy, took the stand at Paul Bernardo's trial. Her voice was high and small, held in like a girl's, but her demeanor was that of a determined woman who'd been through hell without melting. Detachment was her survival technique: passivity forged by a powerful will. She responded to all the questions posed to her, defense or prosecution, without alliance, readily agreeing that her daughter had a "glow" throughout her affair with Bernardo. Her household was a fun-loving and rather permissive place, she agreed: drinks and pool parties for the girls, a stream of friends in and out, long lunches on Sundays, which continued weekly after Karla got married. The parents evidently preferred that their daughters, whom they'd raised on Dundonald Street in Saint Catharines since 1974, grow up in front of them, not behind their backs. "More often than not," Karla said, "our friends would come to our house." Karla's first invitation to Paul Bernardo was, in fact, to come to her house. Within months, Dorothy Homolka and her husband, Karel, a lighting technician, invited the young suitor to sleep on their couch on the weekends so that he didn't have to drive back to his home in Scarborough. By 1990, Bernardo had launched a kind of home invasion, documenting all family frolics with his ever-present camera.

In the video shot the night that Tammy died, the teenagers career about with tropical cocktails in hand, and they are clearly the masters of this multilevel, semi-detached universe. Giggling, they zoom in on Dorothy as she bakes in her small kitchen. "Extreme close-up, Mom, *do* it!" Karla bosses through laughter. Then they tumble downstairs to the shag-rugged rec room, disturbing Karel Homolka as he naps on the couch. He lifts his mild face to them, smiling and blinking. The family's embrace of itself is so tight that one senses how it might have been stifling before Paul came along, the nascent identities of the three girls blurring. Karla, twice displaced by younger sisters, demanded more singular attention. From an early age, her involvement in school was audience-oriented: figure skating, choir, musicals, variety shows, the dance club. She wrote poetry and short stories, and came to love romance novels. In high school, she dressed for attention: multihued hair, miniskirts, jewelry. She bought bridal magazines, fantasizing about the ultimate vanity trip: a woman's "special day." Not that she wanted to be a homemaker. She wanted to be a cop, and wore a pair of handcuffs on her jean jacket as a statement of intent. Homolka was hip to the power to command notice, whatever technique worked, being a bride, being a cop.

At seventeen, she discovered the power of sex appeal. She quit school, went on the pill, and flew off in defiance of her parents' wishes to Manhattan, Kansas, for a two-week rendezvous with an American boy. Three months later, in October 1987, she met Paul Bernardo. If anyone could make Homolka stand out from her sisters on Dundonald Street, it was Bernardo, which may have been precisely his allure. They quickly began having sex in her bedroom off the basement rec room, where her parents watched TV. "I love fucking you with my parents in the house," she raved to her lover in a letter. Soon, their sex included his and her handcuffs, and a dog collar she brought home from the pet store, which he pulled daringly tight around her neck. "I was very physically attracted to him," she would say. "He's got this magnetism. . . . It's his personality. He's very charming." Paul said, "I thought she was really strong-willed and independent and a little weird." She was impulsive, he meant, and sexually unabashed.

She let him take a series of mock-violent fetish shots with a Polaroid, explaining later, "It was important to him, not to me." She stopped wearing miniskirts and fraternizing with boys in her high school; shrugging, she said, "It wasn't that important to me." Ray Houlahan elicited these facts as proof of Karla's physical and sexual abuse. For many people following the case, that was balderdash. Karla permitted Paul's experiments because she was getting what she wanted in return. Bernardo was her perfect subterfuge. On the outside he was everything her parents could want for their dutiful eldest daughter. Privately, he was sexy, lustful, and even a little bit scary, a radical engine for teenage rebellion.

In an FBI survey of seven women who got involved in the crimes of husbands or lovers who were "sexual sadists," researchers noted that, in addition to being uniformly better educated and intelligent than their men, "the women all 'fell' for the men relatively quickly, even though they recognized a sinister side to them." This curious fact was not addressed in the researchers' final analysis. The dynamic was summed up as straightforward male coercion—a process of molding "sexually naive" girls into "compliant victims" through "positive reinforcement (for example, gratitude, compliments, or attention) or negative reinforcement (pouting, ignoring, or rejection) to obtain her compliance for progressively deviant activities."

The FBI paradigm assumes that a woman's stake in deviant behavior can never be self-interest. One could not begin to apply this analysis to the case of Carol Bundy, who teamed up with her sexual sadist in the late 1970s and was ultimately far more articulate about what had happened than either Karla Homolka or the experts. A divorced Valley housewife living in North Hollywood, Bundy met Doug Clark, the degenerate son of a U.S. steel company executive, at The Little Nashville club in 1978. They instantly glimpsed a common bond, which was that they were both sociopathic pseudointellectuals brimming with disdain for the rat race, looking for shortcuts to self-indulgence and dissolution. Well-read, urbane, capable of doing anything they wanted, they delighted, instead, in a mutual venality. At Carol's apartment off Van Nuys Boulevard, near a strip club called The Classy Lady, they got involved in increasingly perverse behavior.

Unlike Hindley and Homolka, both of whom were younger, Bundy made no effort to beautify herself or be sexy. "Carol had big, thick glasses; heavyset, she was a two o'clock tan in a beer bar," says retired detective Leroy Orozco, who investigated the case. "[But] she was flamboyant, very outward, she didn't hide anything." Carol had been an exhibitionist as a teenager, and a peeping Tom—to all intents and purposes, a burgeoning sex offender. Although married for a time to the father of her two children, she kept up a stream of lovers, continuing to see some of them while she dated Clark. She was hardly a "sexually naive girl." Of her sex life with Doug Clark she would say, "He was playing to my fantasies as opposed to me playing to his."

Over time, as with Hindley and Brady, their fantasies began to merge, becoming one shared daydream of immutable outlaw power. They cruised Sunset Boulevard in Carol's beat-up Toyota, looking for prostitutes to assault as a prelude to sex. Eventually, the assaults escalated to homicide, with Bundy slowly shifting from backseat observer to shooter. Within a year they'd killed seven women, beheading one, whose beauty Carol then ghoulishly disfigured with her makeup. Ultimately, two Santa Monica teenagers who'd been hitchhiking fell into their clutches, and the girls' disappearance put the heat on the LAPD. The hunt for the Sunset Strip Killer, as the cops dubbed the man they thought they were tracking, ended in 1980, when Carol Bundy branched off on her own. Returning to the bar she'd met Clark in, she encountered an ex-lover, went parking with him, shot him, and sawed off his head with a boning knife. " 'Doug cut a head off, I cut a head off, and I did it better,' " said Detective Orozco, paraphrasing Bundy's intent. Carol Bundy gave her own summation: "I just sort of went overboard . . . it was a fantasy that just got badly out of control."

The intermingling of two people's fantasies, delusions, or fears is commonly known as folie à deux. Clinically, psychiatrists describe it as shared psychotic disorder. SPD generally refers to cases in which paranoid-delusional persons manage to infuse their lovers (or parents or siblings) with their own insanity. Because they're charismatic, and the person they're with is hyperimaginative and suggestible, their version of reality becomes the dominant one. Contrary to what we might immediately assume about who would be more suggestible, a review of the literature on SPD dating from 1942 indicates that women are, overwhelmingly, the charismatics to whom men or other women succumb.

Why would anyone, male or female, begin to subscribe to a patently insane world view? Why did the Manson girls come to believe so fervently in what Charles Manson said, until it became logical to them to kill? As with cults, the self-imposed social isolation of the couple is a critical ingredient in folie à deux, in that they're removed from reality checks and begin to drift. Substance abuse—booze, pot, cocaine—plays a frequent role in the spiral. Another key is time. One partner is gradually exposed to the other's mindset and accommodates the madness bit by bit. Carol Bundy had never entertained the notion of murder until Doug Clark brought it into her house. In April 1980, he returned to their shared apartment in the wee hours, splattered with blood. Carol said, "It is very difficult to find a reasonable explanation for a man coming home coated with blood, shaking, really, really shaking, and collapsing on the bathroom floor." Clark told her that he led a secret life as a hit man and had been in an altercation with another hit man, named, uh, Nick. "Too many people," Carol scoffed, "tell me that they're hit men." But she let it go. The second time Doug came home covered in blood, Carol came up with an explanation of her own: "I thought maybe he had run over a dog or something. I was willing to give him the benefit of the doubt on that one." But not the next one. "As things progressed, I was forced to accept that murders were going on. Ordinarily, one would not meet a murderer. . . . a person who has murdered two or three or four on up is almost inconceivable."

"Initially," notes clinical psychiatrist Jose Silveira, "there is a state of perplexity and confusion which is uncomfortable and which constitutes a powerful drive to understand the lived experience. Any explanation, even though in itself frightening, appears to be more comfortable than the dread of not knowing." Ultimately, however, there can also be an active wanting at work, a desire to subscribe to the wilder mind, an urge that may be more operative in criminal pairs than in noncriminals who suffer shared psychotic disorder. "Part of me was desperately terrified," Bundy said. "Part of me was drawn to the apparent danger in this, the risk that I was facing. . . . It was sort of a love-hate type of complex. Wanting, yet not wanting. Being afraid, yet being attracted to what I was afraid of."

The most common delusion in folie à deux is persecutory—the belief that someone or something is out to get the couple and destroy them. In the 1994 docudrama *Heavenly Creatures*, two New Zealand girls get so obsessively involved with each other that they murder one of their mothers for fear she'll split them up. Neither girl is violent to begin with. Both are in search of a sense of their specialness, which they find by rejecting reality and reinventing a universe to be masters of. They venture further and further into that world until they reach a point together they never would have mapped out alone. The final scene, in which the murder takes place, is a fascinating portrayal of two people wavering on the brink of moral insanity, unable to pull back as long as the eye of the other is on her, never expecting they would get where they found themselves now.

The second most common delusion in folie à deux is of grandeur, the shared belief that the couple is better, more powerful and glamorous, more *entitled* than those around them. Grandiosity, it would seem, is the shared conceit of some of our most extreme offenders. During Paul Bernardo's murder trial, crown attorneys introduced as evidence a videotape that Paul made in the winter of 1991, one month before he and Karla moved into their house in Saint Catharines. He had returned to his lifelong residence, at 21 Sir Raymond Drive in Scarborough, a house in which he had never felt at home. He was a "bastard" there, he said, because his father, who had recently served a prison sentence for sexual assault, wasn't his sire. His mother had had an affair. He despised her. "Born a bastard, die a bastard!" he often told Homolka. He was driven to create himself anew, and he did so, the videotape revealed, in the sanctuary of his childhood bedroom. The walls of this room were covered with hand-printed cards: "Think Big, Be Big." "Nice Guys Finish Last." "This isn't a democracy, it's a free market." "If We Can Dream It, We Can Do It."

In the midst of this temple to clichés was a picture of his sweetheart. She'd affixed a note: "I love you with all my heart and soul and will." Karla Homolka's will went conveniently AWOL during the murder trial of her ex-husband. But there's little question that it was once as critical to their affair as his own. Attorneys introduced a cascade of Hallmark cards that Karla Homolka had sent to her "Big Bad Businessman," as she'd nicknamed Paul. Homolka frequently referred to herself as "The Princess" in these cards, as in: "The Princess has finally found her Prince." Then she would sign off as the "cute, sexy blonde" who was "runner-up" for the title of "sexiest person in the world." Together they built a temple to status, dyeing their hair blond, dressing like Yuppies, renting a house they couldn't afford. They indulged in the most pretentious wedding never featured in *Vanity Fair*, and riffled through *Who's Who* looking for a last name that was "less ethnic" than Bernardo, settling on the patrician-sounding Teale. After they were arrested, police found these two books in their bedroom: *American Psycho* and *Miss Manners*.

Watching the evidence unfold in the courtroom, some forensic psychologists began to wonder if Homolka wasn't a clinically defined narcissist. Narcissists, according to the DSM-IV, "believe that [they are] special and unique and can only be understood by or should associate with other special or high-status people. Their own self-esteem is enhanced by the idealized value that they assign to those with whom they associate." Narcissists easily attach to psychopaths, who exude a supreme self-confidence and often possess the material flash of success. Bernardo gave Homolka a designer dress and gold jewelry for their first Christmas. She said, "He totally swept me off my feet." Theirs was a pas de deux between grandiose egos, with the narcissist artfully projecting her fantasies of "success, power, brilliance, beauty, or ideal love" on the flat, reflective surface of the psychopathic soul. "We were the envy of everyone," she lamented in a card to her cuddly, murderous rapist as the marriage came crashing down. Paul agreed: "We were the Teales, man, we were winners."

The narcissist's drive for admiration, high self-regard, quick-trigger jealousy, and lack of empathy are the qualities that would prove pivotal in Karla Homolka's initiation into crime. One night in July 1990, Tammy Homolka ran a twenty-minute errand with Paul Bernardo to a liquor store during one of his weekend visits to Saint Catharines. They did not return for six hours, and Bernardo confessed they had been flirting, even kissing, out on the Niagara gorge. Karla was aware of Bernardo's burgeoning attraction to Tammy. But she piously insisted in court that this episode inspired no spark of jealousy. Bernardo contends, on the other hand, that what happened in July sealed Tammy's fate. It was a question of what was at stake for Karla. Three years into the romance, Bernardo was enshrined at the center of her universe. He was what set her *apart* from her sisters.

She appears to have decided that if Paul had designs on Tammy, he was going to have to play them out in Karla's home, in front of her. He was not going to be sneaking off on a clandestine rendezvous behind her back. So, a few days after the incident on the gorge, she served her sister spaghetti with Valium, knocking her out so that Paul could pursue his pleasure. It was a classic act of indirect aggression against a female rival, and one over which she maintained full control. But if Karla hoped that would be the end of it, it wasn't, because Bernardo's infatuation with Tammy went on, as he calculated that it could. Homolka, as a narcissist, craved social approval. Bernardo came to understand that if he stayed by her and played her excellent gentleman in public, he could foray ever more deeply into private perversion without risk of exposure. Exposure was Karla's idea of hell. "I didn't want anyone to think that I shouldn't be with him," she said in court, explaining why she let Bernardo masturbate in Tammy's bedroom in the autumn of 1990 and told no one. Privately, she was tormented by the threat her sister posed and grew increasingly enraged. She struck again at Tammy on December 23, 1990, the night that the teenagers can be seen in Bernardo's family videotape, gamboling about with their piña coladas. Toward the end of Paul's tape, taken at about 7:30 P.M., Tammy is sitting cross-legged on her parents' couch in the festively decorated living room. She is listing to one side and slurring her words, grinning sloppily into the camera, too young to be aware that her loss of control is not the result of the sips she's been taking of her sister's cocktails, but of the powerful tranquilizer called Halcion.

Court spectators awaited the audio portion of Tammy Homolka's rape in an edgy, apprehensive silence. The courtroom speakers spit static. The faint sound of a television or radio drifted out, and then suddenly an adamant, exasperated whisper: "Hurry *up*, Paul."

Further away, somewhere in the Homolka family rec room, comes a distracted "Shut up."

"Please hurry before someone comes *down*," Karla orders in high agitation.

"Shut up," Paul whispers back, concentrating on disrobing Tammy, who has passed out from her evening-long stream of sedatives and alcohol. Then: "Yeah, okay. Here we go. Keep her down."

Karla holds a cloth soaked in Halothane to her sister's face. Then she says, "Put something on," meaning a condom.

"Shhh," says Paul, "you're gettin' all worked up."

"Put it on," Karla repeats, "put it *on*." There's a pause. "Fucking do it," she says. Another pause. "Just *do* it."

Moments later, she realizes that he wants her to participate in the assault, and her irritation shifts to upset. She doesn't want to have sex with her sister. What isn't clear is whether her resistance springs from concern for Tammy, whom she has just forced to inhale six times the amount of Halothane that veterinarians consider safe for dogs, or repugnance: her sister is menstruating. In any event, she complies, and Paul asks her how it tastes. "Fucking disgusting," she mutters. Moments later, the tape goes blank.

The following day, *The Toronto Star* reported the exchange as: " 'Shut up,' Bernardo was heard to yell at Homolka. 'Shut up, Karla,' he repeated later." In *The Toronto Sun*, it read: " 'Do it now,' Bernardo's voice barks on videotapes shown to the jury. 'No. No,' Karla responds in a hushed voice." Reporters were literally unable to perceive Homolka as an active sex offender. Yet, her rape of her sister very much followed the pattern of other women who begin to engage in this crime. In a study of sixteen female sex offenders at the Genesis II Sex Offender program in Saint Paul, Minnesota, three researchers found that 50 percent offended in tandem with men. The solo operators, who had all been sexually abused themselves, reported fantasies prior to the offenses (which usually involved their or their neighbors' children) and arousal during the act. Only two of the partnered offenders were sexually aroused by what they did, but seven of them cited "feelings of anger, revenge, power, jealousy, and rejection [by] other people" as a motive for the assaults.

In court, Karla justified Tammy's rape by saying that Paul threatened her family, although she couldn't think of any examples, and "he kept bugging me and bugging me." As the columnist Christie Blatchford of *The Toronto Sun* wrote so aptly, "Oh, well then." The Crown accepted Homolka's explanation because the trial was really just a high-concept one-liner for them: the guy is worse than the girl. It probably made sense on paper, until it had to play out for three months to a riveted nation, serving not just as legal argument, but Meta Explanation for every bend in a river leading darkward toward Kurtz. Bernardo's defense attorney, John Rosen, challenged Homolka's hapless acquiescence as absurd. "You had nothing to lose but a boyfriend," he told her. But Homolka *wanted* to keep her boyfriend, come hell, high water, or murder. What Bernardo hadn't anticipated, being a psychopath, was the depth of Karla's hostility to her sister. The FBI's concept of "progressive deviance" was less the unfolding of a masculine strategy of coercion than the combustive reaction of his desire and her jealousy.

Three weeks after Tammy's death, Karla and Paul lounged naked on a bed in front of a flickering fire in the basement of her parents' house. As they sipped cocktails, the video camera captured a look of deep serenity between them.

"I loved it when you fucked my little sister," Karla says. She is relaxed and affectionate, laughing softly and often. She prattles as she caresses Paul with Tammy's underwear, and her tone is that of a lover in serenade, sighing ebullient I love yous. "I want you to do it again," she tells him, meaning rape an adolescent girl. "Do you think we can do that? Do you wanna do it fifty times more? Do it every week then?" Paul, who has been lying on his back, struggles up to his elbows and gazes at her, grinning with surprise.

"Why would you want to?" he asks.

" 'Cause I love you," she chirps, " 'cause you're The King." Laughing, she reaches forward and hugs him. "You can take their virginity. They'll be our children."

Homolka's palpable pleasure suggests that she has not only vanquished her sibling rival, but has found a way to make her lover's deviance work in her favor. She will coopt future rivals and remain The Princess, while the rivals are assigned the unthreatening status of "children." It is an effort at both ownership and objectification. Sharing in Paul's fantasies, instead of competing with them, returns her to the center, an effect Carol Bundy's biographer described: "When they talked about it all, everything that was going on, she felt an extraordinary psychological intimacy." On the stand, Paul Bernardo said much the same thing: "After Tammy died, Karla and I were soul mates." With her sister dead and buried, she showed Paul's picture around the Martindale Animal Clinic, basking in oohs and ahs. "I have this ability," she said in court, after viewing herself rape Tammy on the small courtroom monitor, her face fascinatingly impassive, "to watch but not see."

In February, she wrote to her friend Debbie Purdy, "Wedding plans are great. Except my parents are being assholes. They pulled money out saying they can't afford it. Bull*shit!* . . . they are being so stupid. Only thinking of themselves. Screw that . . . if [Dad] wants to sit at home and be miserable, wallowing in Tammy's death, then let him." Karla filled her wedding planner with elaborate notations, and sometime in the spring, the first sex slave stumbled into what John Rosen called "the Venus Fly Trap" of 57 Bayview Drive. The couple had moved there in February, shooting a celebratory video in which Karla bounced around, singing "Our House" by Crosby, Stills, and Nash, and giving a flamboyant tour of her digs with lots of "Ta-dums."

The sex slave was identified in court as "Jane Doe," an adolescent whom Karla had met years before when she worked at a pet shop and Jane Doe came in with her mother. Now Jane was invited over, wined, dined, knocked out, and sodomized before she knew what hit her. ("The fact that the death of Tammy didn't derail the practice of drugging other victims speaks volumes about the character of the participants," psychiatrist Angus McDonald wrote to the court.) Apparently, the catalyst for Jane Doe's rape was a threat that arose unexpectedly when Paul fell for a woman he met in Florida on spring break. He began to reconsider their engagement. A fight ensued, in which Homolka told him acidly that the woman resembled his mother, but he continued to call his Florida belle, and the issue resolved itself only around the time, in late spring, that Karla brought home Jane Doe.

Homolka didn't tell the police about this assault. When it surfaced on the videos, which police and prosecutors first viewed in September 1994, she suddenly "remembered" the incident in "a dream." She wrote to her lawyer, George Walker, "Am I gonna get nailed?" On May 26, 1995, prosecutors decided no. She was a battered woman with repressed memory syndrome. They would let the crime go.

On June 14, 1991, two weeks before the couple's wedding, in

Niagara-on-the-Lake, Paul Bernardo impulsively kidnapped Leslie Mahaffy. Mahaffy was in their home for twenty-four hours, and her ability to identify them threatened everything—Paul's sexual fantasies, Karla's self-image, the couple's freedom, and the facade of what Homolka called "normalcy" in a life that was anything but. For people with such low reserves of empathy, killing wasn't a difficult choice.

It was, however, an extremely radical turn in the life of a young woman who had, only four years earlier, been a fairly ordinary North American teenager. Her own narcissism and taste for power had taken her a certain distance away from "normalcy." Jealousy and rage took her further. And folie à deux, an incremental sort of lunacy, took her to the brink she was standing on now. Homolka agreed to (or possibly committed) Mahaffy's murder as if strangling a young woman who has been in your house overnight—talking to you, eating with you, telling you, because you asked, what her favorite music station was and what she hoped to do when she grew up—was a plausible resolution. If Homolka was haunted, she was able to resume more pleasant dreams through force of will. The next day, she entertained her parents without a hint of upset, and two weeks later, she was on the beaches of Maui, her skin as smooth as peaches and cream, waving to her brand-new husband. The crown contended that Homolka was savagely beaten on this "Honeymoon from Hell." Under cross-examination, Karla scaled it down to a smack on her "buttocks," the only part of her anatomy defense attorneys couldn't see on the honeymoon video. "Hawaii is my favourite place on earth," she gushed to Paul in a card when they got home. "I can't believe it's actually over. I want another wedding!"

The memories of their wedding commingled with shared murder, Karla and Paul found themselves so far down the river there was nothing to do but go on. "Karla and I had evolved so much in our sex lives," Bernardo tried to explain, understating the case to the exact degree that he failed to grasp its enormity. "We were drinking every day and doing drugs." Losing hold of reason. Letting go. The couple drugged and assaulted Jane Doe again that August. They began stalking women they met in bars and restaurants or saw on the street. Other assaults were planned and scrapped. Finally, in April 1992, they engaged in the crazily brazen daylight abduction of Kristen French, dragging her into their car in the middle of a church parking lot. The fifteen-year-old had been walking home from school for Easter weekend.

The videotapes show a progression in Karla's direct involvement in these crimes. By 1992, she is orchestrating much of the action herself. "Suck him now, Kristen," she says at some point during French's three-day captivity. "Good girl." She sounds about as perturbed as a camera assistant on a porn shoot. "Now use your hand. Yeah. Good girl." She proudly tells Paul, "I got some great mouth shots." On Easter Sunday, at Karla's insistence, French was murdered. She was strangled for a full seven minutes, Homolka told the court (for it wasn't taped). She watched. Then she went downstairs to blow-dry her hair. The couple had to go to Easter dinner with her family.

According to Candice Skrapec, "One key to understanding a woman who kills repeatedly may be the recognition that by killing, she experiences herself as someone who matters, as the agent of some substantial happening and, by inference, as powerful. Almost incidentally, she can come to enjoy killing and develop a 'taste' for it." After Carol Bundy's first murder, she thought (as she told Orozco), "Well, I'm ten times as cool as he is, and I don't have half the experience." The rush was undeniable. "After a while, it got to be a joint venture where we were both enjoying it." This seems to be true for less extreme crimes as well. "I was unwilling to at first," one female sex offender recalled, describing her molestation of children, "but then after a while it got to the point where I liked it."

In August 1992, Karla and Paul went to Disneyworld, where she vamped for the camera in a white bikini, unsullied by the beating she would claim to have received. She was tanned almost beyond recognition, her stiff, moussed hair the color of Florida sand. She waved her pretty white bottom, did a campy strip-tease. Paul, mocking the reporters in *Playboy*, asked her what she enjoyed. "Showing off," she said and laughed. "Licking little girls," she added. "Making my man happy." Then she waved the camera away, bored. "End of show." She sauntered out of the frame.

A week later, she and Paul were in a primly decorated room at Trump Plaza in Atlantic City. They'd hired a hooker who looked like a wiser, weather-beaten version of Karla. "She's very good-looking," Karla says appraisingly as the three lounge about, the hidden camera blinking from inside Paul's suitcase. Homolka is not intimidated by this tough street-walker. Paul is. His jokey conversation is nervous and self-conscious. He doesn't know how far he can go. He's tentative, asking her what he's allowed to do, repeatedly losing his way. His apologetic bravado is so familiar to the hooker she barely listens. "Working girls are used to it, Sweetie," she says. She's no fool. "You're rough people, you like [rough sex,]" she points out, surmising the reason he's lost his erection. At one point, as she performs oral sex, he reaches his two hands out as if to hit or strangle her, then leaves them frozen there in midair, lost.

By the autumn of 1992, the Bernardo marriage was imploding from the pressure of its own moral chaos, into violence, paranoia, and loathing. "Events bonded us," Bernardo said at his trial, "but [they] also tore us apart." In an audiotape he recorded after Karla left him, he conceded that he'd treated her "like shit near the end." Indeed, he turned on her with real savagery. Having smashed every boundary of human restraint and gone into crazed dissolution, he went after Homolka like a rabid animal, pulling out her hair, hammering her head with hard objects, forcing her to eat shit.

Bernardo's intense "frustration," as he described it, was fueled by his sudden sense of impotence. He was still unemployed. He was on the lam from the Metropolitan Toronto Police, who would shortly match DNA from blood and hair samples he'd given them to that of the Scarborough Rapist. He hadn't been able to confine himself to legal seduction. He was spurned by both Jane Doe and her successor, another young friend of Homolka's, to whom he had sent a note threatening to kill himself if she didn't sleep with him. She wrote back, indifferent, "Whatever." Humiliated and cornered, Bernardo blamed Homolka. He'd come to depend on her for his crimes, but in the process his perfect wife, his soul mate and accomplice, had been corrupted. Whereas they had once held up mirrors of the other's idealized artifice, the Big Bad Businessman and his swooning Princess, they now reflected back a true depravity, like a pair of Dorian Grays.

It's common for clever serial rapists and killers to suddenly get themselves caught. Criminologists believe this has something to do with psychic exhaustion, that the lie they are living can no longer hold. During the Christmas holidays Bernardo compelled Homolka to announce the sham of their marriage by blackening both of her eyes. It was the one thing he knew he couldn't get away with. He exposed her. After a frantic, unsuccessful search for the videotapes, she allowed her shocked family to take her home.

A doctor who saw Homolka shortly after her flight from Bernardo described her attitude toward him not as fearful so much as "vengeful." She would, and did, arrange his downfall. She has never been candid about this, but Carol Bundy described her own experience: "Going to the police was the final act that I could do to save myself ... the relationship was deteriorating, breaking down, the sense of closeness and rapport that I had initially felt with him, the attraction, was dissipating in the horror of it, and the fear, and a whole lot of things that I wasn't used to dealing with. Just the whole thing was caving in ... I was willing to face my responsibility and ... admit the things that I had done, but if I was going to do that, I damn well was going to take him with me."

Despondent, drinking heavily, Bernardo made a tape for Homolka sometime in January, which he never sent. The police would find it in their search of the house and dub it "The Suicide Tape," because of Bernardo's disingenuous claim that he was going to kill himself. The tape is a striking example of psychopathic expression. It's the clichés. Language borrowed from lonely-hearts ads. Bernardo's lover of five years has vanished from his life, and all he can say, over and over, is "God, you're so beautiful," and whistle along to the theme song of the movie *Free Willie*. He freqently shifts gears. "Okay, check this out!" he says at one point, and then loops his taped statement, just made, pleading undying remorse, like a DJ in a dance hall.

Homolka proved no better than Bernardo at sustaining a sense of grief. After three days in a hospital, she went to Brampton, Ontario, to stay with her aunt and uncle. "I felt like I was seventeen years old again!" she told the police later. "I was so happy, I forgot about Tammy, I forgot about Leslie, and I had a great time." All the while, through the universally sympathetic response she received, Homolka was discovering the imagistic value of two black eyes. For months, she had feared them as her undoing, and now they would be her salvation.

Later, from her prison cell, she wrote to a friend, "I know what you mean about loving Christmas. It's always been my favourite time of year. Of course, since Tammy died things haven't been the same. But one thought I've always held is that she wouldn't want us to live in misery over the holidays." She added, "Life is going to be so great when I'm out of here. I am trying to change myself back into a newer, better version of the person I was before I met Paul . . . I am going to live so differently. I'm going to start horseback riding again. I also want to do volunteer work—I would love to work on the Kids Help Phone." And onward with her daydreams: "Go out on picnics with my friends and sister," and "I really need single girlfriends to go out and meet men with." In another letter, she said she'd just heard that a rape victim had sued her and Bernardo for her physical and emotional suffering. "Wow!" Homolka exclaimed. "I don't know what this woman thinks she's going to get, because Paul and I are broke!"

In the autumn of 1995, Dr. David King, chief of forensic pathology at McMaster Hospital in Hamilton and the man who conducted Leslie Mahaffy and Tammy Homolka's autopsies, telephoned the *Toronto Globe & Mail*. He said that the crown attorney's office had asked him to review Kristen French's autopsy report in preparation for Bernardo's trial. He had done so, and what he found was so at odds with Homolka's account of the murders that the crown refused to call him as a witness to the stand. "I do not think," he told the *Globe*, that "Kristen French died from ligature strangulation and I certainly don't think she died from having an electrical cord tied around her neck for seven minutes. There's no way." The ligature marks on French's neck were shallow and slight, as if, at most, she'd chafed against a cord. "I've been so upset about the whole thing. The prosecution deliberately decided not to use my opinion because it didn't conform with theirs"—that Bernardo, as the man, was the killer.

King found two additional discrepancies between Homolka's testimony and the condition of the bodies. There were two, identical pairs of circular bruises on both girls' backs that could be detected only on the innermost layers of muscle, next to the lowest ribs. They weren't visible on the skin surface, and therefore weren't caused by exterior blows. The findings were consistent with someone perhaps having kneeled on the girls, possibly to suffocate them while their heads were facedown on a soft surface, such as a pillow, an expedient way to kill them if they were too drugged to resist.

Finally, King found severe bruising in a uniform pattern across Kristen's face, as if she had been bludgeoned with a blunt object; the girl had bitten her tongue, and her mouth was filled with blood. King felt this injury was more likely the cause of death than strangulation. He added, because the *Globe* reporter asked him, that the bruising would be consistent with being hit with a mallet—the weapon that Karla Homolka had used to "guard" Kristen French when Bernardo went out.

In September and October, as Americans reeled from the acquittal of O.J. Simpson and argued about what it meant for battered women, Canadians struggled to grasp a different lesson. They (like the British, watching the trial of Rosemary West) had come to realize that Homolka was no battered woman, painfully trying to recover from her trauma. She had become, as Myra Hindley had been at the outset, a totem of pure evil. Those who covered or attended the trial began to have nightmares. Schoolchildren needed to discuss her with their teachers. Conservatives and feminists found themselves, for the first time in this arena, on common ground, frankly outraged at what had gone down. Citizens signed petitions across the nation demanding that Homolka's plea-bargained sentence be overturned. Over three hundred thousand signatures flooded politicians' offices. A senator tried to introduce a bill in the Canadian parliament that would pass a law, exclusive to Karla Homolka, keeping her locked behind bars.

It was too late. The crown decided that a deal is a deal. If it wasn't, none of the thousands of other criminals who plea-bargain in exchange for information would come forward. Homolka can be out horseback riding and picnicking as early as 1997. By the tenth anniversary of Leslie Mahaffy's dismemberment in her basement, the year 2001, it will be mandatory for the state to let her go.

"I have been told that murder is the easiest of crimes to get away with," Carol Bundy wrote to a friend from her jail cell in 1980. "I believe it. If I hadn't confessed . . . ah well. Too late. Too late."

ISLAND OF WOMEN

The World of the Female Prison

A woman in prison is not a dangerous man.

Headline, THE NEW YORK TIMES MAGAZINE, July 3, 1996

An air of viciousness pervaded the whole place. Everyone was frightened of everyone else.

JOSIE O'DWYER, inmate, Borstal and Holloway prisons

When Dorothea Puente was convicted of homicide, she retraced the routes of her migrant childhood, back through the San Joaquin Valley of central California along Route 99, past orchards and almond groves to the Central California Women's Facility, near the town of Chowchilla. From a distance, all one can see of CCWF are giant stadium lights rising in a ring along the flat plateau. Driving closer, along a one-lane highway, a complex of low, red brick bungalows comes into view. The prison is surrounded by two rows of electrified barbed wire fencing, fourteen feet high, nine feet apart, making it feel open and oddly transparent. Chowchilla, as it's called, was built in 1987 to supplement the state women's prison at Frontera, an hour's drive south of Los Angeles. In less than ten years, CCWF's population surged from two thousand to four thousand inmates and a sister facility opened across the highway in 1995. Christened the Valley State Prison for Women, it went immediately into overcrowding as well. In 1994, California women's prisons received 592 new violent offenders, 1,454 property offenders, and

1,696 drug offenders. As of mid–December 1995, the state had 9,162 women in custody, for crimes ranging from armed robbery to drive-by shooting, smoking crack to dealing heroin, embezzlement to serial homicide.

The women at CCWF are divided into five yards, A through E, which consist of double-winged dormitories, each surrounded by an expansive lawn replete with baseball diamond, immovable metal patio furniture, flowerbeds, and gym weights. The only section of CCWF that truly resembles a prison are buildings 503 and 505. Each is two stories high, guarded by watchtowers, constructed of steel-reinforced brick, with narrow, enclosed cement exercise yards and steel-barred gates, which are incongruously painted pale pink. Each building has two floors (the second a catwalk) lined with rows of locked metal doors. Through small viewing windows, one can see the six-by-eight-foot cells, furnished with metal cots and lidless, stainless steel toilets. Building 503 is the gateway to CCWF, housing new inmates, no matter their crimes, for a minimum of five days. The purpose is to dry them out, calm them down, observe their behavior. Who's going to be a troublemaker? Who gets assigned to which yard? Building 505 has two wings, each of which houses forty women at any given time, for two months to a year, after they've committed assaults or other serious infractions in their yards. Guards and visitors here are required to wear protective vests. Women in lockdown are not happy campers.

In the bottom right-hand corner of 505 is a corridor of nine cells with an outer perimeter of bars, which creates a narrow cage for residents to pace. This is death row, the rarest destination in the world for a woman of California. Only four women have been executed in the state in the twentieth century, the last one in 1962. Since the death penalty was reinstated in 1977, no governor has signed a woman's death warrant. When serial murderess Louise Peete taunted the U.S. Supreme Court by saying that "No gentleman would put a lady to her death," she was almost entirely correct. The only four who lost that gamble in California were safely beyond the pale of voter sympathy—Peete herself, plus two notorious organized crime figures, and a woman who killed her husband for his money in the 1950s.

Today, there are six women on death row at Chowchilla. Mary Ellen Samuels hired her daughter's fiancé to kill her Hollywood cinematographer husband. He wanted a divorce, and his life insurance was worth more than his alimony. Samuels then hired additional hit men to kill her daughter's fiancé, and was photographed some months after the murders, lying nude on a hotel bed, in a bath of $100 bills. Rosie Alfaro was a drug addict who stabbed a nine-year-old girl fifty-seven times while robbing her home. Maureen McDermott was a respected nurse who hired a hit man to kill her female roommate for the mortgage on their house. Catherine Thompson killed her husband for his life insurance. Cynthia Lynn Coffman abducted and strangled two teenaged girls during a crime spree with her boyfriend, an ex-con known as the Folsom Wolf. Caroline Young slashed her two small grandchildren to death with a butcher's knife to protest their father's taking custody. (Their mother was in jail on a drug charge and hadn't ever told the father that he'd sired her children. He found out when the state hit him with twelve thousand dollars' worth of back pay for child support, at which point he requested, and gained, custody.) It is a testament to the arbitrariness of the death penalty that both Dorothea Puente and Carol Bundy are milling around in the yards.

To house the general population, all four women's prisons in California are constructed as cottage-style compounds, the theory being that women don't escape by digging tunnels or scaling walls. They don't need to be confined in the sort of stone fortresses built for men. "I think women are escape risks, as much as men. Absolutely. It's just that they don't go over a gate. Here, they enlist help," says CCWF Lieutenant Toby Wong, a convivial, suavely dressed man in his thirties. He is strolling the yards with his visitor, as relaxed and expansive as a real estate agent showing off a house, except that he has a black belt in karate and the house is ringed by scorching wire.

Wong moves through the compound, nodding to guards who sit in bubble-enclosed control booths. He sweeps his gaze back and forth for potential trouble and muses on the special challenges of guarding women. Correctional officers need to struggle with their own prejudices, he explains. They need to resist the sentiments that the Sacramento social work community invested in Dorothea

Puente: that women who come to them, friendly and helpful, are not capable of using that cover to conceal a power play. "I tell my staff, 'Never be alone with an inmate. I don't want you set up, fool,' " says Wong. "Men have a cover officer because they might get hurt. Here, you need one in case you get set up." Indirect strategies of aggression are common in women's prisons, perpetrated not only by inmates but by guards.

It's lunchtime. Out in the yards, dozens of inmates suddenly emerge from the dorms and walk carefully along a prescribed path—no stepping on the grass—to the yard cafeteria, where they can pick up box lunches to take back to their rooms. Mostly in their twenties and thirties, the women's faces are strikingly unhealthy, wan and pockmarked, their hair frizzed, sheenless and limp. They walk in twos and threes, dragging silently on cigarettes. Here and there a pair hold hands, until Wong discourages them with the mimed gesture of a slit throat: "Cut it out," to which they respond with a shrug. Most of the women are dressed in bland, long-sleeved baseball shirts and jeans; others wear the prison-issue muumuu, a shapeless floral-patterned Hawaiian tunic, which resembles a large swath of drapery. One woman so dressed is tall, about five feet, eleven inches, with beefy arms and a hardened face. She walks flat-footed and langorous, like a man made foolish in drag. The youngest women—who are, by all accounts, the toughest and craziest, the quickest to brandish a weapon—flash gang colors, red or blue around their neck or at their hip.

The inmates of Chowchilla reflect the full array of human temperament and desire. They have committed crimes of passion, greed, necessity, and want, because they're unemployed, high, bummed out and fighting back, or because crime is a culture for them—it's what they know. It's estimated that about 20 percent of female inmates in most prison populations are psychopaths, like Dorothea Puente. The rest somehow just got lost along their way. Four in ten have a prior record for violent crime. A third are in prison for drugs. They dealt drugs, or stole for drugs, or committed assault, armed robbery, or homicide while high on drugs. Nationally, one in three women in American state prisons were serving time for drug offenses in 1991. One in four had committed a crime to get money to buy drugs. More women than men had used drugs in the month prior to their arrest, and more women were high at the time of their crime, including a quarter of the violent offenders.

To an inmate—gay or straight, stud or feminine, high or sober—the women of Chowchilla reveal nothing of themselves to the awkward gawker with a visitor's pass. Their expressions are muted, concealed. Lunchtime is no time to reveal the complex relationships that women form within their prison world. "They're not gonna be smiling," says ex-inmate Marti Salas-Tarin. "They don't got time for you. They stick to the schedule. Get up, go to work, go back to the dorm, do drugs." Do a lot of other things, too. Fight, make love, run a thriving illicit economy, launch lawsuits, gather in groups to compare notes on abuse, and arrange themselves into an all-female hierarchy of power that combines masculine and feminine strategies of aggression in a virtually unprecedented way.

Thirty miles from Chowchilla, amid arid miles of ranch land, vineyards, and almond groves, lies the city of Merced, a port of call for the women who are released from CCWF equipped with a bus ticket and a pat on the back. There are no state-run halfway houses for women in Merced, but on a quiet street lined with dogwood and apple trees, a handful of ex-cons live together in a white wooden house with a wide front veranda. The place is called Miracle House, named by its founder, Marti Salas-Tarin, a charismatic and vivacious fifty-year-old who spent twenty years addicted to heroin. Salas-Tarin served one sentence in "the click," as she calls prison, for dealing, which she had an immense talent for—she dealt in prison, too—and three more sentences for "dirty tests," or violating parole on her first conviction. Eventually, she got sick of walking out of prison gates and plunging back into the gutter, so she went back to her Hispanic-Catholic roots, rediscovered church, and dusted herself off.

Now Salas-Tarin zips around Merced in her white Chevy pickup with a bumper sticker that puns, "My hire power is Jesus Christ," fenagling donations of furniture and food from neighborhood businesses, and persuading the Merced County District Attorney's Office to steer women into her one-year halfway house program. She has a glossy tumble of jet-black hair and gorgeously large dark eyes, and when she's on a business run, she dolls herself up in high heels, cherry-colored skirts, and gold hoop earrings. But her preferred form of dress is a turtleneck, jeans, and her own bare feet—a habit she formed when she was shoeless and adrift as a junkie, sleeping in the backs of wrecked cars. What Marti likes to say about her feet, and her drugs, and the noise of brawls and sex in prison, and the fact that she never quite managed to raise her two children, as well as every other detail in two decades of disastrous dishevelment, is this: "You can get used to *any*thing."

Salas-Tarin owns her own home right next door to Miracle House, so she can supervise her "girls" by padding back and forth across the grass. She lives with her electrician husband, Domingo, a soft-spoken sweetheart who stuck by her through her last stints in prison, and their bouncy black lab, Ishaia. In her living room, she sprawls on the sofa, like a down-home Cleopatra, regal and comfortable, one leg trailing the other on the floor, one arm slung over the back, waving her hand in the air. She keeps her big color television set on mute, tuned to a channel that displays the FBI's most-wanted list. Marti's life, her work, her friends, her politics, are dominated by the subject of prison. She hangs out with women who've been in the click, women who should probably have been there except that they never got caught, and women whose boyfriends and fathers and brothers are down at San Quentin or upstate in Pelican Bay.

Her friend Pauline calls collect from jail when Marti's in the kitchen making a soup of tomatoes and tripe called menuto. Pauline's bawling, she's been hauled in with her daughter on a theft-for-drugs charge, and they're both up against their third felony conviction, which, under California's 1994 three strikes law, means that they face a mandatory sentence of twenty-five years to life. "Man," Marti says, when she hangs up the phone, "you gotta pay more at*ten*tion!" She's equal parts mad at Pauline and at the system. Users don't pay much mind to headlines. As a result, a lot of them are getting caught in the dragnet of the three strikes law and being thrown into prison for twice as long as someone like Karla Homolka.

While Marti frets about the fate of Pauline, she's joined by Cat, a quiet woman with a slow, sweet smile who is round and plump, doubtless once voluptuous, now gray and bespectacled on the edge of sixty. Cat was Marti's partner in crime for nearly two decades, both of them totally devoted to their drugs, ripping off whomever they could for a dime bag. Crime, for Cat, is a family business. Her husband is in prison. She hasn't seen her only son in eighteen years, since he got sent to San Quentin, then up to Pelican Bay on a robbery-kidnap charge. She's come to tell Marti that the parole board has turned her son down, again. "I'm glad he's strong," she says, and shows her only photograph of him, taken when he was a boy. "He's a real tough character." Cat's life has been constant chaos, full of mundane deprivation and injustice, but she has her own apartment at the back of Miracle House now, and it's a cozy nest of flowers and family pictures, like any other mother's parlor.

The newest addition to Miracle House is Geita, an energetic platinum blonde with a wrinkled tan and candy-bright jewelry who usually lives in Las Vegas. Geita did time in Nevada for possession of crank, a mixture of crack and speed. Like Marti, she's in her late forties. She has five kids, none of whom has been in touch with her since she went to jail. While her kids were still home with her, Geita's preferred vice was pot smoking. But later, after she got divorced, someone introduced her to crank, and she got herself a steady, four-year shooting addiction, in the midst of which she swung a post-hole digger at her boyfriend, breaking his leg. Now she's doing Marti's program as a court-ordered alternative to a second jail sentence, this time for getting caught with crank paraphernalia in her trailer.

At first, Geita resented being in Marti's program, because Geita hates rules and didn't have much time for straight people, let alone church. But now, after a few months, she's pretty keen on the arrangement. "Church is my new drug," she says with a wide, white-toothed grin, her voice gravelly from cigarettes, "my new high." People for whom addiction is a religion often turn to religion to give up their addiction. If Geita hadn't stayed in Marti's program and gotten clean, she'd have been sent to CCWF or Valley State, in and out again through the revolving door. Women's prisons are no more likely to be filled with new faces than men's prisons. Seventy-two percent of America's female inmates have had prior incarcerations. The American media have a pronounced tendency to depict women in prison as melancholy daughters of virtue who are unjustly sentenced. They don't need rehabilitation because as soon as they get out, they'll rush back to their kids and start saving money for Christmas. The reality is that many of the female inmates are stoned when they're arrested, stoned in the mix, and stoned all over again as soon as they hit the streets. Thanks to Marti, and no credit to the press or the state of California, Geita and Cat are now thinking of starting a beauty parlor. That, for both of them, would be a nice change.

Cat first went to prison in 1963 and has watched with some interest as the landscape around her unalterably shifted. "Back then," she says, "it wasn't but five hundred women. It was empty. The halls echoed. We didn't have radios and TVs. White sheets was contraband. Had to be green. Our rooms was just regular. One woman to a room. It got better and better." She smiles, amused. "I had rugs, curtains, fish. You could have pets. When I went in in 'seventy-nine, the dress code had changed. Women was wearin' mink coats, hats, leather. I mean everything! I thought: 'I gotta dress and get down with 'em,' because I wanted to be like everybody else, dress nice. My mother sent me what I wanted. We ended up havin' a wardrobe there." Now the dorms that echoed when one woman called to another to show off a fancy coat are crowded and increasingly tense, with eight women jammed into cells built for four, sharing one toilet with a chest-high window. Hundreds of other women at CCWF sleep in gray-blanketed bunkbeds in the prison gymnasium, as restless and displaced as evacuees.

No classification system exists for female offenders. Unlike men's prisons, which are divided into different levels of security, most women's prisons are indiscriminately filled with any female who happens to have committed a crime. Multiple murderesses mingle with check forgers, psychopaths share bunks with petty thieves. "I been in a room with a lifer, murderers," says Cat. She crosses her arms. "They very serious." Geita was in prison "with a woman who shot her old man up with Drāno. Another one went on a rampage in Reno and ran a bunch of people down with a car." Imagine the junk bond trader Michael Milken sleeping three feet away from Charles Manson, or J. Gordon Liddy bunk to bunk with Ted Bundy.

Nor do prison officials honor the hierarchy of female transgression. Among inmates, killing children or infants is the least forgivable crime. "They're so many [baby killers] here they could have their own fan club," Lieutenant Wong says. "We have a lot of predatory women, too, a lot of sex offenders." Indeed, one quarter of the women at CCWF are considered "maximum risks." "Baby killers used to be in protective custody away from the population 'cause they caused a lot of violence," says Marti on her sofa in Merced. But overcrowding jettisoned the luxury of separation. At present, only one unit at CCWF holds what Wong calls "disturbed characters," which is to say those who are mentally ill. Otherwise, everyone's shoulder to shoulder, creating an admixture of harmless and highly dangerous women that generates deep unease.

To quell chaos and achieve some semblance of security in a threatening environment, male prisoners create hierarchies of power, inventing a rigid code of conduct that they themselves police. They mete out their own justice, they run their own economy, they fight their own wars. Their laws have nothing to do with the guards' laws or with the values of the world outside. A murderer whom we might revile in society might have very high status in Pelican Bay, while an essentially decent, mild-mannered man may be treated with utter contempt. "It's all the way you carry yourself," says Cat, reflecting on her son's journey through California's toughest lockdowns. "My baby, he went in fightin'. That's how he gained his respect." It's also why he now gets turned down for parole. "My husband, they call him the Professor. They respected him a lot in there. They left him alone."

What men import from the outside is a basic idea of how to build their power structures. Prison gangs, for instance, are no different than the gangs on the streets of L.A. The members know how to follow laws of respect—how to gain it, how to use it as deterrence against unprovoked assaults. Men bring military, corporate, or street experience with them into prison. They know how to vie for status in a strictly impersonal way.

Women, on the other hand, tend to have little or no familiarity with combat in a public arena. They possess no repertoire of in-your-face aggressive postures. Karla Homolka and Myra Hindley and Marybeth Tinning hadn't been socialized to order themselves into an impersonal hierarchy with explicitly enforced rules, based on formal expressions of status rather than relational alliances. Yet when they entered prison, heterosexual femininity was suddenly the least valuable currency. For the first time in many of their lives, women must find a way to build a system of power and privilege that has nothing to do with men.

Although some feminists would argue that no such hierarchy need exist, that women can fall into a healing harmony side by side, the reality is more complex. Female prisoners are not peace activists or nuns who were kidnapped off the street and stuck in jail. They are miscreants, intemperate, willful, and rough. Conflicts flare, and *because* there is no stable hierarchy, they flare with the frequency of brush fires, with no mechanism for containment. Infraction rates against prison rules are extremely high in women's prisons. Nationally, in 1986, female inmates racked up an average of two infractions per year versus 1.4 for males. In England, "the incidence of violence in women's [prisons] is two and a half times higher than in men's." A study of the two female prisons in Texas, Gatesville and Mountain View, found that women committed 3,698 infractions against prison discipline in one year, nearly five times the rate at which male inmates were cited. Among the women's ten most common infractions were striking an officer, fighting without a weapon, damaging or destroying property, and creating a disturbance. More offenses "of a threatening, violent or sexual nature" were cited against women than men.

"You can get into a fight every ten seconds in here if you want to," an inmate at Bedford Hills Correctional Facility in New York State told *Psychology Today*. "I figured that I was going to spend the rest of my life locked up . . . so what the hell? A lot of the women here feel the same way. Just look at them the wrong way and they'll go right for your eyes." Says Marti: "Sometimes the fights are out of the blue, especially when you gonna eat, you don't mess with that. You better not be crowding—a fight will start."

Flare-ups also ignite over trade in the illicit prison economy, in particular the buying and selling of dope. "I seen a woman that's got AIDS shootin' AIDS blood at a woman who can't pay," recalls Cat. "I seen a girl's head put down in one of those industrial kitchen mixers, tore off the top of her head. You can't pay, they're serious." They're serious, but in a much less systematic or decisive way than men are. "My old man was in Folsom," says Geita. "Some of the stories he told me . . . cold-blooded. He's seen men die for a cigarette. Men have an image to live up to. If you're weak, you're through. Women are more into trying to heal each other. Still," she adds, " a deal's a deal. If you say you're gonna do something, do it. Don't play games."

Men in American prisons are far more likely to commit homicide. As their hierarchies are more strict, so, too, are their penalties. "Men stab each other," says Wong, "but here they use weapons to disfigure each other, curling irons, razor blades, locks in a sock. Throwing hot liquids at each other. Their issues are drug-related or lovers' quarrels or sexual misconduct." Both women's weaponry and their "issues" are fashioned from what is at hand, in a world where gender roles and power strategies are suddenly up for grabs.

The sense of urgency women feel when they first enter prison—to locate themselves, connect, find a safe point of reference when the codes are scarily cryptic—leads them to adopt a variety of tactics that are, in effect, wild guesses about how to survive. One tactic is to emulate masculine violence. Josie O'Dwyer entered the British penal system at the age of fourteen, convicted of a relatively harmless robbery. O'Dwyer had never shown a predilection for physical aggression, but when she entered the Borstal prison, she quickly decided that force was her best option for feeling secure. The way she saw it, if she didn't fight the guards, they wouldn't respect her. They'd abuse her privileges. If she didn't fight the other girls, she wouldn't gain any "credit," the ultimate objective being to be left alone. So she fought like hell and achieved a traditionally masculine attitude toward violence. "When I came out of Borstal my ambition in life was to be the top dog, the most hardened criminal, the most vicious," she wrote in her memoir.

According to research in both Britain and the United States, young women are by far the most physically aggressive inmates in their prisons. Maybe they're more insecure, or more impulsive and defiant, but certainly O'Dwyer's tactic was one she was more apt to adopt than older, more seasoned inmates like Marti and Cat. At nineteen, when O'Dwyer was in London's Holloway prison, she took on Myra Hindley. She didn't know how high up Hindley was in the prison hierarchy, only that the famous serial murderess had killed children. She attacked Hindley in a dimly lit hallway. "Her nose was crossed to the left side of her face, I'd split her lip, her knee and her ear, and she had two black eyes." O'Dwyer had, in fact, been set up: Holloway's guards had deliberately exposed her to news clippings about Hindley, then waited for her to explode. Apparently, Myra Hindley was subjected to this kind of set-up every few years. Unlike the prisoners, who could engage in overt aggression, the female guards were still beholden to conventional gender rules. Their aggression was indirect.

Over the years, as O'Dwyer weaved in and out of prison, psychiatrists variously described her as a "paranoid schizophrenic" and "a psychopath." She felt they were completely missing the effect of imprisonment itself on the behavior of women. "They always asked me about my early life but not about what had happened to me in those institutions since the age of fourteen." Prison, for women, can be a transforming experience; in this milieu, it is undeniably culture that dictates how violence bursts forth.

Nevertheless, scholars have generally failed to delve into female inmate aggression, according to criminologist Clemens Bartollas. "Most researchers have focused on the pseudo-family relationships" that women form, their nurturant roles. Apropos of his observation, the one scholar to do a thorough study of Chowchilla's population, the feminist criminologist Barbara Owen, told a criminology conference in 1994 that "women's prison is completely different than men's. The women are all really supportive, really nurturing of each other." Yet one of the few academic studies to focus on hierarchy building in women's prisons confirmed O'Dwyer's experience, in that women who "had established reputations for being able to fight and otherwise physically defend themselves" achieved high status, getting first choice of drugs, for instance, as well as their sexual pick of the new girls. Also high in the hierarchy are white women, who can manipulate preferential guard treatment and get guards to run interference. Men tend to settle disputes among themselves, valuing inmate solidarity above all else. But women will appeal to staff for mediation, or as a means of setting one another up. "You constantly have to watch your back," notes Toni Cato about her own life at the Scott Correctional Facility in Michigan, "because you never know who may wake up wrong or think you're out to take their woman away from them and try and set you up, by putting a razor or stolen food from the kitchen in your room." A study of inmate strategies at Frontera in California found that up to 90 percent of the inmates had acted as snitches. "Women watch each other," says Wong, "who's twisted around whose finger, who's seeing who. Allegations can bury you whether they're valid or not."

Dorothea Puente has solid rank at CCWF, partly because of her crimes, which make her deadly, and partly because she spent a lot of time while *out* of prison sending care packages of Levi's jeans and other prized possessions to the right people *in* prison, so that they'd owe her if she had to go back. Marti Salas-Tarin possessed a similar instinct, which was to grease the wheels: to head her potential combatants off at the pass by offering something they wanted. "You follow the flow there," she explains. "If you think you're better, they'll beat you up. If you don't want to be tough, you become tough, if you're not a lesbian . . . most of the young girls get caught up in that, because they want to be popular. I wasn't a lesbian in there, but I was respected. I hung with all the heroin addicts, and they knew that I worked in the infirmary. I had access to all the needles. So I was their connection."

One of Marti's cellmates was a rich Filipina who'd been caught embezzling. Terrified of prison, she threw money at the problem, buying her safety from Salas-Tarin. "Drugs, food, whatever I wanted—

for protection. 'Cause she was in the click, man! And she was scared. So she paid me to look out for her." Another cellmate was a fortyish blonde from Los Angeles whom everyone called Blondie. For her sense of safety, Blondie opted for the most successful tactic in the outside world, but the most disastrous one in prison: the maiden-in-distress motif. "One of the guards was fucking her for nothing. She saw it as, like, a *romance!*" says Marti, her astonishment vivid on her face. "I said, 'Blondie, you gotta get something *out* of it, girl!' " Sure enough, the guard was shortly transferred to another prison and didn't so much as bid Blondie good-bye.

White women seem more prone to throwing themselves at the mercy of their jailers, whether through sex, romantic manipulation, or by seeking out protection through medical attention. White inmates are reportedly more likely than any other women to receive mental health care in prison and to use prescription drugs. Black women believe this is because whites are more shocked by prison. "Your average drug user knows there's a possibility they'll go to prison," says one African-American inmate, "but a lot of white women are in denial. Prison is something they didn't envision in their future, they're more traumatized by it, more afraid of their sur-roundings. You see a lot more of them in the line-ups for meds." White girls, according to this same inmate, "Jane," are also more likely to seek out and receive protective custody. "Coming in, you have to spend time in reception. They will put white women in a pri-ority cell because they are worried about their safety. Maybe they think they're weaker, or they care more."

Indeed, it is white heterosexual women, with their more tradi-tional guise of femininity and "weakness," whose power plays suc-ceed with prison officials, judges, parole boards, the media. They are the ones who get interviewed by journalists, who get the best jobs working in administration, who get released and go on to lecture others on the conditions of female imprisonment, playing to the script of feminine virtue. "White women get to come out of ninety-day mandatory work schemes quicker," says Jane, "they get into pro-grams quicker, this is commonplace. In the last six weeks, all the white women who came in are now in better jobs with better status—

law library clerk, tutor, administration. White women see themselves as more entitled. Many of them come in with their Jean Harris attitude. They've owned their home, they have strong family ties. Do they see themselves as better? Yes. And I have to say they're better equipped to negotiate the system."

What most women inmates have in common, regardless of race or class, is a desire to be romantically linked to another inmate as the basis for their personal security. If men join gangs in prison to secure their sense of safety, women join "families." They become, to a remarkably high degree, homosexual for the duration of their stay behind bars. Lesbianism in prison has little to do with lesbianism as a sexual preference on the outside. California inmates and correction officers estimate that actual lesbians make up about 20 percent of the yard population. Beyond that particular group, perhaps another 60 percent of inmates "turn" in their yards, forming relationships with other women and going back to their husbands and boyfriends as soon as they're released.

That women, crime, and aggression should come together in many people's minds as an image of Big Betty, the antifeminine butch dyke who couldn't get a man, means, of course, that lesbian stereotypes flourish in popular depictions of prison life. A rash of prison chick flicks in the 1970s, which for some reason always starred Linda Blair of *The Exorcist*, invariably counterposed nice girls with large, leering "lesies" wielding weapons. The iconography angered some feminist cultural critics so much that they vigorously countered the images by arguing that there weren't any lesbians in prison, and if there were, they looked and acted just like other women.

"Common messages gleaned from female prison films, none of which are supported by observations of actual women in institutions," Karlene Faith wrote recently, "include . . . [the messages that] women locked up are masculine, and do routine physical damage to one another" and that a "disproportionate number of women in prison are lesbians," caricatured as "macho heterosexual men." Well, in fact, although the B movies are salacious and cartoonish, and split their characters into a dichotomy of virtuous feminine and amoral unfeminine, the truth is that there *are* inmates in each North

American women's prison who transform themselves into the equivalent of macho heterosexual men. In California, they're known as the stud broads.

There are only two stud broads in B Yard this noontime, one is African American, tall and broad-shouldered, with gnarled rasta hair and a distinctive mustache. She lopes, moving from her shoulders rather than her hips, projecting an air of supreme self-assurance. The other stud is white, with a brush cut and a goatee. She is shorter, but wiry and muscled, like a marine. There is no point in saying she. These are not women imitating men. They don't look campy, like the woman in the muumuu. They have achieved an almost pure masculinity. Their transformation takes your breath away.

"The girls loved the studs to death, man. 'Cause they looked like *men!*" says Marti, explaining what she saw as a pretty obvious equation. "That's your mentality when you're in prison for a while." Women don't want to date women, they want to date men. Moreover, women don't feel secure in an environment as volatile as prison by partnering up with another woman. They feel secure by seeking out the tough, strengthening shelter of a man. "Usually the girls who turn are young," says Marti. "When they walk in, there's like a hundred stud broads standing there fishing. They're like, 'Oh, man, look at that one, I want that one.' And pretty soon they know what room the new girls are in, and they're sending them candy, they're sending them cigarettes, a pair of 501s. . . . And the [young girls] are naive, you know. So they hang onto the stud broads for this stuff, for protection. The cute girls get turned out right away." The relationships may or may not be sexual, depending upon the women. They are rather more marriages of convenience, like political or economic alliances, ceremonially consolidated. "They get married in there, too, you have a ceremony. Another stud that's been there a while will marry you, she's like a priest. They'll just invite certain people."

Which way the cute girls turn—toward the feminine or the masculine—is one of the most fascinating aspects of women's prison culture. "There was this girl named Blanca at Chowchilla," Marti remembers, "she looked exactly like a boy, she was bea-u-tiful. Real cute face. Blond. Every girl in Chowchilla wanted to be with her, that's why they'd go to the chapel, just to see her." Blanca had a boyfriend on the outside, and whenever he came to visit, she kicked off her droopy, slim-hipped men's jeans, pulled off her muscle T-shirt, and slapped on some makeup. She was living two lives, the allure of the feminine, the command of the masculine. "Blanca used to tell me, 'Marti, pray for me. I want to be a man.' "

At Bedford Hills Correctional Facility, stud broads are known as aggressors. One winter afternoon, in the prison's bright, tidy administrative offices, an aggressor named Mohammad strolled in and sat down warily for an interview. Mohammad, whose first name is actually Arlene, is a handsome woman in her forties with crimped hair, cut close to her head, graying at the temples. She sports a tasteful burgundy sweater and an elegant pair of men's tasseled loafers, and plants her feet firmly on the floor when she sits, her hands held loosely in her lap in a posture of relaxed self-possession. Mohammad isn't as flamboyantly masculinized as the California studs. She has no visible facial hair, for one thing. Her sexual preference is more internalized, less connected to the power structure of prison itself. "I'd never heard the word aggressor before I came here in 'eighty-four," she says. "Prior to coming to prison, I'd been called stud, dyke, bull dagger, it changes with the years. I don't change. I've been gay since I was fourteen." Mohammad's experience of being gay on the outside, where homosexuality is not the norm or an arrangement of expedience, makes her particularly sensitive to the negative stereotypes. So, one of the first things she wants known is that aggressors are not the ones who corrupt straight women. "A lot of people think that when a young woman comes in here, she's not given a chance, she's hit on by a bunch of women dressed like men. It's the total opposite. There's so few aggressors (five to eight to a unit) that we're like the woman going alone to a singles bar, who gets hit on. If you happen to be gay before you get in, you're even more popular. People say, 'Hey, she's the real thing.' "

If you're not gay when you go in, then, like Blanca, you find yourself with a choice that no one ever offered you before. "Feminine women are making little aggressors out of the [new girls]," says

Mohammad, "and [because] they haven't been in the world long enough to know their own sexuality," they're responsive. How they dress themselves and what posture they adopt depends to a large degree on the fashion of the times. "The same way you see fads on the street, certain lifestyles, that's carried over to prison." says Mohammad. "You'll find that the younger aggressors have their pants hanging off their butts."

But how deeply do these superficial fads penetrate women's sexual identities? There is a vigorous debate about this within women's prisons. According to Mohammad, women who "turn" in prison will probably continue to explore their bisexuality. "I think a very high percentage will go home to a husband and have, every now and then, a liaison with a woman. They are exposed to something here they didn't know existed before in themselves." To what? A transmutation of sexual boundary, a leveling of the playing field where gender is concerned, an altogether different sensation of power. "When Blanca got outta there," says Marti, "we set her up with Victory Outreach [a Christian, largely Mexican, program]. She completely changed and went back to being a girl, a lady. She goes: 'You know what was the hardest thing for me to do when I went in this program? They told me, "You got to take off those boxers and put on a dress." I cried and cried for about two weeks, and then finally I put the dress on.' "

Mohammad's friend Precious Bedell, who is working on her master's degree while serving time for homicide, wrote a play about the transmutations women undergo in prison. One of the scenes, published in *Prison Life*, involves an aggressor named Moneylove discussing gender with a feminine woman named Sandy, who calls Moneylove "Mr. Career Criminal."

MONEY: That's me, but don't change the gender, baby. Ms. suits me.
SANDY: Oh, so today you want to be a woman?
MONEY: Come on now, baby. I have no illusions about who or what I am. I'm just aggressive and prefer men's attire.

Most stud broads and aggressors view themselves as women, and the physical differences between them and feminine women can be quite subtle, depending upon the individual and the institution. What generates the argument is that some appropriate masculine strategies of domination. "You can use women," Cat points out. "They can do a lot of things that you want done. If you stupid or weak enough to get caught up in that, they'll use you sexually, or make you their maid, or what*ever,* make you run dope." Abuses of power by aggressors are the subject of heated debate for women inmates. "Lesbianism is not the issue," wrote Washington State inmate Veronica Compton (partner of the Hillside Strangler) in a guest editorial in *Prison Life*:

> *Lesbianism is, ideally, women loving other women. What I oppose are women who . . . act as oppressive male figures wielding control and power over other people. . . . What's especially tragic is that a woman finds her misogynist in other women inmates, not just staff.*

Some Bedford Hills aggressors unquestionably replicate the behaviors of misogyny: stringing along three or four girlfriends at a time, making their girls cook and iron for them, smacking them if they step out of line. This, at least, was the observation of former inmate Jean Harris. She recalls one inmate wailing, "What did I do, Tony? I did it all just the way you told me. I can't do any more. How can you be mad at me, Tony?" At least one scholar records that aggressors set up a system of tribute, in the manner of feudal lords.

Stud broads and aggressors may have high status within the inmate social world, but they are not the ones who benefit from guard treatment, because unlike tough heterosexual women or celebrity inmates, their prestige is narrowly confined to their yards. "The famous white girls like Amy Fisher and Pamela Smart, that type, always get into relationships with African-American women," says Jane. "Maybe in their minds they feel safer. But any black girl who goes with them is running a big risk. You got a double whammy of white and celebrity. When a black woman and a white woman get into an argument, and the white woman [tells the guard], 'She made me buy a pair of sneakers,' the black girl goes to lockdown for extortion, even if the truth is exactly the opposite. White girls are believed faster." Where most guards are concerned, African-American aggressors are nothing more or less than the B movie stereotype of butch dykes. "Do we feel [homophobia] in the judicial system?" Mohammad asks. "Most definitely. Are aggressors treated differently than feminine women? Sure. Both inside and outside of prison."

Whether women's conflicts take the form of direct assault or indirect set-up, the emotional currents running through their prisons as a result of relational power structures contribute in large part to the volatility. According to a national survey of correctional officers in America, women inmates were overwhelmingly viewed as more "emotional, temperamental, moody, manipulative, quarrelsome and excitable." Correctional officers in women's institutions have far more complicated relationships with their charges than those in men's prisons, partly because women inmates involve the guards in their politics with other inmates, and partly because the guards get sexually or romantically involved with their charges. The survey found that female officers considered women to be more difficult to manage than men, while for male officers the reverse was true, suggesting that each sex has less tolerance for and less interest in the power plays of its own gender. "Women's view of women differs substantially from men's," says Lieutenant Wong. "Women know when women are lying. Men can get twisted around. Female officers will arrest and cite twice as many women as men do."

Corrections officials, like most people, feel they need to be gentler with women than with men. So instead of enforcing order by roughing up the miscreants, they barrage the women with teensy, stupid rules, adding fuel to a blazing fire. "Possession of contraband" may mean stashing drugs, but it as easily refers to having a postage stamp in one's room (prohibited at Bedford Hills), or candy, or a borrowed comb. "Trafficking" can refer equally to selling heroin, as Marti did, or sharing shampoo in the shower. The regulations can be so oppressively petty that they wind women up to levels of teeth-grating irritability. The effect is compounded by the fact that women tend to be less fearful of their guards.

"My hardest problem has been authority," says Geita. "All the prison guards were *young*."

Marti leaps in: "And they're trying to tell a woman forty-five years old what to do?" She raises her brows.

Responds Geita: "You want to slap 'em. They write the rules in pencil so they can erase 'em and change 'em when they want to."

"You give 'em respect, they'll give you respect," cautions Cat.

Women want to understand the meaning behind a rule and, in prison at least, are more likely to argue its merit. Research on gangs in Los Angeles reveals that girls, too, are less likely than boys to follow a rule just because it exists, and will do something on behalf of the gang only if they judge it to be worth their while. In prison, getting hit with a rule violation for something like sharing shampoo can escalate into an argument between inmate and guard until she gets lockdown for threatening an officer or ripping up her cell. "Negative feelings toward staff lead inmates to respond emotionally to some minor event, which serves to confirm the staff in its perceptions" of women as moody and quarrelsome, notes the author of the study on infraction rates in the two Texas prisons for women. Interestingly, however, the study found that the one difference between the two prisons studied was that the maximum-security facility had fewer problems than the facility with all different sorts of inmates mixed together.

The Prison for Women in Kingston, Ontario, to which Karla Homolka was assigned in 1993, resembles an old stone dungeon. Until it shut down in the summer of 1996, the prison held 120 women, nearly 25 percent of whom were serving life sentences for violent crime, in extremely restive conditions. On April 22, 1994, six inmates attacked four guards in a preplanned escape attempt outside B Range, a high-security segregation area like CCWF's Building 505. The guards, all of whom were female, were put in chokeholds, punched in the face, kicked in the stomach, stabbed with a hypodermic needle, and assaulted with scissors and a telephone ripped from the wall. When one guard went to another's aid, inmate Joey Twins grabbed her around the throat and went for her keys: "Don't push me, Boston," Twins warned, "I've got a shiv and I'll stick you." A male guard arrived, tried to subdue her, and got kicked in the testicles. The guards finally regained control by using Mace. They returned the inmates to their cells but forgot to strip-search them for weapons.

P4W (as Prison for Women is called) rapidly lost control of the situation; the hostility between the guards and the prisoners grew so intense that B Range geared up to full revolt, with noise levels so loud that "cell bars were vibrating." The inmates set fires, flung urine, and threatened guards' lives. One woman tried to hang herself. Another slashed her body with scissors, getting bloodier and bloodier and demanding that the guards let her out of her cell.

On April 26, guards demanded that the warden bring in an "Institutional Emergency Response Team" from the nearby men's prison. The demand was to result in a national scandal. The all-male IERT stormed in, strip-searched eight inmates, and placed them, half-naked, in full-body restraints, all of which they videotaped, as was standard procedure in the prison that the IERT members worked in. Because the inmates were women, however, the strip-search became front-page news. "I felt very degraded," Brenda Morrison, who was serving five years for armed robbery and aggravated assault, told a federal commission of inquiry. "How can they walk in there, rip my clothes off and say it's okay? I don't know how any man could do that to a woman and say it was their job. As far as I know, it's a crime." Reporters covering the inquiry described Morrison as "dabbing at tears" while she gave her account. An expert who saw the IERT videotape described what they had done as "a little like shoving a gun down the mouth of a woman—I mean, it's a very phallic act."

According to the *Toronto Globe & Mail*, an internal inquiry into the uprising "paint[ed] a picture of the prison as a place that has tended to view women as victims, and so has been ill prepared to deal with inmates who are manipulative and capable of serious violence." Ultimately, all the guards involved took prolonged mental health leave. Two transferred out of the prison, and one quit the business. "Noting the inevitable problems posed by trying to house prisoners requiring different levels of security in one institution," the *Globe* reported, "the report [also] recommends that violent inmates be housed in a facility separate from the general population." Yet in 1996, P4W's inmates were farmed out to smaller institutions. None of them were maximum-security. Canada's federal department of corrections opened a new facility in Edmonton, Alberta, for all the prairie region's female inmates, and designed it along minimum-security guidelines, responding to arguments made by Canada's Elizabeth Frye Society that women are only in prison because of men's abuse, and that if you treat them with respect, they'll conduct themselves with dignity. No security fence was erected around the perimeter, and no locks were put on the "bedroom" doors. Within the first six months, 25 percent of the inmates escaped. One inmate was apparently hanged in her room by others who simply let themselves in.

Since the P4W uprising, according to Irving Kulik, deputy commissioner of Corrections Canada, federal prison policy has been to back away from the rigid rules for minor infractions so apt to fan inmate frustration. Women, the deputy said, are not charged if they're caught with small amounts of drugs. Although this sounds compassionate and rational, letting women dope themselves so that they'll remain passive in prison is not a new managerial strategy. "Mostly everybody that wasn't a heroin addict [before] was on heroin in Chowchilla," points out Marti. "That is the god honest truth. I had girls that were, like, 'Do me, do me.' Everyone's strung out." The same is true, apparently, at New York's Bedford Hills. "I lost a friend to AIDS," reflects Mohammad, "after she got addicted to drugs in here." Perhaps it's just a coincidence that the one drug that agitates the addict—crack—is nowhere to be seen in prisons, whereas drugs that pacify, such as heroin and hashish, are abundant. Coincidence or no, the fact that so many women do time in the first place for drug-related crime is hardly assisted by their continuing substance abuse in the mix. "Why do you think the courts send me the girls?" Marti demands. "Because they *know*. They ain't gonna learn nothing in there. You know what I'm saying? It's a big old game." In the absence of a rational corrections strategy for handling female inmates, doping them may be the only unofficial alternative. The use of prescription drugs like sedatives and tranquilizers is five times higher in female prisons than in male prisons. Drugs, according to British scholar Alexandra Mandarakka-Sheppard, are "for the purpose of social control and not for the genuine help of prisoners."

· · ·

When we focus our scant attention on female prisoners, fixating almost exclusively on wrongly imprisoned battered wives, we generate the impression that women just sit around looking pensive and fragile, awaiting rescue, like Rapunzel from her tower. It is not a blessing for female inmates to be viewed this way, because we don't ask if they're receiving parenting skills, vocational training, drug treatment, or adequate security. We don't provide them with halfway houses upon their release, and we don't care that they're all thrown together into homogeneous compounds—the most violent and volatile in the mix with those who are sane and kind. We may hope to give "wrongly punished wives" a benevolent, cottage-style purgatory from which they can escape as soon as they file an appeal, but for corrections departments across North America, that vague sentiment translates into a mandate for warehousing. Lieutenant Wong spelled out the approach of his institution: "Our obligation is to safely house inmates. Curing them, as adults, is nearly impossible. They have so few resources on the street that they have it better in here."

Where this presents a particular problem is in the rise of violence by younger women, in terms not only of numbers but degree. "There're a lot of younger girls now, coming in from the gangs," says Marti. "Yesterday, I saw a girl that was in for a drive-by shooting. She shot a girl. She's gonna do a long time. The gang girls think they're tough, they think they're bad. When you go into the prison, you can do your time easy, or you can do your time hard. And we did easy. Never wanted to beat anybody up. [These girls] make weapons with razor blades. They're tough, man. They don't want to go straight. They're rebellious."

"Prison very much reflects the world," says Mohammad. "As society becomes more chaotic and violent, so does prison. When I came in, you respected those inmates who were older. Now, [new inmates] tend to be drawn to one another, to run in groups. There *was* no older person in their life, so there's disrespect. I hear it every day. There was no father, the mother was an alcoholic or a drug addict. They lacked the love. A lot of them are mothers themselves now, they're twenty-year-olds leaving four children behind in foster

care. They don't know the first damn thing about parenting."
Increasingly disconnected from the network of kinship that supposedly endows women with an ethic of care and keeps their aggression
suppressed, these young women are game to display physical violence. Neither prison officials nor the unstable female prison hierarchy are prepared for the effect that a young, violent inmate
population will have. "We don't have the role models we used to,"
says Mohammad. "Aggressors look to me for advice and as a role
model. But there are less and less of us. To know that [in the future]
there won't be any mentoring is scary."

One can predict with some confidence that Mohammad will be
left to grapple with that concern on her own in the future. Like battered men and lesbians, female inmates are outcasts on a barren
island in our thinking about violence. Myths about female nature
govern the way they are treated and guarded, to their own detri-
ment. Should it matter? Is the problem so large? Male inmates, after
all, fall victim to rape, assault, and murder, and we consider it the
price that they pay for their crimes. But male inmates expect to pay
that price, and have acquired the skills for survival. What do female
inmates expect? Perhaps, if they knew, Mohammad's future would
be a little less scary.

LET THE GUN SMOKE

Holding Ourselves Accountable for Our Deeds

To Aileen Wuornos and all the women who have been vilified, pathologized and murdered for defending themselves by whatever means necessary.

Dedication by cultural critic LYNDA HART in *FATAL WOMEN: LESBIAN SEXUALITY AND THE MARK OF AGGRESSION*, 1994

We must choose with great caution the folk heroes we present to one another and the qualities they embody, for they shall surely return to haunt us.

ELLIOTT LEYTON, anthropologist, 1996

On a Saturday morning, bright and hot, eleven well-heeled Los Angeles women stand in a circle at the LAX Firing Range and shout: "Get the fuck away from me!" Then they bellow, "No!" And pick up volume. *"No!"* This eruption of hostility is a rehearsal. The women, in their twenties and thirties, have signed up for a daylong course called "Women's Empowerment in the '90s." The day begins with "what to shout at men who walk too close behind you on the sidewalk" and ends by pumping fifty rounds of live ammunition into paper silhouettes of men. Laid out on a table at the front of the class are stun guns, pepper sprays, reinforced steel door jams, and small black police batons, which you can hang from your key chain and swing at a face.

"Women, by definition, are targets," says the petite, golden-haired instructor, whose bearing is low-key and self-assured. Her name is Paxton Quigley. She was "very antigun" until a friend of hers was raped in Beverly Hills, even though the friend called the police when she heard the intruder break in. Quigley went over at 2:00 A.M.

and drove her to the hospital. "Do you think you could have stopped him if you'd had a gun?" she wanted to know. The friend wasn't sure. Quigley did some research and wrote a book called *Armed and Female.* Her main point was that women needed to foster in themselves the psychological entitlement to use weapons so that they could feel more powerful, more defended, even if they never had to shoot. Shortly after, Quigley became a spokeswoman for Smith & Wesson.

Her students look grim, resolved. "I want to be mentally prepared for violence," says a dark-haired actress in black, steel-toed boots. A housewife with two children offers that she just bought a .22 Ruger: "I went through that whole feeling of 'Could I shoot somebody?' And I decided that I could." The classroom is festooned with posters of guns: a Beretta, two Smith & Wessons, and a snub-nosed revolver accompanied by the curious slogan, "A terrific Taurus afternoon." It's illegal to carry guns concealed in California, but there are holsters on the market all the same. "Now, I want you to know that I am not endorsing an illegal activity," Quigley cautions, "but here's a purse with a holster inside it. You just say to the guy, 'I can waste this purse, and I can waste you.' " Next, she brandishes a "bra holster," which resembles a large white bandage. Removing her tailored jacket, she shows how to wear it, high up around the ribs, beneath a fluffy sweater, say.

"Now, I never use the word 'kill' in this class," Quigley says. "I say stop. You want to be able to stop your attacker. So you go for the center of mass." She hits her chest with her fist. "If the police ask you what you did, say you shot to stop." After the women have learned how to load and aim their .38s with sweaty palms, the talk turns to how women are much better shooters than men. "We don't get into pecker contests," says a soft-voiced blonde who used to be married to a Texan. "We're more controlled." As soon as they file into the range, outfitted with metal earmuffs and goggles, all the men hanging around at the firing range that afternoon line up at the window and grin.

On the range, twelve booths face down a hundred-foot alley of steel and cement. Each one has a paper target hanging down from a ceiling track, so that it can be moved as close or as far as you want. Quigley stands behind the line with a megaphone, barking out carefully paced commands. One-handed shooting is the hardest exercise. Some can't pull the trigger without bracing. "Squeeze!" Quigley commands, but instead of a line of sharp bangs, there's a series of puffs and grunts. Then there is a point-and-shoot, in which they must fire off five rounds as fast as they can, as they would in a dark house or alley, with an assailant fast approaching. With every bullet spent, the gun's power ebbs.

"Okay," comes the command. "Now I want you to shoot to the head."

"*Yeah!*" yells the actress, and you imagine her paper target has turned into an ex-boyfriend's smirk.

"Wow," notes Quigley, "we have a real stopper here."

For just under four seconds, the range is a deafening chaos of gunfire. "Okay," Quigley says, "let's see the damage." The target silhouettes waft forward with a mechanical whirr. There are bullet holes clear through each head. "*Hot!*" Quigley laughs. Behind the glass partition, not a few manly grins fall away.

In 1975, a criminologist named Freda Adler shook up her field by publishing a book called *Sisters in Crime*, in which she proposed, with undeniable excitement, that female aggression and criminality were going to catch up with men's. As the opportunities opened up by feminism led women to assert themselves, they would adopt more traditionally masculine methods of self-empowerment. Adler envisioned the change primarily in economic terms, as one in which women went for the gold, just as men did, legitimately or illegally, depending upon what avenues were open to them. If their only means were deviant, due to poverty or lack of skill, then their self-assertion would take place within the context of crime. The traditionally higher involvement of African-American women in criminal enterprise would be balanced as white women joined them. White-collar women might engage in embezzlement or insider trading; unemployed women would settle for extortion, trafficking, or robbery. But it would happen. As support for her argument, Adler pointed to the rising crime rates of young women, and to the outbreak of women's prison riots, among other 1970s trends.

Her proposal came to be known as the liberation hypothesis.

Over the next two decades, a great deal of energy went into disproving Adler, partly because the notion that women's crime could be linked to women's liberation was too politically dangerous. The liberation hypothesis would be—and was—gleefully appropriated as a weapon by conservatives to discredit the feminist agenda. For instance, an *Alberta Report* column on the rising crime rates recently gloated: "Women only have themselves to blame." It is a perspective that harks back to the nineteenth–century view of women as inherently corrupt: Unbridle them from confinement, and they'll give their baser desires free reign, unfettered by masculine reason, and fall lower into depravity than any man could. It is a repugnant view, and most feminist scholars reflexively shy away from any perception of women that plays this way into misogynist hands.

Adler's hypothesis also became unpopular because of overall trends in her culture: The exuberant antiestablishment energy of the 1960s and 1970s, which was what she tapped into in envisioning female aggression, gave way to the culture of victimhood. By the 1980s, it was no longer a badge of honor to make a fist and wave it; it was more prestigious to weep in a therapist's office. Therefore, women couldn't want to do something so antisocial and frankly offensive as crime. Women were not to be held as men's equals in villainy, they were to be shown as men's victims.

In the 1990s, the wisest rejoinder to Adler lies somewhere between the poles of reaction and counterreaction, between male prejudice and feminist sentiment. Women's equality cannot "cause" women to be aggressive, destructive, or coercive, because they had that capacity all along. Female aggressive strategies alter according to cultural practice, according to how women are permitted to channel their impulses. Girls today not only live in a generally more violent society, but their models are more assertive, in every realm from female rock to primetime TV to movie stars. The capacity to be physically forceful and volubly angry is much more evident to these girls, as it is to young women in other Western nations. Finnish psychologist Vappu Viemero has documented changes in girls' aggression over the last decade in her country and found the gap between boys' and girls' aggression to be narrowing considerably. "In some of the aggression measures, the girls score even higher than the boys," she notes. At the level of role playing and "doing gender," the shift for girls from indirection to straightforward conflict appeared to be a good thing to Viemero. "Aggressive behavior seems to be something positive in girls' social setting, something that makes the girl feel powerful, strong, and makes her popular."

The *severity* of aggression committed by girls, whether indirectly or in-your-face, has less to do with shifting sex roles than with broader social stress. Violence by either sex intensifies in times of transition—such as in wartime, or during an upheaval of cultural norms. At the end of the twentieth century in North America, women are changing their patterns of aggression, but they are also, at the margins, engaging in violence more intensely. When Mohammad observed that prison reflected the world, she did not mean the feminist world, she meant one in which poverty, drug abuse, and family dissolution are tilting us all toward chaos.

In New York City in 1994, girls committed one third of all serious offenses—assault, robbery, harassment—against teachers. In 1991, they were arrested for more than one thousand felonies. Los Angeles now counts about six thousand female gang members, and research on the gangs finds that girls are engaging in vandalism, narcotics, assault, battery, rape, burglary, extortion, robbery, and murder. Perhaps most significantly, the shift is visible across the demographic landscape, from New York and L.A. to suburbs of Canadian cities like Toronto. "There's an increase in the intensity of violence," says Toronto youth worker Lew Golding. "Before, a girl might have pulled hair. Now she has a knife. It's not necessarily more, it's what they're doing. We see girls who had to transfer schools because other girls were going to beat them up. That's leading them to form gangs, and then they discover the power, [which is] something the guys have already been through. Girls are getting physically and mentally tougher."

In general, girls appear to be committing the most severe acts of violence in groups, suggesting that they, like partners in crime, still need group permission to break their feminine taboos. For instance: In October 1995, two Maryland girls were charged with armed carjacking; in Lorrain, Ohio, two girls were charged with conspiracy to murder their teacher; in L.A., three sisters fatally stabbed an elderly woman in an apparent thrill kill; in Brooklyn, three teenage girls shot and killed a livery cab driver; in Calgary, in the same month, two teenage girls committed the identical crime.

"In the late 'seventies, you got a pattern, more women were getting involved in crimes," says Leroy Orozco. "It's increased, the robberies, the gang violence. They always had gals in the gangs, when I grew up in East L.A., but never like now. They'll go out on their own. This is the bank robbery capital of the world, and it's always been just guys, maybe had a woman driver, and then it seemed like the last couple years women were participating. They'd shoot guards. We had one where the bank caught it on video, two girls shot an old lady."

If the modus operandi of the teenaged girl is shifting, so, too, are the targets and motives of adult violent offenders. In a review of prison records of homicidal women in Julia Tutwiler Prison in Alabama from 1929 to 1985, the criminologist Penelope Hanke found that 95 percent of the stranger homicides committed by white women had occurred after 1970, as well as 60 percent of both family and friend murders. For black women, the nonfamily/business category had also increased. Ralph Weisheit, of Illinois State University, reviewed the records of 460 murderesses incarcerated between 1940 and 1983 and found that the most important change over time was motive. Murder in the course of robbery jumped from 18 percent of cases to 42 percent, while domestic violence fell from 22 percent to 17 percent. Refuting the feminist/economic basis of the liberation hypothesis, Weisheit found no differences in whether the women were married or single, or what kind of postfeminist employment opportunities they had—most murderesses were, and are, unemployed. In Coramae Richey Mann's study of homicide in six U.S. cities, over half of the victims of women turned out not to be cheating lovers and abusive husbands but children, friends, siblings, and acquaintances. More than half of the homicide offenders had prior arrest records, and more than a third had violent arrest records.

Under the circumstances, which suggest a widening diversity in women's aggressive behavior, it is increasingly urgent that our culture acknowledge violence as a human, rather than gendered, phenomenon. This is true not only as it applies to family violence research, and biocriminology, and studies of youth crime, but also in the way it applies to women themselves. Women have reached a dangerous crossroads. On the one hand, we are discovering our capacity for explicit masculine-style aggression. On the other hand, even as we commit traditionally male acts of violence, a chorus of voices rises to proclaim our innocence. We assert our victimhood. We champion our righteous rage. We are acquitted in the courts and by the community for lashing out at our husbands and lovers, at strangers, at men as symbols of our oppression.

Now that more than twelve million American women own handguns, we must develop a vocabulary of motive that incorporates concepts of female power and accountability. It is essential that the paper silhouettes on the firing range don't evolve into flesh-and-blood targets; that men do not become the targets of our guns purely on the basis of their maleness. Consider such slogans, circulating in the early 1990s on bathroom walls: "Dead men tell no lies." "Dead men don't rape!" "The way to a man's heart is through his chest." "So many men. So little ammunition." The individual man is not relevant; all men serve as symbolic targets. And this is true along a wide continuum, from permissibly sexist jokes about men to the applause garnered by women who kill. The message being conveyed is that women, being blameless, are entitled to victimize without consequence. It was in that context that Aileen Wuornos killed, and in that climate of sanctimonious wrath that she gained her sympathizers. As Candice Skrapec observed in 1993, in an essay about female serial killers, "A woman's anger and need for empowerment will be directed at the power-brokers, those she has experienced as victimizing her. She will seek to punish them for being men." With what result? "The victim becomes the victimizer."

• • •

Betty Broderick, a heroine in parts of America for shooting her husband dead, breezes into an interview room at Frontera Prison for Women in southern California with all the aplomb of the celebrity she has become, tossing jokes over her shoulder to the public relations woman who follows cheerfully behind. Broderick wears an expensive and sporty baby-blue track suit, a paler shade of her impossibly wide blue eyes. Her bobbed blond hair flips pertly at each earlobe, and she is plump and healthy and high-spirited, apparently unaffected by the first four years she has spent incarcerated for double homicide.

She plops down on a cushioned leather chair and throws her elbows onto the table, fixing her interviewer with a high-beam smile. The room, adjacent to the warden's office, appears to be a meeting room for prison officials, with business and management books strewn about. Broderick has received everybody who's anybody, from Oprah Winfrey to *Vanity Fair* writer Bella Stumbo. "I have visits from very far a*way*," she says, "like Pennsylvania, Ohio, North Carolina, and Canada and—not professional people, just normal people who want to spend money to visit me!" Her gestures are exuberant and oddly teenaged, with exaggerated sighs and rolled eyes, as if the currency of her charm as a San Diego housewife, married to an esteemed medical malpractice lawyer, was to be irrepressibly cute.

"Anyway," she continues, "my out-of-town visitor this weekend had a very interesting thing to say. He doesn't think the real, true Betty Broderick story can ever be told until I'm dead, because society does not allow women to protect themselves and their children, to use self-defense. In fiction," she explains, "you can have a Rambo character. But in reality, you cannot tell the real Betty Broderick story where I come out to be the hero in the end, because I withstood incredible forces for so long, and then did this outrageous thing, because I'm real, and you can't applaud a real person." She sits back in her armchair to emphasize her point.

Broderick has, however, been widely applauded for her violence. For a giddy spell of two or three years, she was the toast of California housewives, a heroine on the talk-show circuit, the subject of a major true-crime biography. Many San Diego residents wrote approvingly on her behalf to the newspapers. "She worked hard to send her husband through law school," read one letter to the *San Diego Tribune*, "and how did he reward her? He traded her in for a younger model." Ergo, he and the younger model had to pay.

One quiet, sea-scented dawn in her hometown of La Jolla, California, Betty Broderick awoke to reread another letter from her ex-husband's lawyer, quarreling with her about yet another fractious point in their wildly bitter custody battle. Infuriated, stressed to the breaking point, feeling very black indeed, Broderick drove her GMC Suburban from her newly purchased condo to her ex-husband's home. She broke in, fumbled her way around through the shadows, found the bedroom, and shot him dead. His young wife, Linda, whom Broderick still refers to as "that cheap bimbo nothing," died beside him in the bed.

The violence of November 1989 was the culmination of hostilities between Daniel and Elisabeth Broderick dating from the start of that decade, when Betty first suspected he was having an affair with his legal assistant, twenty-two-year-old Linda Kolkena. Initially, her response to her husband's affair was to burn his clothes, wreck their bedroom, and break the windows to their home. She spray-painted the walls; she smeared cream pies on his sweaters and shirts. Daniel Broderick coldly refused to respond. He kept being her husband; he kept having his affair. The tension grew extreme, and so did the displays of temper. Finally, Dan filed for divorce. The experience was shattering. In many ways, Broderick's life mirrored the world in which millions of women once dwelled. It was Betty Friedan's world, described in *The Feminine Mystique* as one in which country clubs, cocktails dos, and well-tended gardens passed for wifely fulfillment. The women who entered this world in the 1950s and 1960s, after educations at Smith and Vassar and Radcliffe, left their intellectual passions behind in exchange for a vow. Although it may have been unconscious and was certainly unspoken, the vow they expected their husbands to give them was this: "I will remain true to you, and to the life that we build, in honor of what you invested." When that vow was broken, which in so many cases it was, women felt a degree of betrayal and fury that far exceeded their objective predicament—one that often involved the end of a loveless marriage, and an alimony settlement that helped them build their lives anew.

In her late thirties, when her husband left, Broderick was a beautiful and literate woman. It wasn't difficult for her to start a new life. There are photos of her at Club Med in Tahiti; taking her sons camping in the Rocky Mountains; palling around with a girlfriend up the coast in San Francisco. She began dating a new man. "I met Brad two weeks after my husband walked out, and Brad is a major babe. He's just a really nice guy." Was all that enough to carry her through from the generational frustration articulated by Betty Friedan to the freedoms championed by subsequent feminists? It's hard to outgrow one's paradigm, one's model for survival.

So it was that a woman who was granted sixteen thousand dollars a month in alimony in the aftermath of her divorce felt entitled to say: "He took my home . . . and my money," and to ram her car through Daniel Broderick's new front door. "There's lots of men out there who would love to wad the ex-wife up in a ball and throw her in that trash can," she says, lowering her voice. "Well, you can't do that. Can you?"

After the murders, Broderick began to assemble an account from the vocabulary of motive, describing herself alternately as a mama bear defending her cubs and a battered wife fighting back. "I didn't go there in a rage," she says, of what happened on that catastrophic morning, "I didn't go there like, 'I've had it with these two.' I went there—unfortunately for the feminists, because they'd love to think I just, 'Blam' [she laughs], and I guess it makes a better movie—but I went there as such a wreck, and I was literally going to go down to the beach and just blow my brains out, and I just thought of my kids. Because if I did that . . . I'd leave them with *him*. And I couldn't do that. So I'm going to go over there and I'm going to talk to that son of a bitch one more time, human being to human being, not in court where he was the big shot and I was spit."

Broderick insists that she was actually going to kill herself but shot in the bedroom out of panic. "I didn't aim at those people, I aimed at the telephone. They were going for the telephone and they *moved* into the line of fire!"

Broderick's rage, however, is abundantly evident in a conversation (recorded on Dan's answering machine) with her youngest son, Danny, which would later be played in court:

Sobbing, the boy asked her, "Don't you think being mad for two years is enough, Mom?"

Her response was unequivocal. "No . . . that money is mine. I earned it for twenty years of hard work and total shit from that asshole."

Danny wails, "What else do you care about besides your money and your share of things to own?"

Broderick responds, "I put up with shit in my face and you kids never even knew it. You never knew he was fucking Linda while he was married to me, did you?"

"No," the boy says, "but now, you know, if you care about your family you would stop saying bad words."

But Broderick had lost what was sacred; now all is profane: "I'd rather be a lady and wonderful person and call a cunt a cunt . . . I wish he'd just die. I wish he would get drunk and drive his fucking car . . . then he'll be gone off the earth."

Broderick is a study in the contradiction between script and reality for women in her generation. Socialized to behave without ego, she is completely unaware how strongly she displays one; socialized to be sunny and supportive, she is totally unaware of how destructive she has been. By interpreting herself as girlish, kind of incompetent, vulnerable to abuse, and supremely maternal, she incorporates many of the self-exonerative dodges of her sex, even while her fury and indignation shine through. "Never for a moment," she says about Linda Kolkena, "was I jealous [of her]." Yet the woman is dead by her hand.

Broderick's behavior is hers alone, but her account of it, and the way that account was received, reflects a widely accepted idea in this era about permissible female aggression. The idea, and the perceptions it springs from, haven't evolved since the case of Jean Harris, who shot her lover Herman Tarnower in 1980. If the roles had been reversed in that case, with Tarnower arriving at Harris's home in darkness, armed with a .38, leaving her bloodied corpse in the bedroom, we would have a straightforward instance of violence against women. Instead, many women hailed Harris's deed as judicious revenge against men who throw older women over for younger lovers. The fact that Harris claimed her intent was suicidal, that somehow the gun ended up pointing at Tarnower, did not prevent her, like Broderick, from accepting kudos for her deed. After receiving clemency from New York Governor Mario Cuomo, she embarked upon a vigorous lecture tour. In 1994, when she flew to Toronto to talk in a "Unique Lives" series presented by female celebrities, she was shocked to find herself turned back at Pearson International Airport for her record as a felon. "They're treating me like a criminal!" she huffed. Her supporters loudly protested. Yet what Harris had benefited from all along was not a feminism that applauds women for standing on their own two feet, but a deeply paternalistic view of white, middle-class women as good girls with good manners, who couldn't possibly have the guts to blow someone away in a rage.

Then came Lorena Bobbitt, emasculating her husband, blaming it on madness, and finding herself feted both in the United States and in her native Ecuador. Aileen Wuornos was honored with art exhibits and protests in *The New York Times*. When the Miss Canada International beauty queen punched another woman out in a bar in September 1996, knocking her victim's tooth out, she held a press conference blaming the incident on her own sexual abuse, and supporters flooded her with mail. Lesser-known women gained support within their communities all over the continent for this illogical psychological couplet of standing up and lying down. Shoot with a bang and dodge with a whimper. Bravo to the violent and pity them. Do women have no better way to stake their claim?

Insofar as female violence is incorporated into a victim-feminist heroic, the failure to take explicit responsibility for our actions poses a conundrum whose implications extend well beyond the lot of the criminal woman. Cheering on people who gain fame through sensational crime yet fail to concede their own culpability directly undermines what good can come of women's recognition of their capacity for aggression. It sabotages the credibility of every female cop and combat soldier; every battered wife who stands up to abuse and wants to own it; every criminal woman—from Marti Salas-Tarin to the death row inmate Guinevere Garcia—who wants to concede the destruction she has caused and promote herself as a rational actor; every teenaged girl who knows herself to be powerful, but can only articulate her status as victim. Women have virtually no access to anger management counseling, sex offender therapy, child abuse prevention programs, and prison security—all because we won't concede their fundamental agency.

At her trial, Broderick's defense team argued that she had been the victim of domestic psychological abuse. "I made up a term that applies to me," she explains. "It's white-collar domestic violence. A normal guy feels frustrated, losing control, and he physically intimidates and threatens. My husband didn't have to resort to that. He could use the system." Broderick recently organized a letter-writing campaign among her supporters, urging that notes be addressed to the Board of Prison Terms in Sacramento, to argue for her release on the basis of the new California law that authorizes commutation of sentences when "evidence of battered woman syndrome" is found. The evidence has been newly defined to include "the effects of physical, emotional, or mental abuse upon the beliefs, perceptions, or behavior of victims of domestic violence where it appears the criminal behavior was the result."

When Broderick first entered Frontera, several dozen women were members of a group called Convicted Women Against Abuse, founded by Brenda Clubine, who attacked her husband with a bottle and then killed him with a gun. Thirty-four of the women in the group have applied to Governor Pete Wilson for clemency. Clubine also helped to start the California Coalition for Battered Women in prison, in San Francisco. Across the country, a movement toward clemency for battered women gained momentum in the early 1990s, resulting in releases and pardons in a number of states. It was and is a valid movement, rectifying the wrongs that had been done to these women when their entrapment was misunderstood by the courts.

But it also spread into the general prison population as a mantra of self-justification and self-pity. "A lot of women do not act accountable," Lieutenant Wong says of the inmates at Chowchilla, where Broderick spent her first two years. "They're all saying they're battered women. It's a hell of a stretch. It's in vogue."

Well, what else can they say? What other model for redemption has been offered them? "Various factions within the [male] prisons have their spiritual leaders," Veronica Compton wrote from Washington State in *Prison Life* magazine. "They claim to follow Martin Luther King, Jr., Malcolm X, Zapata, Great Grandfather, Jesus, Marx . . . the list has no women. Why? Where are they? Gloria Steinem, Maya Angelou, Betty Friedan? Are they out there?"

"Women don't need heroines," Arlene Mohammad counters. "Their needs are different. What they miss from their lives is different. Men tend to think about self. [Male prisoners] look to self-growth. Their world revolves around them, whether it's weight lifting—physical improvement—or studying in the law library—intellectual improvement. Females are nurturers, their world revolves around others." With all due respect to Mohammad, an articulate, measured person, she herself is in prison for committing the ultimate antinurturant act of murder. Most women in prison are there because they took an antisocial, antirelational stand. At the moment of their crimes, their world did not revolve around their children, their families, or their community. It revolved around themselves. Of 254 female killers at Bedford Hills in 1994, only 12 percent had killed in a domestic dispute. Ten percent had killed children through "abuse or neglect." The others shot or stabbed in drug-related conflicts, sexual rivalries, or for some other reason. Across New York State, 420 women were convicted of murder or manslaughter between March 1992 and May 1993. Of a cross section studied, 58 percent murdered people outside the family. A quarter murdered husbands or lovers, and 12 percent murdered children. For myriad reasons, these women rebelled against the relational universe in which their sex is expected to perpetually orbit. To perceive themselves solely as nurturers is to live a life exiled from their own experience.

When anthropologist Victoria Burbank talked to the Aboriginal women of Australia about their use of aggression, it struck her that there was something immensely positive in, simply, their awareness of their own power. "In being aggressive," she mused, "[women] potentially augment rather than diminish themselves." By taking "an aggressive stance," they express their determination not to be victimized, not to be "acted upon." They stop subscribing to a romantic view of their own submission, cease threatening to fling themselves into rivers of masculine pity, and start owning their own strength, ingenuity, and guts. In his memoir of boyhood aggression, the novelist Richard Ford concluded: "And in the end, it seems simply better and more generally informative that I know at least this much about myself—and learn caution from it, forbearance, empathy—rather than know nothing about it at all."

One Friday night at Miracle House in Merced, seven women, Latina and white, gather in Marti's living room for their weekly motivation session. They are trying to learn the lessons their own lives have taught them without the benefit that Richard Ford had, of behavior being culturally acknowledged. It is late February. The air outside is soft and fragrant and damp, and the women sit on plush brown carpet and two donated sofas, with their notebooks scattered on the plywood coffee table. Over the nonworking fireplace hangs a big, framed photograph of the participants: Marti, Lisa, Tina, and Cat all decked out on a Sunday afternoon, grinning into the camera with newfound pride.

Earlier in the day, Marti took her youngest charge, twenty-year-old Yvette, to court to appear for a sentencing hearing. Yvette is olive-skinned, doe-eyed, and demure; she was arrested for possession of crank. "Man, can a woman fool men," booms Marti. "You get up there, dress nice, put a smile on. Man!" Everyone chuckles.

Yvette says that that's why Marti's program is so good: "I never had nobody discipline me before." She means somebody looking her in the eye, saying, "Yo, girl, don't pull that shit with me. Respect yourself."

Tina, a graduate of Marti's program, is a tough-minded twenty-eight-year-old former crank dealer, now a working citizen with a trim nine-to-five hairdo and spiffy new glasses. She's impatient and shrewd and deems a lot of stuff around her to be bullshit. Tina had contempt for the counselors in prison, "with their degrees and their big words." She didn't think they got it. "Come to me on *my* level," she told them, "then we'll talk." Marti had a hard time bringing Tina into line: "It took me sixty days to break her." Tina says it's because the one thing she had to learn was to "humble" herself: "You ain't runnin' nothing but your mouth," she told herself in the mirror, deciding to cooperate with Marti. Tina thinks Marti's program is terrific, not for the Christian part, per se, more for Marti's strength of personality and her insistence on personal responsibility.

Themes of self-restraint and accountability are uppermost in these women's lives. They do not perceive themselves to be victims. They see themselves as having gone willfully and rebelliously down the wrong road, damaging themselves and their families en route. As one—an ace drug dealer at Chowchilla who dealt a dime bag over the wall as she was being released—tells the others: "The wisdom, I always had. But I didn't have the constructive motivation to use it." She is borrowing the term from an ex-con turned motivational speaker named Gordon Graham, who is something of a guru to these women. On Friday nights, Marti has her girls watch his videos, which come in seven sessions, with a workbook to use in between as homework.

"We give up accountability," Gordon Graham says on his video, addressing a classroom of cons, "and then we're always waiting for somebody else to fix it for us. It's not *my* fault. Society did it." A thin man, balding and bespectacled, Graham sports a short-sleeved plaid dress shirt and looks like a high school math teacher. The last time he got arrested for robbing a bank, he tells his class, he never dreamed it was his own fault. All his fury focused on the fact that his partner hadn't *told* Graham that he couldn't drive standard, the knucklehead, and foiled their getaway. If the cops showed up, that wasn't his fault, either. The cops were cheating. Marti grins; she knows what he means. She remembers her own busts for heroin. "You get it so twisted around," she says, "it's like the cops' fault for *being* there if you get caught."

Gordon Graham's point is that anybody can play the part of a victim, even when they're victimizing. It's guilt-free. It's also a dead end. "You gotta make your own choices," he says, "or you're always going to have somebody jerking you around. You cannot get motivated by looking at losing." The Miracle House women nod, as if to say Amen. They are strong, these women, and opportunistic, ever hip to their own advantage. Perhaps they are victims, in a broad systemic sense, but merely broadcasting that fact has given them nothing to work with, just righteous air to breathe. What interests them is finding a way to act constructively. In the absence of any sort of feminist conversation about women's responsibility, they wound up cobbling together their own script. The church gives them a way to struggle openly with their conscience and promote their own complexity in a manner that is not preoccupied, exclusively, with how they are acted upon. God lets them own their mistakes. Gordon Graham, a guy on a video, gives them a way to address them.

After the session, the conversation turns to this and that, anecdotes and musings, and, after some prodding, disinterested reflection on the famous women they served time with in the mix: Broderick, the Manson girls, Dorothea Puente, Carol Bundy, none of whom are half as titillating or inspiring to ordinary inmates as they are to the world beyond. Then someone brings up another woman, now seeking clemency, who also had her time in the sun: forty-one-year-old Ellie Nesler. In the spring of 1993, a middle-aged man who had been accused of molesting several boys at a summer camp, including Nesler's son, sat quietly, shackled, at his preliminary hearing in Jamestown, California. Also sitting in court, Nesler thought she saw the accused man smirk. She left the courthouse, got a gun, somehow evaded the metal detectors on her return, and shot Daniel Driver five times, point-blank, in the head. Overnight she became a heroine, an applauded representative of what one op-ed writer called "the spontaneous eruption of American motherly virtue." Fundraisers were held to raise money for her defense; telegrams and letters arrived; talk shows offered her star appearances. The fervor died down somewhat when reporters discovered that "Mrs. America" had a criminal record for auto theft. She retained a strong contingent of feminist and provigilante supporters and was found guilty of manslaughter rather than murder. At her sentencing, on January 16, 1994, Nesler said: "I don't want my little boy growing up thinking it's okay to kill someone."

Surely she has just taught him that it's so.

Our deeds have long spoken for us. It is time that we found the right words.

The consequences of our refusal to concede female contributions to violence are manifold. It affects our capacity to promote ourselves as autonomous and responsible beings. It affects our ability to develop a literature about ourselves that encompasses the full array of human emotion and experience. It demeans the right our victims have to be valued. And it radically impedes our ability to recognize dimensions of power that have nothing to do with formal structures of patriarchy. Perhaps above all, the denial of women's aggression profoundly undermines our attempt as a culture to understand violence, to trace its causes and to quell them.

NOTES

GIRLS WILL BE GIRLS

2   Letters from Anthony Riggs to Tina Killie: Paul Srubas, " 'Angel Tina' loved letters from Riggs," Gannett News Service, March 23, 1991.

3   "the great American tragedy": Brenda Ingersoll, "Relatives stunned that soldier slain after returning from war," *Detroit News*, March 19, 1991.

3   "during every 100 hours on our streets": James Gannon, "U.S. faces another war—in the streets of America," Gannett News Service, March 23, 1991.

4   "a new war needs to be fought on the home front": Yolanda Woodlee, Heidi Mae Bratt, "City mourns Gulf soldier slain 2 days after return," *Detroit News*, March 23, 1991.

4   "I can't believe I've waited": Cato Riggs interviewed by Brenda Ingersoll, "Relatives stunned that soldier slain after returning from war," *Detroit News*, March 19, 1991.

6   "what I did, I did for a soldier": Holley quoted by Bill Nichols, "A not-so-random slaying?" *USA Today*, March 27, 1991, p. 1. The same article reported the rumors about Toni Cato Riggs.

8   Primate origins of human aggression: Richard Wrangham and Dale Peterson, *Demonic Males: Apes and the Origins of Human Violence* (New York: Houghton Mifflin, 1996).

8   "their greater endowment of aggression": Anthony Storr, *Human Aggression* (New York: Penguin, 1968), p. 85.

8   "authority, control": James Messerschmidt, *Masculinities and Crime: Critique and Reconceptualization of Theory* (Lanham, Md.: Rowman & Littlefield, 1993), p. 85.

8   testosterone, the oldest chestnut: J. Archer, "The Influence of Testosterone on Human Aggression," *British Journal of Psychology* 82 (1991). For additional refutation of causative effects, see M. Haug et al., eds., *The Aggressive Female* (Den Haag, The Netherlands: CIP-Gegevens Koninklyke Bibliotheek, 1992); David Adams, "Biology Does Not Make Men More Aggressive Than Women," in Kaj Björkqvist and Pirkko Niemela, eds., *Of Mice and Women: Aspects of Female Aggression* (New York: Academic Press, 1992), pp. 17–25.

9   psychologist David Benton: "Hormones and Human Aggression," in *Of Mice and Women*, p. 42.

9   head injury: "Woman Blinded by Spring from Truck," Lindsay Scotton, *Toronto Star*, April 10, 1995.

9   "bullying, vandalism . . .": Herbert Needleman, Julie Riess, Michael Tobin, Gretchen Biesecker, Joel Greenhouse, "Bone Lead Levels and Delinquent Behavior," *Journal of the American Medical Association* 275 (February 7, 1996), 363–369.

10   rodent version of soccer hooligans: Natalie Angier, "Gene Defect Tied to Violence in Male Mice," *The New York Times*, November 23, 1995.

10   "chronically low levels of arousal": Adrian Raine, Mark Williams, and Peter H. Venables, "Better Autonomic Conditioning and Faster

Electrodermal Half-recovery Time at Age 15 Years as Possible Protective Factors Against Crime at Age 29 Years," *Developmental Psychology* 32:4 (July 1996), 624.

11   primate loyalty: Sarah Blaffer Hrdy, *The Woman Who Never Evolved* (Cambridge, Mass.: Harvard University Press, 1981), p. 173.

11   primate killing and exclusionary tactics: Reijo Holmström, in Björkqvist and Niemela, eds., *Of Mice and Women*, pp. 297–305.

12   "there is very little support in the psychological literature": Anne Colby and William Danon, "Listening to a Different Voice: A Review of Gilligan's *A Different Voice*," in M. R. Walsh, ed., *The Psychology of Women: Ongoing Debates* (New Haven: Yale University Press, 1987).

12   Seventy percent of respondents to a 1968 survey: R. Stark and J. McEvoy III, "Middle-Class Violence," *Psychology Today* 4 (November 1970): 52–65.

12   Every year since 1976: Sourcebook of Criminal Justice Statistics (Washington, D.C.: United States Department of Justice). In 1991, more than twice as many men as women responded "yes" to this question: 52 vs. 22 percent. Nearly twice as many American men as women were the victims of violent crime of any kind. Moreover, in 1994, 13 percent of men, vs. 10 percent of women, answered "yes" to the question "When you were growing up, do you remember any time when you were punched or kicked or choked by a parent or guardian?"

12   "culture of honor": Richard E. Nisbett and Dov Cohen, *Culture of Honor: The Psychology of Violence in the South* (Boulder, Colo.: Westview Press, 1996).

13   British men follow a different cultural model: Elliott Leyton, *Men of Blood: Murder in Everyday Life* (Toronto: McClelland & Stuart, 1996).

13   women engage publicly in physical aggression: Victoria K. Burbank, "Female Aggression in Cross-Cultural Perspective," *Behavior Science Research* 21 (1987), 70–100. Burbank found that adultery was one of the most frequent reasons for women's physical aggression against mates. She also found that other women were by far the more frequent targets of female

aggression, noted in 91 percent of the 137 societies, whereas men were targets in only 54 percent. See also V. K. Burbank, "Cross-Cultural Perspectives on Aggression in Women and Girls: An Introduction," *Sex Roles* 30:3/4 (February 1994).

13   Margarita Island, off the coast of Venezuela: H. B. Kimberley Cook, "Matrifocality and Female Aggression in Margariteno Society," in Björkqvist and Niemela, eds., *Of Mice and Women*, pp. 149–61.

14   Aboriginal women in Australia: V. K. Burbank, *Fighting Women: Anger and Aggression in Aboriginal Australia* (Berkeley: University of California Press, 1994), pp. 98–104.

14   aggressive strategies on the island of Vanatinai: Maria Lepowsky, "Women, Men and Aggression in an Egalitarian Society," *Sex Roles* 30:3/4 (February 1994), 199–213.

15   female rulers have mysteriously disappeared: Antonia Fraser, *The Warrior Queens* (New York: Alfred A. Knopf, 1988).

16   At the height of international terrorism: Richard W. Kobetz and H. H. A. Cooper, "Target Terrorism: Providing Protective Services" (Risk International, 1979). See also Eileen MacDonald, *Shoot the Women First* (London: Arrow Books, 1991).

16   slaughter at Kubaye Hill: "Prison Nuns Exemplify Dimensions to Carnage," Vincent Browne, *Irish Times*, October 2, 1996; Rwanda: "Women Turned Killers," *The Guardian*, August 26, 1995.

16   "I have no illusions": Carol Tavris, *Mismeasure of Woman: Why Women Are Not the Better Sex, the Inferior Sex or the Opposite Sex* (New York: Touchstone/Simon & Schuster, 1992), p. 91.

17   Of 314 studies on human aggression: A. Frodi, J. Macaulay, and P. R. Thome, "Are Women Always Less Aggressive Than Men?" *Psychological Bulletin* 84 (1977), 634–660.

17   "In our view": Claudia Frey and Siegfried Hoppe-Graff, "Serious and Playful Aggression in Brazilian Girls and Boys," *Sex Roles* 30:3/4 (February 1994), 249–269. See also J. Condy and D. Ross, "Sex and Aggression: The

Influence of Gender Label on the Perception of Aggression in Children," *Child Development* 56 (1985).

17   indirect aggression defined: Björkqvist and Niemela, eds., *Of Mice and Women*, p. 8.

17   what girls did to compete with rivals: Kaj Björkqvist, Karin Osterman, and Ari Kaukiainen, "The Development of Direct and Indirect Aggressive Strategies in Males and Females," Björkqvist and Niemela, eds., *Of Mice and Women*, p. 51–63.

18   high school girls most afraid of "other girls": Frederick Mathews, *The Badge & the Book: Building Effective Police/School Partnerships to Combat Youth Violence* (Ottawa: Solicitor General Canada, 1995), p. 11.

19   modes of female aggression: Ilsa M. Glazer and Wahipa Abu Ras, "On Aggression, Human Rights, and Hegemonic Discourse: The Case of a Murder for Family Honor in Israel," *Sex Roles* 30:3/4 (February 1994), 269–302.

19   "When I was a leader of a gang": Frederick Mathews, *Youth Gangs on Youth Gangs* (Ottawa: Solicitor General Canada, 1993), p. 26.

19   Polynesian aggression: Rolf Kuschel, "Women are Women and Men Are Men: How Bellonese Women Get Even," in Björkqvist and Niemela, eds., *Of Mice and Women*, pp. 173–185.

20   "It seems unlikely": Colin Wilson, *The Mammoth Book of True Crime* (London: Robinson Publishing, 1988), p. 175.

20   "criminality of women is largely masked criminality": Otto Pollack, *The Criminality of Women* (New York: A. S. Barnes, 1961), p. 3.

22   trauma reenactment syndrome: Dusty Miller, *Women Who Hurt Themselves: A Book of Hope and Understanding* (New York: Basic Books, 1994).

23   tattooing: Mary Valentis and Anne Devane, *Female Rage: Unlocking Its Secrets, Claiming Its Power* (New York: Carol Southern Books, 1994), p. 85.

23   "schizophrenic . . .": Miller, *Women Who Hurt Themselves*, p. 154.

23   female suicide attempts: *Youth Risk Behavior Surveillance Survey* (Washington, D.C.: National Center for Health Statistics, 1992).

27   African-American women have a different experience of violence: Laura T. Fishman, "Slave Women, Resistance and Criminality: A Prelude to Future Accommodation," *Women & Criminal Justice* 7:1 (1995), 35–63. "The slave women who struck back did not suffer a paralysis of fear," Fishman notes; "it was not unthinkable to stand up and fight." See also Lamb and McDermott (*Criminology* 23:4 (1985), 81–97), who conducted a study with the National Crime Survey on juvenile offenders from 1973 to 1981. The data support the proposition that differences by sex in violent criminal behavior are greater among whites than among blacks, and that differences by race are greater among females than among males.

28   Cato's school experience: Correspondence with author.

29   homicides in Chicago: Carolyn Rebecca Block and Antigone Christakos, "Partner Homicide in Chicago Over 29 Years," *Crime & Delinquency* 41:4 (1995).

29   female homicide in six U.S. cities: Coramae Richey Mann, "Black Female Homicide in the United States," *Journal of Interpersonal Violence*, June 1990, pp. 176–197.

30   "resource for self-protection": Nancy C. Jurik and Russ Winn, "Gender and Homicide: A Comparison of Men and Women Who Kill," *Violence and Victims* 5:4 (1990), 227–242.

30   AP wire stories: "Woman Charged with Killing Infant Nephew with Stun Gun"; "Woman Sentenced to Prison for Killing Infant Son"; "HIV-Infected Woman Sentenced After Biting Elderly Man"; "Daughter Accused of Setting Fatal Housefire Because of Dispute with Mom"; "A Daring Escape, a Trip, a Capture"; "Mother Charged with Lighting House Fire That Killed Her Two Children." November 23, 1994.

31   robbery arrest rate for women: Darrell Steffensmeier and Cathy Streifel, "Trends in Female Crime, 1960–1990," in Concetta C. Culliver, ed., *Female Criminality: The State of the Art* (New York: Garland, 1993), pp. 368–74. By 1990, the arrest rate was 31 per 100,000 women. By 1992, the arrest rate had increased to 50 per 100,000 women: U.S. Department of Justice,

"Crime in the United States," FBI Uniform Crime Reports, 1992, Washington, D.C.

32   aggravated assault and robbery rates for girls, 1960 and 1990: FBI Uniform Crime Reports, 1992.

32   felony arrest rates for girls, 1991 and 1992: FBI Uniform Crime Reports, 1992.

32   proportion of arrests: FBI Uniform Crime Reports, 1992.

32   suicide drop: Centers for Disease Control, Atlanta, Georgia.

MAYBE YOU MISTOOK ME FOR AN ANGEL

33   Margaret Drabble, *The Waterfall* (London: Weidenfeld and Nicolson, 1969)

36   "You're innocent. You're the victim:" Quoted in Scott Burnside and Alan Cairns, *Deadly Innocence* (Toronto: Warner Books, 1995), p. 354.

37   "Women will try to use their femininity": Interview with the author.

37   police identifying female offenders with their mothers, sisters, or daughters": H. Allen and C. Simonsen, *Corrections in America* (New York: Macmillan, 1986).

37   women least likely to be processed beyond arrest stage: M. D. Krohn, J. P. Curry and S. Nelson-Kilger, "Is Chivalry Dead? An Analysis of Changes in Police Disposition of Males and Females," *Criminology* 21 (1983), 417–438. Police are particularly unlikely to arrest if there are children at home and no alternative caretaker. See Meda Chesney-Lind, "Judicial Paternalism and the Female Offender: Training Women to Know Their Place," *Crime and Delinquency* 35 (1977).

40   vocabulary of motive: Allison Morris, *Women, Crime and Criminal Justice* (Oxford: Basil Blackwell, 1987), p. 50. The vocabulary of motive was first proposed in 1940 by C. W. Mills: "Situated Actions and Vocabularies of Motive," *American Sociological Review* 5 (1940), 904.

41   menstruation studies: Morris, *Women, Crime and Criminal Justice*, p. 50.

41   Rikers Island inmates: Robert J. Kelley, "Vindictive Vindications: Crime Causation from the Inmates' Standpoint," *The Keeper's Voice* 17:2 (1996), 9–13.

42   "They appear to have a distinct problem in self-consciously acknowl-edging . . . rage": Jack Katz, *Seductions of Crime: Moral and Sensual Attractions in Doing Evil* (New York: Basic Books, 1988), p. 50.

42   premenstrual syndrome as homicide defense: Morris, *Women, Crime and Criminal Justice*, p. 51.

44   "Many women who kill their abusers start out intending to commit sui-cide": Lenore Walker, cited by Alene Kristal, "You've Come a Long Way, Baby: The Battered Woman Syndrome Revisited," *New York Law School Journal of Human Rights* 9 (1991), 111–160.

44   suicide rates in Chicago: Block and Christakos, "Partner Homicide in Chicago."

45   "Some severely depressed parents": John McCormack, *Newsweek* cover story, November 14, 1994.

46   "It is a crucial moment": John Glenn Gray, *The Warriors: Reflections on Men in Battle* (New York: Harper Torch Books, 1970), p. 184.

46   psychiatrists' reports: All cited by Kirk Makin, "Bernardo Might Have Killed Homolka, Doctors Say," *Toronto Globe & Mail*, September 5, 1995, p. 10.

47   Carol Bundy to Doug Clark: Quoted by Louise Farr, *The Sunset Murders* (New York: Pocket Books, 1993), p. 216.

47   a book she was reading in prison: Christine McGuire and Carla Norton, *Perfect Victim: The True Story of "The Girl in the Box" by the D. A. Who Prosecuted Her Captor* (New York: Dell, 1988).

48   case of Francine Hughes: Faith McNulty, *The Burning Bed: The True Story of Francine Hughes—A Beaten Wife Who Rebelled* (New York: Harcourt Brace Jovanovich, 1980).

49   Sturm: David France, "Life After Death: Battered Women Who Killed Their Husbands," *Good Housekeeping*, July 1995.

50   learned helplessness: Lenore E. Walker, *The Battered Woman* (New York: Harper & Row, 1979), p. 49.

50   "only men kill in anger": Walker, cited by Gerald Caplan, "Battered Wives, Battered Justice," *National Review*, February 25, 1991.

51   domestic violence not an appropriate example of learned helplessness: Christopher Peterson, Steven F. Maier, and Martin E. P. Seligman, *Learned Helplessness: A Theory for the Age of Personal Control* (London: Oxford University Press, 1993), p. 239.

51   "reasoning doesn't explain how women who are that helpless": Gerald Caplan, "Battered Wives, Battered Justice."

53   men in war: Paul Fussell, *Wartime: Understanding and Behavior in the Second World War* (New York, Oxford: Oxford University Press, 1989), p. 281.

54   survey of California's female prisoners: Barbara Owen and Barbara Bloom, "Profiling Women Prisoners: Findings from National Surveys and a California Sample," *Prison Journal* 75:2 (1995), 179.

54   sample of 1,880 female offenders: J. Crawford, "Tabulation of a Nationwide Survey of State Correctional Facilities for Adult and Juvenile Female Offenders" (College Park, Md.: American Correctional Association).

54   women incarcerated in Florida: William Blount, J. Kuhns, and Ira Silverman, "Intimate Abuse Within an Incarcerated Female Population: Rates, Levels, Criminality, A Continuum and Some Lessons About Self-Identification," in Culliver, ed., *Female Criminality*, p. 413.

55   standpoint epistemology: women have "a more complete view of social reality": Joyce McCarl-Nielson, ed., *Feminist Research Methods: Exemplary Readings in the Social Sciences* (Boulder, Colo.: Westview Press, 1990), p. 10.

55   "centrality of consciousness raising": See Mary Margaret Fonow and Judith A. Cook, eds., *Beyond Methodology: Feminist Scholarship in Lived Research* (Bloomington: Indiana University Press, 1990).

55   Veronica Compton, guest editorial, *Prison Life*, September/October 1995, p. 12.

56   Coramae Richey Mann on abuse and self-defense as rationale: "The Battered Woman Syndrome Is Not a Legitimate Defense," in *Violence Against Women: Current Controversies* (San Diego, Calif.: Greenhaven Press, 1994), pp. 292–300.

56   1848 manifesto: Seneca Falls Convention, "Declaration of Sentiment," cited by Naomi Wolf, *Fire with Fire: The New Female Power and How It Will Change the 21st Century* (New York: Random House, 1994), p. 201.

57   Presentence investigations reports: Kathleen Daly, *Gender, Crime and Punishment* (New Haven, Conn: Yale University Press, 1994), p. 83.

60   Guinevere Garcia described in *The New York Times*: Don Terry, "Hours Before Execution She Sought, Illinois Woman Is Given Clemency," *The New York Times*, January 17, 1996, p. 10.

61   ACLU to *Christian Science Monitor*: James Tyson, "Woman's Pending Execution Revives Death Penalty Furor," January 16, 1996, p. 3.

61   "serious crimes" data for 1987: Rita Simon, "Women in Prison," in Culliver, ed., *Female Criminality*, p. 375.

61   Phoenix, Arizona, study: J. B. Johnston, T. D. Kennedy, and I. Shuman, "Gender Differences in the Sentencing of Felony Offenders," *Federal Probation* 51 (1987).

61   Average sentences for spousal homicide: Patrick A. Langan, U.S. Department of Justice, Bureau of Justice Statistics, October 1995.

62   Men 11 percent more likely than women to be incarcerated: Darrell Steffensmeier, John Kramer, and Cathy Streifel, "Gender and Imprisonment Decisions," *Criminology* 31:3 (1993), 411–446.

    C. Frazier, E. Bock, and J. Henretta, "The Role of Probation Officers in Determining Gender Differences in Sentencing Severity," *Sociological Quarterly* 24 (1983), 305–318. Authors found a 23 percent discrepancy between male and female sentences, with women more likely to be described in psychological terms.

62   1987 review of London crown courts: Hilary Allen, "Rendering Them Harmless: The Professional Portrayal of Women Charged with Serious Violent Crimes," in Pat Carlan and Anne Worrall, eds., *Gender, Crime and Justice* (Philadelphia: Milton Keynes, 1987), pp. 81–94.

For additional research see: Hilary Allen, *Justice Unbalanced* (Oxford: Open University Press, 1987). The argument is frequently advanced that women receive greater lenience because they are often mothers with sole responsibility for their children. But a 1989 study of male and female offenders in the Seattle and New York courts found that the courts were more lenient to the women supporting families than to the men supporting families even if the women were separated or divorced and without the children. Kathleen Daly, "Neither Conflict, Nor Labelling, Nor Paternalism Will Suffice: Intersections of Race, Ethnicity, Gender and Family in Criminal Court Decisions," *Crime & Delinquency* 3:1 (1989). Daly, like other scholars, points to women's childcare responsibilities as perhaps the single greatest argument to keep them out of jail. But to say that women should be freed because they have children is to make too eager a generalization. Some women are in prison because they assaulted or killed their children. A third are there for drug offenses that involved a lifestyle in which their children were the least of their priorities. According to Ralph Weisheit, "What information was available indicated that nearly half of the mothers with children did not have custody of those children at the time of the offense. Surprisingly absent from the reports of prison psychologists were references to distress over separation from children." Ralph Weisheit, "Female Homicide Offenders: Trends over Time in an Institutionalized Population," *Justice Quarterly* 1:4 (December 1984), 471–488.

62   "This is a masculine system": Interview with the author.

The Problem That Still Has No Name

64   "With regard to the public": Quoted in Donna Osborne, "The Crime of Infanticide: Throwing the Baby Out with the Bath Water," *Canadian Journal of Family Law* 6 (1987), 52.

64   "power of the mother": Adrienne Rich, *Of Woman Born: Motherhood as Experience and Institution* (New York: W. W. Norton & Company, 1986), p. 68.

70   killing of infant children between 1985 and 1988: Karen McCurdy and Deborah Daro, "Child Maltreatment: A National Survey of Reports and

Fatalities," *Journal of Interpersonal Violence* 9:1 (1994), 75–94. According to the National Center on Health Statistics, the homicide rate for children under one year old rose 55 percent between 1985 and 1988, climbing to 8.2 per 100,000 children. But, say McCurdy and Daro: "It should be noted that these figures undercount the actual incidence. . . . Research has consistently found that some percentage of accidental deaths . . . and SIDS cases might be more appropriately labeled a child maltreatment death if comprehensive investigations were routinely conducted."

There is evidence that child homicide and infanticide are on the rise in the United States. Reports of child abuse increased 50 percent nationwide between 1986 and 1992, with a total of 2,936,000 children allegedly abused in 1992, of whom 1,160,400 were confirmed as abused by investigators—a 10 percent increase over 1991. Child fatalities rose 49 percent between 1985 and 1992, from 1.3 per 1,000 children to 1.94. Forty-six percent of all child fatalities were infants.

70   data on infanticide compiled by WHO: Katherine K. Christoffel and Kiang Liu, "Homicide Death Rates in Childhood in 23 Developed Countries: U.S. Rates Atypically High," *Child Abuse & Neglect* 7 (1983), 339–345. The median homicide rate for children under one year of age was 1.7 per 100,000, as compared with a median rate of 1.2 homicides per 100,000 for all age groups. Japan had the highest rate, at 8.6 infants killed per 100,000. The U.S. homicide rate for male children under the age of one year was 4.8 per 100,000; for female children it was 3.3. Adding in possible homicide, the rate became 8.7 infants per 100,000, compared with a rate of 8.2 homicides per 100,000 for *all* ages. "The incidence of infanticide, unlike the incidence of child homicide, tends to be as high [as] or higher than the rate of homicide for adults." The data, conclude the authors, "may indicate that the susceptibility to infanticide is reinforced by features of our society, perhaps particularly social isolation of parents." See also Murray Straus, "State and Regional Differences in U.S. Homicide Rates in Relation to Sociocultural Characteristics of the States," *Behavioral Sciences and the Law* 5 (1987), 61–75.

71   "neonates are discarded but not found": Patricia M. Crittenden and Susan E. Craig, "Developmental Trends in the Nature of Child Homicide," *Journal of Interpersonal Violence* 5:2 (June 1990). In Dade County, Florida, between 1956 and 1986, 171 child murders were recorded by police. Mothers accounted for 86 percent of newborn deaths, 39 percent of infant deaths, 22 percent of toddler deaths, 23 percent of preschooler deaths, and

8 percent of child deaths. These figures don't include the 22 percent of cases where the perpetrator was unknown, or possible child homicides where no body was found. "Should a mother decide either to end the neonate's life or to dispose of a body which she believed to be dead, there would be no observers or official records of the death." This would follow from the fact that in seven of the thirteen neonate cases, "the murder was discovered only when the infant's body was accidentally found after being discarded."

71   "Infanticide Increasing, Experts Fear": Martha Shirk, *St. Louis Post Dispatch*, April 7, 1991.

73   *Long Island Newsday* editorial: "Compassion fits this crime, not punishment," March 22, 1991.

73   Suffolk County Detective Lieutenant Gierasch: Interview with the author.

75   extrapolating from animal behavior to human mothers: An in-depth account of this research is cited in Diane Eyer, *Mother-Infant Bonding: A Scientific Fiction* (New Haven, Conn.: Yale University Press, 1992).

75   skin-to-skin bonding: Ibid. Although this sort of bonding is still being touted in pregnancy and birth books, many researchers have rejected its significance, pointing out that mothers with premature infants, as well as adoptive mothers, have no trouble bonding with their offspring in the long term.

75   Dr. Stuart Asch: Interview with the author.

76   Letters to the editor: *Suffolk Times*, "Ellwood Case: Unequal Justice," March 28, 1991; *Newsday*, "Questions in Ellwood Case," March 4, 1991.

76   "Under Christianity": Adrienne Rich, *Of Woman Born*, p. 259.

77   Thirty-three percent of Paris women: William Langer, "Infanticide: A Historical Survey," *History of Childhood Quarterly* 1 (1974), 353–374.

77   Infant abandonment and killing in Greece and Rome: Shari Thurer, *The Myths of Motherhood: How Culture Reinvents the Good Mother* (New York: Houghton Mifflin, 1994).

78   "a preschool-age stepchild is 100 times more likely": Margo Wilson and Martin Daly, "Evolutionary Social Psychology and Family Homicide," *Science* 242:4878 (1988), 519.

78   A new name for Medea: Ira Daniel Turkat, "Divorce Related Malicious Mother Syndrome," *Journal of Family Violence* 10:3 (1995), 253–263.

78   maternal resentment and infanticide in ancient Greece: Thurer, *Myths of Motherhood*, p. 77.

78   infanticide in colonial America as "revolutionary": Ann Jones, *Women Who Kill* (New York: Fawcett Crest, 1980), p. 55.

78   Personal impulses in the murder of infants: Brandt F. Steele, "Psychology of Infanticide Resulting from Maltreatment," *Child Abuse & Neglect* 120:1 (1987), 76–85.

79   "women who commit infanticide run a wide spectrum": Stewart interviewed by the author. See also C. Erlick Robinson and Donna E. Stewart, "Postpartum Psychiatric Disorders," *Canadian Medical Association Journal* 134 (January 1, 1986).

80   Infanticide Act: K. O'Donovan, "The Medicalisation of Infanticide," *Criminal Law Review* 5 (1984). In two reviews of the act—by the Butler Committee (1975) and the Criminal Law Revision Committee (1980)—its medical basis was challenged, and social stress was conceded. Noted members of the Butler Committee: "the operative factors in child killing are often the stress of having to care for the infant, who may be unwanted or difficult." And: "mental disorder is probably no longer a significant cause of infanticide." The CLRC went beyond that concession and recommended that the act be revised to include "environmental or other stresses," including poverty, incapacity to cope with the child, and failure of bonding. Nevertheless, as O'Donovan notes, "the Committee was careful to link such factors to 'the fact of the birth and the hormonal and other bodily changes produced by it.' Thus, to enable the court to take account of socio-economic factors, yet still forgive women, the medical model was retained" (p. 263).

80   link between postpartum hormones and violent behavior: See, for example, Robinson and Stewart, "Postpartum Psychiatric Disorders." "Despite terms like lactational psychosis," note the authors, "researchers have been

unable to confirm a link between postpartum psychosis and levels of prolactin or for that matter, levels of thyroxine, estrogen, progesterone, adrenal corticoids, follicle-stimulating hormones or B-endorphins."

80   coroner's inquests: Cited in O'Donovan, "The Medicalisation of Infanticide."

80   "courts regularly returned 'not guilty' verdicts": Osborne, "Crime of Infanticide."

80   defending the diagnosis of lactational insanity: J. H. Morton, "Female Homicides," *Journal of Mental Science* 80 (1934), 64–74.

80   "studies linking life history to depression": Michael O'Hara, Janet Schlechte, David Lewis, Michael Varner, "Controlled Prospective Study of Postpartum Mood Disorders: Psychological, Environmental, Hormonal Variables," *Journal of Abnormal Psychology* 100:1 (February 1991), 63; Steven E. Hobfoll, "Depression's Birth in Poor Women," *Science News* 147:24 (June 17, 1995), 381; Phyllis Zelkowitz and Tamara Milet, "Postpartum Psychiatric Disorders: Their Relationship to Psychological Adjustment and Marital Satisfaction in Spouses," *Journal of Abnormal Psychology* 105:2 (May 1996), 281; Susan B. Campbell and Jeffrey Cohn, "Prevalence and Correlates of Postpartum Depression in First-time Mothers," *Journal of Abnormal Psychology* 100:4 (November 1991), 594.

81   fathers and postpartum depression: E. J. Anthony, "An Overview of the Effects of Maternal Depression on the Infant and Child," in H. L. Morrison, ed., *Children of Depressed Parents: Risk Identification and Intervention* (New York: Grune & Stratton, 1983), pp. 1–17. See also W. V. Diskin et al., "Postpartum—After the Baby is Born," in *Our Bodies, Ourselves* (New York: Simon & Schuster, 1976), pp. 297–316.

82   Kathleen Householder: "Why Mothers Kill Their Babies," *Time*, June 20, 1988; Josephine Mesa: "Women Who Killed Child Remains Free," Tom Gorman, *Los Angeles Times*, April 26, 1989; Sheryl Massip: "Judge Won't Confine Massip," Andrea Ford, *Los Angeles Times*, March 11, 1989.

82   depression and psychosis less severe in early twentieth century: Katherine Dalton, *Depression After Childbirth* (New York: Oxford University Press, 1989).

83   Harris and Thompson on "Oprah Winfrey" show episode: "Mothers Who Killed Their Children," February 6, 1991.

84   account of professional woman giving birth to twins: Robinson and Stewart, "Postpartum Psychiatric Disorders."

85   "the parent may decide it is a hopeless task": Steele, "Psychology of Infanticide," 83.

86   "I was like I gotta do this": Paula Sims to Audrey Becker, *Dying Dreams: The Secrets of Paula Sims* (New York: Pocket Books, 1993), p. 328.

87   Of eighty-eight infanticidal women in a 1988 study: Martin Daly and Margo Wilson, *Homicide* (New York: Aldine de Gruyter, 1988).

87   women admitted to Broadmoor: Patrick McGrath, "Maternal Filicide in Broadmoor Hospital, 1919–69," *Journal of Forensic Psychiatry* 3:2 (1974).

87   "morbid and mistaken maternal solicitude": J. Baker, "Female Criminal Lunatics," *Journal of Mental Science* 48 (1902), 13–28.

88   men in Brixton prison convicted of infanticide: P. D. Scott, "Fatal Battered Baby Cases," *Medicine, Science and the Law* 13 (1973), 197–206.

88   Jennifer Uglow on Toni Morrison: "Medea and Marmite Sandwiches," in Katherine Grieve, ed., *Balancing Acts: On Being a Mother* (London: Virago, 1989), pp. 148–159.

89   average prison sentence: Mann, *When Women Kill*, p. 150. Thirty-seven percent of the women convicted of killing their offspring in Mann's study were sentenced to prison. The remainder received probation, were remanded for psychiatric treatment, or were dealt with in some other manner.

89   British imprisonment rates for infanticide: Allison Morris and Ania Wilczynski, "Rocking the Cradle: Mothers Who Kill Their Children," in Helen Birch, ed., *Moving Targets: Women, Murder and Representation* (London: Virago, 1993), pp. 198–217.

89   Phillip Resnick interviewed by *Long Island Newsday*: Carolyn Colwell, "The Pregnancy Denial Defense," March 11, 1991.

90   number of U.S. cases involving postpartum psychosis defense: G. Lav-
erne Williamson, "Postpartum Depression Syndrome as a Defense to Criminal Behavior," *Journal of Family Violence* 8:2 (1993), 151–164.

91   Dade County, Florida, prosecutions: Crittenden and Craig, "Developmental Trends."

91   use of postpartum psychosis as a reason why women shouldn't vote:
O'Donovan, "The Medicalisation of Infanticide."

91   "myth-making by legislation": Nigel Walker, *Crime and Insanity in England. Volume I: The Historical Perspective* (Edinburgh: Edinburgh University
Press, 1968), p. 121.

MEDEA IN HER MODERN GUISE

92   "ideal mother": Cited in Thurer, *Myths of Motherhood*, p. xxvii.

92   "powerless women": Rich, *Of Woman Born*, p. 38.

94   MSBP as "a 'career' pursued by ostensibly wonderful mothers": Herbert A. Schreier and Judith A. Libow, *Hurting for Love: Munchausen by Proxy
Syndrome* (Guilford, Conn.: Guilford Press, 1993), p. 88.

95   "The disorder is far from rare": Ibid. p. 38.

95   "substantial challenge: "Munchausen Syndrome by Proxy," *The FBI Law
Enforcement Bulletin* 64:8 (August 1995), 5–7. A clearly coercive, instrumental
form of self-directed violence is Munchausen syndrome. It has been noted that
such individuals can often shift the direction of their aggression, becoming
threatening or physically violent toward medical staff. See, for example,
Donald A. Swanson, "The Munchausen Syndrome," *American Journal of Psychotherapy* 35:3 (July 1981). Women with Munchausen syndrome by proxy often
threaten to commit suicide. The FBI Bulletin on MSBP investigation notes that
60 percent of the women in a sample of the disorder had attempted suicide.

96   "Because I'm a woman": Joyce Egginton, *From Cradle to Grave* (New
York: William Morrow and Company, 1989), p. 99.

97   MSBP as a "form of psychopathy": Schreier and Libow, *Hurting for
Love*, p. 53.

97   analysis of psychopathic speech patterns: Interview with author. See also Robert Hare, *Without Conscience: The Disturbing World of the Psychopaths Among Us* (New York: Pocket Books, 1994).

97   psychopath described: Hervey Cleckley, *Mask of Sanity*, 5th ed. (St. Louis, Mo.: C. V. Mosely, 1976).

97   psychopath's brain likened to a reptile's: J. Reid Meloy, *The Psychopathic Mind: Origins, Dynamics and Treatment* (Northvale, N.J.: Jason Aronson, 1988), p. 34.

98   Psychiatrist's interview with psychopath: Patricia Pearson, "Frankenstein's Orphan," *Saturday Night*, November 1991.

98   women more likely than men to perpetrate child neglect: Leslie Margolin, "Fatal Child Neglect," *Child Welfare* LXIX:4 (July-August 1990), 309–318. Two-thirds of fatal neglect victims are male. See also Nino Trocme, "Ontario Incidence Study of Reported Child Abuse & Neglect" (Toronto: Institute for the Prevention of Child Abuse, 1994). This investigation of child abuse and neglect in Ontario tracked 46,683 cases. Child neglect involved a mother as the perpetrator in 85 percent of the cases. In abuse, mothers were responsible in 39 percent of cases, as compared with 40 percent for fathers.

98   "Neglect is continual": Dr. Mindy Rosenberg, in testimony at the sentencing hearing of Dorothea Puente.

98   "soul murder": Alice Miller, *For Your Own Good: Hidden Cruelty in Child-Rearing and the Roots of Violence* (New York: Noonday Press, 1990), p. 248.

99   "inability to socialize": Meloy, *The Psychopathic Mind*, p. 35.

100   "a baby was an extension of herself": Egginton, *Cradle to Grave*, p. 188.

100   "You could paper the walls": Ibid., p. 326.

100   "projective containers": Meloy, *The Psychopathic Mind*, p. 51.

101   "I've seen psychopaths cry like a baby": Bill Tillier, interviewed by the author.

101   "doing his best to elicit a confession": Egginton, *Cradle to Grave*, p. 225.

103   "the Roman mother's use of her own sons": Thurer, *Myths of Mother-hood*, p. 78.

103   "A woman whose rage is under wraps": Rich, *Of Woman Born*, p. 206.

103   anomie theory: Virginia Morris, review of Allison Morris, *Women, Crime and Criminal Justice*, in *Women & Criminal Justice* 1:1 (1989). Morris was quoting Eileen Leonard, from *Women, Crime and Society*, p. 93.

104   scientific mothering: Rima D. Apple, "Constructing Mothers: Scientific Motherhood in the Nineteenth and Twentieth Centuries," *Social History of Medicine* 8:2 (1995), 161–178.

106   comments about Genene Jones: Peter Elkind, *Death Shift* (New York: Viking Penguin, 1989).

107   "That we have so much difficulty seeing these mothers": Schreier and Libow, *Hurting for Love*, p. 102.

107   Roy Meadow research: "Suffocation, Recurrent Apnea, and Sudden Infant Death," *Journal of Pediatrics* 117:3 (September 1990), 351–357; see also C. P. Samuels et al., "Fourteen Cases of Imposed Airway Obstruction," *Archives of Diseases in Children* (1992); Ian Mitchell et al., "Apnea and Factitious Illness," *Pediatrics* 92:6 (December 1993), 810; W. Alexander and R. Smith, "Serial Munchausen Syndrome by Proxy," *Pediatrics* 86:4 (1990); Diana Brahms, "Video Surveillance and Child Abuse," *The Lancet* 342:8877 (October 16, 1993). See also W. Alexander and R. Stevenson Smith, "Serial Munchausen Syndrome by Proxy," *Pediatrics* 86:4 (1990).

108   Chicago study of crib deaths: K. K. Christoffel, E. J. Zieserl, and J. Chiarmonte, "Should Child Abuse and Neglect Be Considered When a Child Dies Unexpectedly?" *American Journal of Diseases of Children* 39 (1985), 876–880.

109   SIDS concealing homicides: See, for example, John S. Emery and Mary Newlands, "Child Abuse and Cot Deaths," *Child Abuse & Neglect* 15 (1991), 275–278; Robert M. Reece, "Fatal Child Abuse and Sudden Infant Death Syndrome: A Critical Diagnostic Decision," *Pediatrics* 91:2 (1993).

109   Martha Woods case: V. DiMaio and J. D. Bernstein, "A Case of Infanticide," *Journal of Forensic Sciences* 34:2 (1975).

110   "A lot of doctors are very naive about these cases": DiMaio interviewed by Egginton, *Cradle to Grave*, p. 203.

110   proposed genetic cause of SIDS: A. Steinschneider, "Prolonged Apnea and the Sudden Infant Death Syndrome: Clinical and Laboratory Observations," *Pediatrics* 50 (1972), 646–654. When Connie Chung asked Steinschneider about his article's influence, he replied: "Not the paper. I'm influential. I'm a big man"; from "Eye to Eye with Connie Chung," June 16, 1994.

110   account of Deborah Gedzius: "Eye to Eye with Connie Chung," June 16, 1994.

111   child abuse rates nationwide: Karen McCurdy and Deborah Daro, "Child Maltreatment: A National Survey of Reports and Fatalities," *Journal of Interpersonal Violence* 9:1 (1994), 75–94.

111   mothers more likely than fathers to commit child homicide: Fifty-five percent of parental-child (under-twelve) killings were carried out by mothers. U.S. Department of Justice, "Murder in Families" (Washington, D.C., 1993). The figures were based on prosecution and convictions, and some critics charge that they don't tell the whole story. It's possible that fathers, stepfathers, and boyfriends have a greater propensity than mothers to kill the children in their care; by the same logic, of course, it's equally possible that mothers have a higher rate than reported. For child homicide in England, see Morris and Wilczynski, "Rocking the Cradle," in Birch, ed., *Moving Targets*, p. 201.

111   smaller samples: According to Murray Straus, Richard J. Gelles, and S. K. Steinmetz, *Behind Closed Doors: Violence in the American Family* (Garden City, N.Y.: Anchor Books, 1980), mothers had a 62 percent greater rate of physical child abuse than fathers. Mothers beat their children nearly twice as often as fathers do, and fathers are less likely than mothers to throw objects at, slap, spank, or hit their child with objects. See also Leslie Margolin, "Child Abuse by Mothers' Boyfriends: Why the Overrepresentation?" *Child Abuse & Neglect* 16 (1992), 451–551. Margolin notes that the majority of physical abusers are women.
Sexual abuse rates are the most difficult of all to determine, because the whole framework of inquiry is geared toward the assumption that men molest children. Only recently have data emerged to challenge that assumption. See, for example, David Finkelhor and Diana Russel, "Women as Perpetrators: Review of the Evidence," in Finkelhor, ed., *Child Sexual Abuse*. See

also F. F. Knopp, F. F. Lackey, and L. B. Lackey, *Female Sexual Abusers: A Summary of Data from 44 Treatment Providers* (Orwell, Vt.: Safer Society Press, 1987); K. Faller, "Women Who Sexually Abuse Children," *Violence and Victims*, 2 (1987); K. L. Kaufman et al., "Comparing Female and Male Perpetrators' Modus Operandi: Victims' Reports of Sexual Abuse, *Journal of Interpersonal Violence* 10:3 (1995); R. L. Johnson and D. Shrier, "Past Sexual Victimization by Females of Male Patients in an Adolescent Medicine Clinic Population," *American Journal of Psychiatry* 144:5 (1987).

111   "Women are linked more intimately": Steffensmeier and Streifel, "Trends in Female Crime," in Culliver, ed., *Female Criminality.*

112   "When a person cannot talk": Miller, *For Your Own Good,* p. 242.

112   influence of child abuse on subsequent criminal behavior: Several studies of wife-assaulters reveal that these men were abused as children and that the abuser was as likely to be the mother as the father. See, for example, Lynn Caesar, "Exposure to Violence in the Families-of-Origin Among Wife-abusers and Maritally Non-violent Men," *Violence and Victims* 3:1 (1988), 49–63; C. Cappell and R. B. Heiner, "The Intergenerational Transmission of Family Aggression," *Journal of Family Violence* 5 (1990), 135–52.

Cathy Spatz-Widom's research on the relation between child abuse or neglect and adult arrest for crime shows that 16 percent of girls who were abused (in her sample) were later arrested for adult crime, twice as many as girls who were not abused. "Child Abuse, Neglect, and Adult Behaviour: Research Design and Findings on Criminality, Violence, and Child Abuse," *American Journal of Orthopsychiatry* 59:3 (1989).

112   impact of sexual abuse on subsequent sex offending: A. Nicholas Groth, "Sexual Trauma in the Life Histories of Rapists and Child Molestors," *Victimology* 4:1 (1979): 10–16; Freda Briggs and Russell Hawkins, "A Comparison of the Childhood Experiences of Convicted Male Child Molestors and Men Who Were Sexually Abused in Childhood and Claimed to Be Nonoffenders," *Child Abuse and Neglect* 20: 3 (1996): 221–33; David Finkelhor and Diana Russel, "Women as Perpetrators: Review of the Evidence," in David Finkelhor, ed., *Child Sexual Abuse: New Theory and Research* (New York: Free Press, 1984).

113   "Defenselessness and helplessness find no haven": Ibid., p. 117.

BALANCING THE DOMESTIC EQUATION

114   "shameful secrets": Ann Jones, *Next Time, She'll Be Dead: Battering and How to Stop It* (Boston: Beacon Press, 1994), p. 236.

114   "responsibility of women in domestic abuse": Judith Shevrin and James Sniechowski, "Women Are Responsible, Too," *Los Angeles Times*, July 1, 1994.

117   lesbian abuse: See Claire Renzetti, *Violent Betrayal: Partner Abuse in Lesbian Relationships* (Newbury Park, Calif.: Sage Publications 1992); Nancy Hammond, "Lesbian Victims of Relationship Violence," *Women and Therapy* 8 (1989), 89–105; M. J. Bologna, C. K. Waterman, and L. J. Dawson, "Violence in Gay Male and Lesbian Relationships: Implications for Practitioners and Policy Makers," paper presented at the Third National Conference of Family Violence Researchers, Durham, N.H., 1987 (the authors found that 18 percent of gay men and 40 percent of lesbians admitted to being victims of aggression in their current relationship); Gwat-Yong Lie and S. Gentlewarrior, "Intimate Violence in Lesbian Relationships: Discussion of Survey Findings and Practise Implications," *Journal of Social Service Research* 15 (1991), 41–59 (in their 1990 survey of 1,099 lesbians, Lie and Gentlewarrior found that 52 percent had been victims of aggression by their partners); G. Y. Lie et al., "Lesbians in Currently Aggressive Relationships: How Frequently Do They Report Aggressive Past Relationships?" *Violence and Victims* 6:2 (1991).

118   percentage of severe violence in spousal abuse: Straus, Gelles, and Steinmetz, *Behind Closed Doors*, p. 40.

119   male approval of spousal assault: Murray Straus and Glenda Kaufman Kantor, "Change in Cultural Norms Approving Marital Violence from 1968 to 1994," paper presented at the annual meeting of the American Sociological Association, Los Angeles, August 1994.

119   survey of family violence: Straus, Gelles, and Steinmetz, *Behind Closed Doors*, pp. 40–41.

120   research "patriarchal": See, for example, M. Bograd and K. Yllo, eds., *Feminist Perspectives on Wife Abuse* (Newbury Park, Calif.: Sage Publications, 1988).

120   resurvey of family violence: Murray Straus and Richard J. Gelles, "Societal Change and Change in Family Violence from 1975–1985 as Revealed by Two National Surveys," *Journal of Marriage and the Family* 48 (1986), 465–479. "We found that among couples where violence occurred, both partners are violent in about half of the cases, violence by only the male partner occurs one-quarter of the time, and violence by only the female partner occurs one-quarter of the time. . . . These results cast doubt on the notion that assaults by women on their partners primarily are acts of self-defense or retaliation." In terms of damage done, the study found that levels of medical care, days off work, and time spent bedridden were not significantly different between the sexes (162–163). Women, however, reported much higher levels of depression.

See also "Physical Assaults by Wives: A Major Social Problem," in Richard J. Gelles and Donileen R. Loeske, eds., *Current Controversies in Family Violence* (Newbury Park, Calif.: Sage Publications, 1993).

120   study of young American military couples: J. Langhinrichsen-Rohling, P. Neidig, and G. Thorn, "Violent Marriages: Gender Differences in Levels of Current Violence and Past Abuse," *Journal of Family Violence* 10:2 (1995), 159–175.

121   new books on the self-help market: See, for example, Patricia Evans, *Verbal Abuse: Survivors Speak Out on Relationship and Recovery* (Holbrook, Mass.: Bob Adams, Inc., 1993).

121   high degrees of female verbal hostility by women in violent marriages: See, for example, D. Vivian and K. D. O'Leary, "Communication Patterns in Physically Aggressive Engaged Partners," paper presented at the Third National Family Aggression Research Conference, University of New Hampshire, July 1987.

121   battered husband syndrome: S. K. Steinmetz, "The Battered Husband Syndrome," *Victimology* 2:3/4 (1977).

121   familiar with Murray Straus as a man: Pat Marshall's remarks described by David Lees, "The War Against Men," *Toronto Life*, December 1992. Lee quotes Marshall as saying: "I know Murray. . . . I was speaking at an international conference a few years ago in Jerusalem. . . . Met a woman there and . . . didn't know her name . . . I have never met a woman who looked so victimized. Never in my whole, whole life. By coincidence, it happened to be Murray Straus's wife. I have never met somebody who

was trying so desperately to be invisible in the space that she occupied. I mean, it was just dramatic."

121   Kentucky Commission on Violence Against Women: M. Schulman, "A Survey of Spousal Violence Against Women in Kentucky" (Washington, D.C.: Government Printing Office, 1979). The raw data were reviewed by C. A. Hornung, B. C. McCullough, and T. Sugimoto, "Status Relationships in Marriage: Risk Factors in Spouse Abuse," *Journal of Marriage and the Family* 43 (1981), 675–692. The authors found that 38 percent of the violent attacks in the Kentucky survey were by women—against men who had not assaulted them.

121   emergency medical admissions in Detroit: Christina Hoff Sommers, *Who Stole Feminism: How Women Have Betrayed Women* (New York: Simon & Schuster 1994), p. 201.

122   violent dating: Walter DeKeseredy and K. Kelly, "The Incidence and Prevalence of Woman Abuse in Canadian University and College Dating Relationships: Preliminary Results from a National Survey," unpublished report to the Family Violence Prevention Division, Health and Welfare Canada, 1993.

122   physical aggression by young women in premarital romance: See, for example, D. B. Sugarman and G. T. Hotaling, "Dating Violence: Prevalence, Context and Risk Markers," in M. A. Pirog-Good and J. E. Stets, eds., *Violence in Dating Relationships: Emerging Social Issues* (New York: Praeger, 1989); Diane Follingstad et al., "Sex Differences in Motivations and Effects in Dating Relationships," *Family Relations*, 40 (January 1991), 51–57: Two and a half times more women than men cited "control" as a motive for assaults. More males cited jealousy. Twenty percent of females said they had the right to use violence, whereas no males did. See also A. DeMaris, "Male vs. Female Initiation of Aggression: The Case of Courtship Violence," in E. Viano, ed., *Intimate Violence: Interdisciplinary Perspectives* (Bristol, Pa.: Hemisphere Publishing, 1992); P. Marshall and L. Rose, "Gender, Stress and Violence in Adult Relationships of a Sample of College Students," *Journal of Social and Personal Relations* 4 (1987); Sarah Ben-David, "The Two Facets of Female Violence: The Public and the Domestic Domains," *Journal of Family Violence* 8:4 (1993).

For female sexual coercion in dating relationships, see, for example: L. O'Sullivan and S. Byers, "Eroding Stereotypes: College Women's Attempts to Influence Reluctant Male Sexual Partners," *The Journal of Sex*

Research 30 (1993); Kate Fillion, *Lip Service: The Truth About Women's Darker Side in Love, Sex and Friendship* (Toronto: HarperCollins, 1996).

122   survey on alcoholism and domestic violence: Reena Sommer, "Male and Female Perpetrated Partner Abuse: Testing a Diathesis-Stress Model," unpublished doctoral dissertation, University of Manitoba, 1994. See also R. Sommer, G. E. Barnes, and R. P. Murray, "Alcohol Consumption, Alcohol Dependence, Personality and Female Perpetrated Spousal Abuse," *Personality and Individual Differences* 13:12 (1993), 1315–1323.

123   Therapist Michael Thomas: Interview with the author.

125   differences among women: Mildred Pagelow, *Family Violence* (New York: Praeger, 1984).

126   "specious notion": Susan Brownmiller, "Hardly a Heroine," *The New York Times*, February 2, 1989, p. 25.

126   Nussbaum: Jones, *Next Time, She'll Be Dead*, pp. 167–198.

127   "search for causation a wild-goose chase": E. Wilson, *What Is to Be Done About Violence Against Women?* (London: Penguin, 1983).

127   "If a man abuses his wife": Final Report of the Federal Panel on Violence Against Women, Ottawa, Canada, 1993, p. 8.

127   "same old crap": Ann Jones, "Where Do We Go From Here?" *MS.*, September/October 1994, p. 57.

129   "For men, abuse is a double whammy": Murray Straus, in interview with the author.

130   "slapping the cad": Straus, "Physical Assaults by Wives: A Major Social Problem," in Gelles and Loeske, eds., *Current Controversies in Family Violence*, p. 58.

130   "I suspect that some academic": Jones, *Next Time, She'll Be Dead*, p. 81.

131   abused lesbians unable to go to local shelter: Renzetti, *Violent Betrayal*, pp. 93–94.

131   "When shelter workers": Hammond, "Lesbian Victims," 95.

131   no "lesbian utopia": Barbara Hart, "Preface," in Kerry Lobel, ed., *Naming the Violence: Speaking Out About Lesbian Battering* (Seattle: The Seal Press, 1986), p. 10.

131   "tactics may look the same": "Women Who Batter Women," *Ms.*, September/October 1994, p. 53.

132   "Women use the same rationalizations": Laurie Chesley, interview with the author.

132   patriarchal attitudes about marriage: P. Burke, "Gender Identity, Self-Esteem, and Physical and Sexual Abuse in Dating Relationships," in Pirog-Good and Stets, eds., *Violence in Dating Relationships.*

132   distinction between "strength" and "power": Renzetti, *Violent Betrayal*, p. 117.

132   "many . . . believe": Walker, *The Battered Woman*, p. 96.

133   "I was his one-eyed teddy bear": Quoted in Joyce Johnson, *What Lisa Knew: The Truth and Lies of the Steinberg Case* (New York: Zebra Books, 1990), p. 209.

133   "intense displays of rage": Arlene Istar, "The Healing Comes Slowly," in Lobel, ed., *Naming the Violence*, pp. 163–172.

134   female abusers with "personality disorders": L. K. Hamberger and J. Hastings, "Characteristics of Male Spouse Abusers Consistent with Personality Disorders," *Hospital Community Psychiatry* 39 (1988), 763–770.

134   "Violence is a learned behavior": Debbie DeGale, in interview with the author.

135   children who are beaten by their mothers more likely to become victimizers: Langhinrichsen-Rohling, Neidig, and Thorn, "Violent Marriages." See also J. Malone and A. Tyree, "Cycle of Violence: Explanations of Marital Aggression and Victimization," paper presented at the 86th Annual Meeting of the American Society of Anthropology, Cincinnati, Ohio, 1991.

In R. Sommer, unpublished doctoral dissertation, 1994, 34.78 percent of males and 40.91 percent of females who perpetrated physical abuse had observed their mothers hitting their fathers, a higher rate than for those who had observed fathers hit mothers.

135   "Domination begins with the attempt to deny dependency": Jessica Benjamin, *The Bonds of Love: Psychoanalysis, Feminism, and the Problem of Domination* (New York: Pantheon Books, 1988), p. 52.

136   "dependency" for lesbians: Renzetti, *Violent Betrayal*, p. 116.

136   "couples' violence ultimately results from partners' insecurities": William A. Stacey, Lonnie R. Hazlewood, and Anson Shupe, *The Violent Couple* (Westport, Conn.: Praeger, 1994), p. 104.

136   "dance of mutual destructiveness": Shevrin and Sniechowski, "Women Are Responsible Too."

136   "spent most of their time drinking": Eve Lipchik, "Spouse Abuse: Challenging the Party Line," *The Family Therapy Networker*, May/June 1991.

137   case of Favell and Pelly: For a different interpretation of the relationship, see Lisa Priest, *Women Who Killed*, p. 15.

137   "abuse aimed at the men's resources or abilities": Stacey et al., *The Violent Couple*, p. 63.

137   "According to former patrol officer": R. Kim Rossmo, in interview with the author.

137   Green and Julio: "the official victim is the one who submits": Jeanne P. Eschner, *The Hitting Habit* (New York: The Free Press, 1984), p. 21.

138   "As one Austin woman": Stacey et al., *The Violent Couple*, p. 63.

WOMAN AS PREDATOR

146   Epigraph quotes: Camille Paglia, *Sexual Personae: Art and Decadence from Nefertiti to Emily Dickinson* (New Haven, Conn.: Yale University Press, 1990, p. 247. Toppan cited in Eric Hickey, *Serial Murderers and Their Victims* (Belmont, Calif.: Wadsworth, 1991), p. 124.

153   percentage of serial killers who are women: Hickey, *Serial Murderers*, p. 107.

153   nicknames of multiple killers: Ibid.

153   "We can be fascinated without being afraid": James Alan Fox and Jack Levin, "Female Serial Killers," in Culliver, ed., *Female Criminality*, p. 260.

154   gender differences in serial murder superficial: Candice Skrapec, "Female Serial Killer," in Birch, ed., *Moving Targets*, p. 263.

154   twenty-two killers arrested between 1972 and 1992: Belea T. Keeney and Kathleen M. Heide: "Gender Differences in Serial Murderers: A Preliminary Analysis," *Journal of Interpersonal Violence* 9:3 (September 1994). Keeney defined serial homicide in her 1992 master's thesis as "the premeditated murder of three or more victims, committed over time in separate incidents, in a civilian context, with the murder activity being chosen by the offender" (unpublished, University of South Florida, Tampa, Fla.).

156   use of guns by female serial killers: Hickey, *Serial Murderers*, p. 117.

157   FBI definition of serial murder: R. Ressler, A. Burgess, and J. Douglas, *Sexual Homicide* (Lexington, Mass.: Lexington Books, 1988). For account of BSSU research, see also R. Ressler and Tom Schactman, *Whoever Fights Monsters* (New York: St. Martin's Press, 1992).

159   "routine activities theory": See, for example, R. V. Clarke and M. Felson, eds., *Routine Activity and Rational Choice* (New Brunswick, N.J.: Transaction, 1993); D. K. Rossmo, "Targeting Victims: Serial Killers and the Urban Environment," in T. O'Reilly-Fleming and S. A. Egger, eds., *Serial and Mass Murder: Theory, Research and Policy* (Toronto: University of Toronto Press, 1994).

160   female serial killers average a greater number of victims: Hickey, *Serial Murderers*, p. 126.

162   "white male drifters": Phyllis Chesler, "A Double Standard for Murder?" *The New York Times*, January 8, 1992, p. 19.

162   Serial killer as henchman: Jane Caputi, *The Age of Sex Crime* (London: Women's Press, 1987).

162   "the State says . . .": Susan McWhinney, "Petite Treason: Crimes Against the Matriarchy," in Amy Scholder, ed., *Critical Condition: Women on the Edge of Violence* (San Francisco: City Lights Books, 1993), pp. 48–51.

165   "Many years ago, I was a boy drowning in the sea": Nilsen quoted by Brian Masters, *Killing for Company: The Story of a Man Addicted to Murder* (New York: Dell, 1993).

166   quotes from Sharon Smolick and inmates at Bedford Hills: Interviews with Matthew Scanlon, "Women in Prison," *Psychology Today* 26:6 (November-December 1993).

167   function of temperament: H. J. Eysenck, *Crime and Personality* (London: Routledge and Kegan Paul, 1964), p. 91.

168   right man syndrome: Colin Wilson, *Written in Blood: A History of Forensic Detection* (London: GraftonBooks, 1989).

170   "nightmare artworks": Joyce Carol Oates, *The New York Review of Books*, March 24, 1994.

171   "Poisoning is a cloak-and-dagger kind of crime": Quoted by Tom Kuncl, *Death Row Women* (New York: Pocket Books, 1994), p. 190.

WHAT'S LOVE GOT TO DO WITH IT?

176   women "the distaff half of a murderous couple": Joyce Carol Oates, "I had no other thrill or happiness," *The New York Review of Books*, March 24, 1994, p. 52.

176   account of Hindley and Brady: Emlyn Williams, *Beyond Belief: The Moors Murderers* (London: Hamish Hamilton, 1967).

178   "In 1967": Diana Bryden, "Monsters and Virgins," *Fuse* 18:3 (1995).

179   "soft touches for clever men": Henry Weinstein, "Woman bandit's sentence to be restudied," *Los Angeles Times*, July 8, 1991, p. 1.

179   "a woman who would do anything for love": Farr, *Sunset Murders*.

179   "only wanted to be loved": Dan Darvishian, "Blood Ties," *Sacramento*, April 1984, p. 29.

179 Homolka a "brutalized" victim: Susan G. Cole, "Homolka Not Like Bernardo," *Now*, July 13–19, 1995, p. 11.

179 Lord Astor: Patricia Pearson, "How Women Can Get Away with Murder," *Toronto Globe and Mail*, August 18, 1993, p. 9.

180 "compliant victims": Roy Hazelwood, Park Dietz, and Janet Warren, "Compliant Victims of the Sexual Sadist," *Australian Family Physician* 22:4 (April 1993), 1–5.

180 "Women like us": Farr, *Sunset Murders*, p. 207.

180 sample of co-killers with one or more women: Hickey, *Serial Murderers* p. 175.

180 Rosemary West: "In Darkest England," *National Review*, November 6, 1995; Judith Neely: Candice Skrapec, "The Female Serial Killer"; Tina Powell, Gwendolyn Graham, and Diedre Hunt: all three cases discussed in Tom Kuncl, *Death Row Women*.

181 "I killed the bitch": Hickey, *Serial Murderers*, p. 179.

181 "Learning crime": Morris, *Women, Crime and Criminal Justice*, p. 76.

181 account of Karla Faye Tucker: Beverly Lowry, *Crossed Over: A Murder, A Memoir* (New York: Alfred A. Knopf, 1992).

185 FBI survey of seven women involved with sexual sadists: Hazelwood, Dietz, and Warren, "Compliant Victims."

186 comments by Carol Bundy: Testimony at the trial of Douglas Clark.

186 shared psychotic disorder: Jose M. Silveira, M.D., and Mary V. Seeman, M.D., "Shared Psychotic Disorder: A Critical Review of the Literature," *Canadian Journal of Psychiatry*, October 1995.

191 study of sixteen female sexual offenders: Ruth Mathews, Jane Kinder Matthews, and Kathleen Speltz, *Female Sexual Offenders: An Exploratory Study* (Orwell, Vt.: The Safer Society Press, 1989).

192 "When they talked about it all": Farr, *Sunset Murders*, p. 123.

195   "One key to understanding a woman who kills repeatedly": Skrapec, "Female Serial Killer," in Birch, ed., *Moving Targets*, p. 263.

195   "I was unwilling to at first": Mathews, Matthews, and Speltz, "Female Sexual Offenders," p. 15.

198   "I felt like I was seventeen years old again!" Letters published by *Toronto Sun*, September 12, 1994, pp. 3–5.

198   "I do not think Kristen French died from ligature strangulation": Kirk Makin, "Homolka Testimony Challenged," *Toronto Globe & Mail*, September 5, 1995, p. 1.

200   "too late, too late": Farr, *Sunset Murders*, p. 208.

ISLAND OF WOMEN

201   "air of viciousness": Josie O'Dwyer in Pat Carlan, ed., *Criminal Women: Autobiographical Accounts* (London: Polity Press, 1985), p. 143.

204   percentage of inmates who are psychopaths: K. Howells and C. Hollin, eds., *Clinical Approaches to Mentally Disordered Offenders* (New York: Wiley, 1993). See also S. B. Guze, *Criminality and Psychiatric Disorders* (New York: Oxford University Press, 1976).

204   data on female inmates and drug use/drug crimes: Bureau of Justice Statistics, "Special Report: Women in Prison."

208   recidivism rates: Ray Belcourt, Tanya Nanners, and Linda Lefetarve, "Examining the unexamined: Recidivism among female offenders," U.S. Department of Justice Report, April 12, 1996.

210   U.S. infraction rate for 1986: Bureau of Justice Statistics, U.S. Department of Justice. A study comparing male and female inmate misconduct in North Carolina found that "non-violent sexual offenses" and "escapes" were more common among the women. Craddock, "Misconduct Careers," *The Prison Journal*, March 1996.

210   British infraction rates: Morris, *Women, Crime and Criminal Justice*, p. 121.

210   infraction rates in two Texas prisons: Dorothy Spektorov McClellan, "Disparity in the discipline of male and female inmates in Texas prisons," in *Women & Criminal Justice* 5:2 (1994), 71–97.

211   four in ten inmates have prior record of violent crime: Washington, D.C., Bureau of Justice Statistics, "Special Report: Women in Prison," 1991.

211   "You can get into a fight every ten seconds here": Interviews with Scanlon, "Women in Prison."

212   "When I came out of Borstal": O'Dwyer in Carlan, ed., *Criminal Women*, p. 147

212   O'Dwyer attacking Hindley: Ibid., p. 164.

212   "Scholars have generally failed": Clemens Bartollas, "Little Girls Grown Up: The Perils of Institutionalization," in Culliver, ed., *Female Criminality*, p. 471.

213   hierarchy building: Imogene Moyer, "Leadership in a Women's Prison," *Journal of Criminal Justice* 8 (1980). See also A. Mandaraka-Sheppard, *The Dynamics of Aggression in Women's Prisons in England* (London: Gower Press, 1986).

213   Frontera study on snitches: D. Ward and G. Kassebaum, *Women's Prison: Sex and Social Structure* (Chicago: Aldine, 1965), p. 33. See also Vergil Williams and Mary Fish, *Convicts, Codes and Contraband: The Prison Life of Men and Women* (New York: Ballinger, 1974), p. 118.

215   "Common messages gleaned from female prison films": Karlene Faith, *Unruly Women: The Politics of Confinement and Resistance* (Vancouver: Press Gang Publishers, 1993).

219   "Lesbianism is not the issue": Veronica Compton, *Prison Life*, September/October 1995, p. 12.

219   account of Bedford Hills aggressors: Jean Harris, *"They Always Call Us Ladies": Stories from Prison* (New York: Charles Scribner's Sons, 1988), p. 112.

220   national correctional officer survey: J. M. Pollock, *Sex and Supervision: Guarding Male and Female Inmates* (New York: Greenwood Press, 1986), p. 35.

221   gang behavior in Los Angeles: George T. Felkenes and Harold K. Becker, "Female Gang Members: A Growing Issue For Policy Makers," *Journal of Gang Research* 2:4 (Summer 1995), 1–8. Asked to reply "yes" or "no" to the statement "If you have a good reason, you don't have to obey the law," 71.8 percent of girls said "yes" versus 54.1 percent of boys. The law, apparently, also applied to the rules of the gang. Boys were much more likely than girls to say they would kill or commit some other crime specifically if asked to do so by the gang, although 50 percent of the girls *had* committed a crime. A majority of both sexes said they were not forced to join the gang against their will.

221   "Negative feelings toward staff lead inmates to respond emotionally": McClellan, "Disparity in the Discipline of Male and Female Inmates in Texas Prisons," *Women & Criminal Justice.*

221   account of P4W riot: Commission of Inquiry into Certain Events at the Prison for Women in Kingston, Madam Justice Louise Arbour, presiding, March 1996.

222   "a place that has tended to view women as victims": Henry Hess, "Report Vindicates Women's Prison Staff," *Toronto Globe & Mail,* January 21, 1995.

223   drugs "for the purpose of social control": Mandaraka-Sheppard, *Dynamics of Aggression,* p. 134. See also Concetta C. Culliver, "Females Behind Prison Bars," in Culliver, ed., *Female Criminality,* p. 397.

LET THE GUN SMOKE

226   Lynda Hart, *Fatal Women: Lesbian Sexuality and the Mark of Aggression* (Princeton, N.J.: Princeton University Press, 1994).

226   Elliott Leyton, *Men of Blood: Violence in Everyday Life* (Toronto: McClelland & Stuart, 1996).

228   liberation hypothesis: Freda Adler, *Sisters in Crime: The Rise of the New Female Criminal* (New York: McGraw-Hill, 1975).

229   "Women have only themselves to blame": Jim McDowell, "You've Come a Long Way, Baby," *Alberta Report,* July 31, 1994, p. 24.

230   Finnish girls' aggression: Vappu Viemerö, "Changes in Patterns of Aggressiveness Among Finnish Girls over a Decade," in Björkqvist and Niemela, eds., *Of Mice and Women*, p. 105.

230   New York City girls' offenses against teachers: United Federation of Teachers, New York chapter. A corroborating number was requested from the New York City Board of Education, Department of Safety, but was never supplied.

230   L.A. gangs: See Felkenes and Becker, "Female Gang Members"; see also Mary Harris, *Cholas: Latino Girls and Gangs* (New York: AMS Press, 1988); James Diego Vigil, *Barrio Gangs* (Austin: University of Texas Press, 1988). Vigil confirms that the kind of violence engaged in has grown more severe for both males and females, although males still command the most respect and seniority.

231   homicidal women in Julia Tutwiler Prison: Penelope J. Hanke, "A Study of Victim-Offender Homicide Relationships," paper presented at annual meeting of the American Society of Criminology, Miami, Fla., November 1994.

231   study of homicide in six U. S. cities: homicidal women, change in motive—Weisheit, "Female Homicide Offenders."

231   Mann, *When Women Kill.*

232   male-bashing slogans: Cited by Tama Starr, *Eve's Revenge: Saints, Sinners and Stand-up Sisters* (New York: Harcourt, Brace, 1994).

232   "anger and need for empowerment will be directed at the power-brokers": Skrapec, "Female Serial Killer," in Birch, ed., *Moving Targets*, p. 265.

237   "They're treating me like a criminal!": "Canadian Immigration Bar 'Foolish,' Activist Says," *Toronto Star*, February 20, 1994.

239   "Various factions . . . have their spiritual leaders": Compton, *Prison Life*, September–October 1994, p. 12.

239   of 254 female killers at Bedford Hills in 1994: Henry H. Brownstein et al., "The Evolution of Motive and Circumstance in Homicides by Women,"

paper presented at the annual meeting of the American Society of Criminology, Miami, Fla., November 1994.

239   New York State statistics: Ibid.

240   Burbank, *Fighting Women*, p. 274.

240   Richard Ford, "In the Face," *The New Yorker*, September 16, 1996.

242   Ellie Nesler: "Mother Gets 10 Years for Slaying Molester Suspect," *The New York Times*, January 8, 1994.

INDEX